University of
Chester **LIBRARY**
Warrington Campus

Telephone: 01925 534284

International Communications
Series Editor: Philip M. Taylor

This is the first comprehensive series to tackle the fast-expanding subject of International Communications.

This multi-disciplinary subject is viewed as a field of enquiry and research that deals with the processes and impact of the transfer of information, news, data and cultural products as well as other forms of transborder communication between nation-states within the wider context of globalisation. As such it is not only a field of study in its own right but also directly connected to international history, international politics, international affairs and international political economy.

Most writers in these more 'established' fields are agreed that communications have come to play an ever more significant part in relations between states at the political, economic, diplomatic, military and cultural levels. This series will show *how* communications serve to influence those activities from the points of transmission to those of reception.

Enormous breakthroughs in communications technologies – satellite communications, computer-mediated communications, mobile personal communications – are now converging, and the possibilities which this might present are forcing a reconsideration of how established patterns of inter-state relations might adapt to, or be influenced by, this latest phase of the information age.

Debates relating to international regulation, censorship, public diplomacy, electronic democracy, cross-cultural communications and even information warfare all reflect the sense that communications are transforming the nature and practice of government, education, leisure, business, work and warfare. Information has become the lifeblood of this globalising set of patterns.

Books in the series reflect this phenomenon but are rooted in historical method, even when tackling more contemporary events. They are truly international in coverage. The range of books reflects the coverage of courses and teaching in international communications and they are carefully aimed at students and researchers working in this area.

Nazi Wireless Propaganda

*Lord Haw-Haw and British Public Opinion
in the Second World War*

M. A. Doherty

Edinburgh University Press

© M. A. Doherty, 2000

Edinburgh University Press Ltd
22 George Square, Edinburgh

Typeset in 10 on 12 point Ehrhardt
by Hewer Text Ltd, Edinburgh, and
printed and bound in Great Britain by
The Cromwell Press, Trowbridge, Wilts

A CIP Record for this book is
available from the British Library

ISBN 0 7486 1363 3 (paperback)

Contents

List of Tables

Schedule of German Broadcasts
on Compact Disk Insert

Track	Broadcaster	Date of Recording	Synopsis of content
1	William Joyce	14 January 1940	*'Germany Calling . . .'*
2	William Joyce	20 January 1940	*Fate of British cruiser* Exeter.
3	William Joyce	21 January 1940	*Germany denies British and French claims that she has designs on the Balkans.*
4	William Joyce	18 February 1940	*Churchill's message to Captain of* HMS Cossack *after* Altmark *episode, 'the height of cynicism'.*
5	William Joyce	27 February 1940	*English women wearing hats of tin, to protect them from splinters from German bombs.*
6	New British Broadcasting Station	5 March 1940	*Disorganisation and chaos of evacuation of children classic example of confusion. Popularity of German radio due to its truthfulness.*
7	William Joyce	9 April 1940	*Operations concerning occupation of Denmark and Norway have proceeded to plan. German minister in Norway has warned that resistance is futile.*
8	William Joyce	1 June 1940	*Belgian surrender – commentary.*
9	William Joyce	June 1940	*Plutocratic caste who provoked war are abandoning 'doomed' island.*
10	William Joyce	1 June 1940	*'Bloody and battered fragments' of the BEF drift back in wreckage to England.*
11	William Joyce	1 June 1940	*Churchill an 'unclean and miserable figure'.*
12	William Joyce	18 September 1943	*Commentary on rescue of Mussolini.*

13	Eduard Roderich Dietze	8 September 1943	*Commentary on the fall of Italy. America acquires body and soul of England from Churchill.*
14	Margaret Joyce	11 February 1944	*Commentary on unemployment problem in the democracies – 'What on earth is this war being fought about?'*
15	'Lancer' (Norman Baillie-Stewart)	March 1944	*Commentary on 'invasionitis' – Jews profit from armaments boom.*
16	'Lancer' (Norman Baillie-Stewart)	29 August 1944	*Russian rule – Bolsheviks bring unemployment, terror and Jews.*
17	Edward Bowlby	31 August 1944	*Terror raids by RAF will be avenged by total war effort.*
18	Messages from British Prisoners in Germany	1 September 1944	*Messages from British prisoners-of-war in Germany.*
19	John Amery	16 September 1944	*Anti-German resistance no more than Jewish-run terrorists.*
20	Edward Bowlby	4 September 1944	*The Jewish problem.*
21	Workers' Challenge	2 December 1944	*What workers could have done with money wasted on war.*
22	William Joyce	Unidentified	*Savage hoards of Bolshevism threaten European civilisation.*
23	William Joyce	Unidentified	*American domination of Canada.*
24	William Joyce	30 April 1945	*Joyce's last drunken valedictory talk – unbroadcast.*

Acknowledgements

This book was developed from research undertaken towards my doctoral thesis at the University of Kent at Canterbury. During that time and subsequently I was assisted by many individuals and institutions to whom I am greatly indebted. In particular I would like to acknowledge the help of the following: the School of Social and Behavioural Sciences at the University of Westminster; the staff at Riding House Street Library, University of Westminster; the *Deutscher Akademischer Austauschdienst*; the Imperial War Museum (in particular Mr Terry Charman); the British Library of Political and Economic Science; the Public Record Office; the Wiener Library; the BBC Written Archives Centre (in particular Mr Jeff Walden); the BBC Monitoring Service; the BBC Sound Archive; the National Sound Archive; the Tom Harrisson Mass-Observation Archive at the University of Sussex (in particular Ms Joy Eldridge); Mr Vladimir Rubinstein; Mr Nigel Acheson; Mrs Gweneth Neill; Mrs Lorna Swire; Mrs Sally Biggs; Miss Barbara Crowther; Mr James Clark; Mr Horst Bergmeier; Mr Alan Fish. Special thanks I owe to Professor D. J. Oddy, Professor Keith Phillips, Dr Lewis Johnman and Mr Anthony Gorst of the University of Westminster; Professor Philip M. Taylor, Director of the Institute of Communication Studies, University of Leeds; Professor David Culbert of the Department of History, Louisiana State University; Professor Hugh Cunningham of the University of Kent at Canterbury; Dr Brian Brivati of the University of Kingston; Ms Nicola Carr of Edinburgh University Press; and Ms Eileen Roberts.

Finally, I owe my greatest debt to my doctoral supervisor, Professor David Welch, Director of the Centre for the Study of Propaganda at the University of Kent at Canterbury. Professor Welch inspired my original interest in propaganda and remained consistently supportive over the many long years that it took me to produce some ideas of my own. Needless to say, responsibility for errors or omissions in what follows lies only with me.

Mass-Observation material is reproduced with permission of Curtis Brown Ltd, London. Copyright the Trustees of the Mass-Observation archive at the University of Sussex.

Martin Doherty
London, 1999

Abbreviations used in the text

AA	*Auswärtiges Amt* [German Foreign Office]
AGP	Analysis of German Propaganda
BBC	British Broadcasting Corporation
BBC DD	BBC Daily Digest of Foreign (World) Broadcasts
BBC MR	BBC Monitoring Report
BBC WAC	BBC Written Archives Centre
BIPO	British Institute of Public Opinion
BREM	Station Bremen
BRES	Station Breslau
CAL	Station Calais
COLOG	Station Cologne
CPM	Christian Peace Movement
DES	*Die Deutschen Europasender*
DEUT	*Deutschlandsender*
DGP	Development of German Propaganda
DPP	[British] Director of Public Prosecutions
DÜS	*Die Deutschen Überseesender*
FBIS	[US] Foreign Broadcast Intelligence Service
FCC	[US] Federal Communications Commission
FO	[British] Foreign Office
FRANK	Station Frankfurt
FRIES	Station Friesland
HAM	Station Hamburg
HILV	Station Hilversum
IAFSA	In Afrikaans for South Africa
IDFH	In Dutch for Holland
IEFA	In English for Africa
IEFAFE	In English for Australia and the Far East
IEFE	In English for England
IEFENA	In English for England and North America
IEFFE	In English for the Far East
IEFSA	In English for South Africa
IEFUK	In English for the UK
IEFUSA	In English for the USA
IFFF	In French for France
IGFFE	In German for the Far East
IGFG	In German for Germany

IGFUSA   In German for the United States
IPFP   In Polish for Poland
ISFLA   In Spanish for Latin America
LUX   Radio Luxemburg
MO   Mass-Observation
MoI   Ministry of Information
MUN   Station Munich
NBBS   New British Broadcasting Station
OKW   *Oberkommando der Wehrmacht* [German Army High
            Command]
PODE   Station Podebrady
PRO   Public Record Office
PWE   Political Warfare Executive
RC   Radio Caledonia
RMVP   *Reichsministerium für Volksaufklärung und Propaganda*
            [German Propaganda Ministry]
RN   Radio National
RRG   *Reichsrundfunkgesellschaft* [German Broadcasting Company]
STUTT   Station Stuttgart
WC   Workers' Challenge
ZEE   Station Zeesen

Introduction

Few political operators in the modern world have had as high a regard for propaganda as the German National Socialists. Certainly the Nazis regarded themselves as unrivalled masters of the art of modern political propaganda, and this image was perpetuated by their friends and enemies before, during and long after the period in which they dominated the German and European political landscape. And when Britons of a certain age hear the word 'propaganda', the name which often comes to mind is 'Lord Haw-Haw', the English voice of wartime Germany, the laughable Nazi traitor, who supposedly kept everyone amused during the blackout with his ridiculous propaganda broadcasts from Germany. 'Lord Haw-Haw' of course was merely a gimicky nickname for German wireless broadcasts in English dreamt up by a tabloid journalist in 1939 to poke fun at the humourless Germans at a stage of the war when the two sides threw insults at one another but not much else. The nickname caught on, and one publicity-loving fascist exile from England, William Joyce, happily let it catch on to him. It was Joyce's good luck and ultimately his misfortune that almost by chance he was given the opportunity to display his particular talents for vituperation and his obsessive anti-Semitism on a world-wide stage in historical circumstances in which political propaganda, and especially radio propaganda, had assumed an extraordinarily heightened significance. The 'twenty years' crisis' had exploded into a European and then a global war of terrifying proportions and possibilities, a war in which it seemed for a time that the 'totalitarians' – the Nazis, the Fascists and the Soviets, with their machine-men armies and blaring propagandists, had the tide of history upon their side. These were the circumstances which lifted William Joyce from the margins of political fanaticism and obscurity in Britain, and transformed him into a world-wide propaganda celebrity whose fate was inexorably linked with the fate of regime which he served so assiduously.

And of course, in the end it was Joyce's fame which was his undoing. Captured by the British in 1945, and after a series of high-profile trials and unsuccessful appeals, he was hanged as a traitor in 1946, in spite of the fact that he wasn't British and never had been. No doubt the quite widespread and even guilty feeling in Britain that Joyce was hanged more for the sake of vengeance than for the sake of justice has contributed to the longevity of the myths which surround him. And it is at least arguable that Joyce and his one-time colleague John Amery, also executed for broadcasting from Germany, were scapegoats whose deaths performed a sort of catharsis for many Britons. Both men, and large numbers of the lesser known British individuals who worked with them, held political views which most people today rightly find reprehensible. Nevertheless, sixty or seventy years ago their views were widely held to a greater or lesser extent throughout Europe. So what *had* these men done to deserve execution, while others escaped whose guilt as traitors was much more real? What message had they broadcast over the ether from Germany at Britain, to what purpose, with what effect? What lessons can historians learn about Nazi Germany from the story of her anti-British wireless propaganda campaign? As important, what lessons can they learn about Britain and the British in the Second World War, a conflict which they continue to regard as their finest hour? These are the questions to be addressed here.

To my knowledge, this book represents the first monograph devoted exclusively to the analysis of the Nazis' radio war effort against the United Kingdom. The task is to present the propaganda in context, to determine the purpose or purposes which lay behind it, to identify the changing patterns, themes, styles and techniques over the whole period of the war, and to assess the impact upon the target audience and upon its morale. The issue of morale and its connection with the receptivity of the audience is crucial. For in a sense, propaganda operates like a gas introduced deliberately into a particular environment. But it is a gas which depends for its potency upon the presence of suitably reactive elements in the atmosphere, and in the weakness or absence of counteracting material. Otherwise, it is harmless and inert. In the end, the British failed to succumb to the stupefying effects of Nazi propaganda, and they traditionally congratulate themselves upon the national unity which immunised them against it. It will be argued here that this traditional view disguises a more complex, less appealing reality.

Organisation of
Nazi Wireless Propaganda for the UK

In the twenty years which elapsed between the first working system of wireless telegraphy, pioneered by Marconi in 1895, through the first sound transmissions (wireless telephony) by Reginald Fessenden in 1906, to the establishment in 1920 by Westinghouse of the first public broadcasting service, radio was transformed from a primitive system of point-to-point communication to a medium of mass communication. Alongside the development of mass literacy and mass circulation newspapers, and at least as important as its more glamorous rival the cinema, radio was a formative influence in the creation of 'mass society' in the industrialised and urbanising west. By the end of the 1920s, the decade in which for the first time the majority of Americans lived in towns or cities, nearly one half of American households contained a radio receiver. The appeal of radio for the American urban masses lay primarily in its ability to entertain, chiefly through the transmission of musical programmes. For the broadcasters, its appeal lay in its ability to sell, through the advertising interspersed between the musical and entertainment items.

In Britain, too, there was in the 1920s a remarkable growth in broadcasting technology, organisation and reception. In 1922, the Postmaster-General permitted the formation of a British Broadcasting Company, organised by the six major wireless manufacturers, to give regular programmes of entertainment from various stations. Initially there were only five stations, at London, Birmingham, Manchester, Newcastle and Cardiff, but gradually a nationwide network was built up. While in the United States the broadcasters engaged in ruthless and chaotic cut-throat competition, in Britain the Lloyd George coalition granted a monopoly of the ether to the BBC, the system to be funded by the wireless companies, plus half the receipts from a licence fee. There was even a suggestion from some of the newspapers that the proceedings of Parliament be broadcast, creating a 'wireless Hansard' for the benefit of electors, an early opportunity for political propagandising of which Parliament declined to avail itself. By the mid-1920s 'radio', as it was now being commonly called, had ceased to be the private realm of the technical faddist and was insinuating itself into the daily life of the mass of the population. In 1927, after its staunch support of the government in the General Strike, the BBC, under Sir John Reith, was granted a Royal Charter and elevated to the status of a Corporation, nominally independent of government, funded by the licence fee, but an institution tied firmly within the British constitution.

By the 1930s there was evidence that the widening availability of radio was altering the settled patterns of domestic life in Britain. In regional as well as national services, through news broadcasts and talks, 'serious' as well as popular music, features and variety shows, dramas and serials, radio listening was as much a part of daily life for the average family in interwar Britain as was television by the 1970s. The number of radio licences increased dramatically, from just over two million in 1926 to over nine million by 1938.[1] Thus, while in 1924 licences were held by only 10 per cent of British households, by 1930 30 per cent had a licence, 48 per cent by 1933 and 71 per cent by 1939.[2] This did mean that by the outbreak of war in 1939, some 13½ million people, the great majority of whom were from the working classes, did not have direct access at home to a wireless set. On the other hand, there were numerous opportunities for collective access to radio, even for the poorest sections of society, in public houses, in the homes of friends and family or through 'Group Listening' sponsored by the BBC, local education authorities and various charitable organisations.

In spite, however, of the great leaps forward in broadcasting and reception technology and of the greatly increased range, quality and variety of BBC programming, the Corporation had its critics, many of whom regarded Reith's self-proclaimed mission to raise educational and cultural standards as elitist, patronising and dull. Moreover, many in the Labour movement regarded the Corporation as avowedly reactionary, socially conservative and biased against Labour. As the number of licences increased, for many the BBC too often provided a dull fare, especially on Sundays, when programming was 'gloomily puritanical' and listeners in their millions tuned in to *Radio Luxemburg* and *Radio Normandie*, stations providing light music and variety turns. Thus in the 1930s was the habit established in Britain of listening in to foreign stations for diversion from the staid offerings of the BBC.

In Germany too, radio was a reasonably well-established mass medium prior to the Nazis' accession to power in 1933. Before that date, however, broadcasting in Germany was highly decentralised and politically neutral, controlled only loosely by the various *Länder*. Fifty-one per cent of the capital of the *Reichsrundfunkgesellschaft (RRG)*, the German equivalent of Britain's BBC, was owned by the *Reichspost*, while the remaining 49 per cent was owned by the nine regional broadcasting companies.[3] Moreover, the central authority had no say over programme content, a factor which caused considerable tension as Germany moved closer to authoritarian government in the early 1930s. One of the last acts of the von Papen administration in November 1932 had been to install a second Broadcasting Commissioner nominated by the Ministry of Interior, to undermine the programming autonomy of the regions, a move which met with fierce resistance from the *Länder*.

By the time of the Nazi takeover, however, radio was still a relatively young medium when compared with other media, and the Nazis found it considerably easier to take unified control of broadcasting than they would, for example, of the press. The nature of Hitler's rule through overlapping, competing and often mutually antipathetic state and party agencies could and did result in bitter struggles for mastery of particular organisations and institutions, the long battle which Goebbels fought and lost with Dietrich over control of the press being a case in point. His control over the domestic wireless system was always much more secure, and his instrument was his Propaganda Ministry.

The Ministry, which carried the grand title of *Reichsministerium für Volksaufklärung und Propaganda* (*RMVP*), was the first new ministry to be established after the Nazi takeover. Hitler's insistence, against Goebbels' better judgement, on the inclusion of the word 'propaganda' in the title, reflected the Führer's obsession with propaganda as a vital instrument in the seizure and consolidation of political power. As is well known, he had devoted two chapters of *Mein Kampf* to the subject, and while his theory of propaganda was hardly sophisticated – amounting really to no more than the endless repetition of simple, easily graspable ideas, until one's target (always the untutored masses) had come to accept them as gospel – he considered propaganda a deadly weapon in skilled hands. Hitler was equally convinced that propaganda could be as effective in international conflict, an idea which again was not original, but was part of a good deal of German pseudo-psychological and militaristic discourse in the interwar years. Something of a minor international sensation had been caused, for example, by the publication in 1931 of Ewald Banse's *Raum und Volk im Weltkriege*, a book which accurately forecast Nazi techniques of domestic and international psychological manipulation. Banse had written:

> Applied psychology as a weapon of war means propaganda directed towards influencing the mental attitude of the nations to a war . . . It is essential to attack the enemy nation in its weak spot (and what nation has not its weak spots?), to undermine, crush, break down its resistance, and convince it that it is being deceived, misled and brought to destruction by its own government, in order that it may lose confidence in the justice of its cause and that thus the opposition at home (and what nation is without one?) may raise its head and make trouble more successfully than before. The originally well-knit, solid, powerful fabric of the enemy nation must be gradually disintegrated, broken down, rotted, so that it falls to pieces like a fungus when one treads on it in a wood.[4]

Whether or not Hitler knew of Banse's work, his own views on the coming use of psychological warfare were strikingly similar. According to Hermann Rauschning, Hitler had said in 1933 that in a future war, psychological dislocation of the enemy through revolutionary propaganda would replace artillery preparation before an attack:

> The enemy must be demoralized and driven to passivity . . . Our strategy is to destroy the enemy from within, to conquer him through himself. Mental confusion, contradictions of feeling, indecision, panic – these are our weapons.[5]

When Hitler got around in June 1933 to providing a legislative foundation for the new ministry, its brief was to undertake all tasks of spiritual national indoctrination, of promotion for state, culture and economy, of public instruction about these tasks at home and abroad, and the administration of all facilities which served these purposes. As Michael Balfour has rightly pointed out, this was a typically elastic formulation, characteristic of the Third Reich, which could stretch and contract in scope, depending upon the political muscle of the man in charge. Goebbels certainly was determined on stretching it to its utmost, but, as will be seen, was not without opposition.[6]

As far as wireless was concerned, a Broadcasting Division was established within the *RMVP*, charged with the task of overseeing the work of the *RRG*, the entire stock of shares in which, by the summer of 1933, was owned by the Propaganda Ministry.[7] Control over German broadcasting had been centralised for Goebbels by Eugen Hadamovsky, departmental head of the Reich Propaganda Office of the Party (*Reichspropagandleitung der NSDAP*), and from 1933, effective head of the *RRG*. The management of the *RRG* was entrusted to a triumvirate of directors, responsible for programming, administration and technical matters, who operated through the General Managers (*Intendanten*) of the nine regional stations. Hadamovsky, as Chief Programme Director, was the key individual in the use of broadcasting as a political weapon in Nazi Germany. He was in 1933 still in his twenties.[8] The directors were controlled directly by the Broadcasting Division of the *RMVP*. The posts of Broadcasting Commissioners were abolished. Control over artistic creativity was supposedly exercised through the *Reichsrundfunkkammer* of the *Reichskulturkammer* (*RKK*), although this organisation too was abolished in October 1939. Its administrative functions were taken over by the *RRG*, while artistic staff were distributed throughout the other chambers of the *RKK*.[9]

Just as the Bolsheviks had expected that the wordless magic of the silent cinema would win the illiterate Russian masses over to socialism, the Nazis believed that the astonishing communicative power of wireless could help build their People's Community (*Volksgemeinschaft*) in Germany. In 1934 Hadamovsky had written:

> The men who are moulding the new German radio are fighters. They value radio as a key element in the political battle, and the vanguard of their *Weltanschauung.* For them, radio is the most modern, most powerful and most revolutionary weapon which we possess in the struggle against an old and perishing world, and in the struggle for the new Third Reich.[10]

But Hadamovsky was certain too of the power of radio as a means of international propaganda: 'We spell radio with three exclamation marks because we are possessed in it of a miraculous power – the strongest weapon ever given to the spirit – that opens hearts and does not stop at the borders of cities and does not turn back before closed doors; that jumps rivers, mountains, and seas; that is able to force peoples under the spell of one powerful spirit.'[11] For Goebbels, radio was 'the most modern and the most important instrument of mass influence that exists anywhere . . . With this instrument', he told the heads of German radio, 'you can make public opinion'.[12]

Even in peacetime though, the difficulties encountered by Goebbels in establishing a monopoly of information and propaganda production within Germany were mirrored in overseas propaganda. Especially following the appointment of von Ribbentrop as Foreign Minister in 1937, the operation was hampered by wrangles and petty struggles between the competing official and party agencies, including the *RMVP* itself, the Foreign Office (*Auswärtiges Amt (AA)*), Hess's Party organisation for Germans abroad, the *Volksdeutscher-rat*, and later the military High Command (*Oberkomando der Wehrmacht (OKW)*). That these agencies should be keen to establish control over international broadcasting is scarcely to be wondered at. As broadcasting had developed in Europe in the 1920s, domestic programming had inevitably been picked up by foreign listeners, and by the 1930s such listeners were deliberately targeted by cultural and political propagandists as the almost unlimited potential of this uniquely unstoppable, uncensorable medium became apparent. By 1939, over twenty-five nations had international services, and by the end of the Second World War, fifty-five nations were broadcasting internationally.[13]

Moreover, because of its unique properties, radio was bound to appeal to an aggressive nation like Nazi Germany, and in particular one whose leaders were obsessed with the manipulative power of political propaganda. German language broadcasts for overseas listeners actually pre-dated the Nazi takeover, as part of a service for German minorities abroad, run under the auspices of the *RRG*'s Home Service. In April 1933, however, short-wave services were begun in German and English, the latter, consisting mostly of news bulletins about Germany, being aimed primarily at the United States.[14] A Spanish service was begun in 1933 and a Portuguese one in 1937. The 1936 Berlin Olympics provided the additional incentive to upgrade Germany's broadcasting network and from fourteen hours a week in 1933 German foreign broadcasts rose to fifty-eight hours by 1939, by which time ten short-wave transmitters were in use operating on twenty-eight wavelengths, with a total strength of 300kW.[15]

However, Hitler had long since made plain that Britain was the key nation with which he would need to come to terms in his determination to restore Germany to her rightful position as a European and a world political power. From the days of his earliest political musings, he saw Britain as a potential ally against the French, and against the Jewish world-enemy, if only traditional British statesmanship could 'break the devastating Jewish influence'.[16] To the end, he clung to the hope that, in the absence of an alliance, he could persuade, cajole and threaten the British into staying out of his quarrels on the European mainland. It is in this light that one needs to consider the fact that, as Anglo-German tensions increased during 1938 and 1939, each country began regular medium-wave transmissions targeted at the other's populations. Both governments tried to convince opposing domestic audiences of the merits of their case, and to weaken the resolve of their opposite numbers to stick to their guns, as they circled each other warily in an atmosphere of growing suspicion and tension, particularly after the German annexation of Bohemia and Moravia in March 1939.

The BBC had begun a regular German service in September 1938, while regular medium-wave transmissions in English started from Hamburg on 22 March 1939.[17] In Germany, the build-up of an aggressive radio service aimed abroad did not progress entirely smoothly. Shortly after the beginning of the regular English service, Hitler agreed in May 1939 to a request from von Ribbentrop for the establishment of an *AA* Radio Division. Here was another attempt by von Ribbentrop to expand his empire into an area which Goebbels regarded as his bailiwick, an attempt which, after an unseemly row involving the ejection of *AA* officials from the *RRG* offices, was resolved for the time being by Hitler in Goebbels' favour.

Upon the outbreak of Anglo-German hostilities on 3 September, the tactics in the ether war shifted, although the strategic aim for both powers remained much the same: to conclude hostilities as soon as possible, but − naturally enough − on their own terms. The British were anxious to convince the German people, and through them the German government, that they had not wanted war, but now that it had been thrust upon Europe by the Nazis, the united British people were determined to see it through to final victory. The Germans, for their part, were anxious to convince the British people that they had not wanted war, but now that it had been thrust upon Europe by the British government and the Jews, the united German people were just as determined to see it through to final victory. For both sides, radio was to be a highly valued weapon, and no single event more clearly signals the Nazis' regard for the power of international radio propaganda than the ban imposed in Germany on 1 September 1939, on listening to foreign radio broadcasts, an offence punishable by penal servitude or imprisonment.[18] The penalty for the spreading of news emanating from foreign wireless broadcasts was death, and the justification given by the German government for these extraordinary measures explains in itself their determination to make vigorous use of radio against their enemies:

* In modern warfare, the belligerent does battle not only with armed force, but also with methods which can influence and wear down the minds of the people. One of these methods is radio.[19]

Moreover, in the absence of any really serious fighting between Britain and Germany, the importance accorded to the ether war significantly increased. By the end of the first month of hostilities, the *RRG*'s foreign language output had increased to 113 hours in fourteen languages per day.[20] By the end of 1939, transmissions in English were given daily from Hamburg on 331.9 metres, usually coupled with Bremen (395.8 metres) and Zeesen DJA (31.45 metres), carried along landlines from the Berlin headquarters of the *RRG*, the *Funkhaus*, in Berlin. Each English broadcast lasted for up to fifteen minutes, beginning at 10.15, 14.15, 17.15, 18.15, 20.15, 21.15, 22.15, 23.15 and 00.15. The extent each day was up to two and a quarter hours. The 10.15, 14.15, 17.15, 20.15 and 00.15 bulletins consisted of news items and quotations from supposedly neutral sources, supporting by their cumulative effect the main propaganda points which were developed in the 21.15 and 23.15 bulletins and the 22.15 talks.[21] In addition, a secret organisation code-named *Büro Concordia*, began in February 1940 a series of 'black' propaganda broadcasts aimed at the UK, with a number of stations purporting to represent disaffected Britons hostile to their nation's war against Germany. By January 1940, Germany was broadcasting news in twenty-two languages, as compared with the BBC's fourteen, while by 1943 transmissions were being made in fifty-three languages compared with the BBC's fifty-four.[22]

Control of the ever-expanding foreign services of the *RRG* was settled by Goebbels on Dr Adolf Raskin, formerly *Intendant* at Saarbrücken, and the mastermind of the successful radio campaign directed in 1935 at the Saar. Raskin was killed in an air crash in November 1940, and his successor, Dr Toni Winkelnkemper was, at thirty-five, another typically young and able Goebbels protégé. Subordinate to Winkelnkemper, was Walter Kamm, head of the short-wave services, who, following their establishment as a separate division in early 1941, became head of the European Services (DES). Kamm had personally interviewed the exiled British National Socialist William Joyce in mid-September 1939, and had agreed to give him a try as a newsreader.[23] Joyce's immediate superior was Eduard Roderich Dietze, a German born in Glasgow, who had joined the *RRG* as a reporter in 1932. In time Dietze became one of Germany's best radio journalists, becoming in 1933 the BBC's Berlin commentator, fulfilling, from 1936, the same function for NBC. In October 1939, he was prevailed upon by the *AA* to begin work at the England Section of the Wireless News Agency with a view to becoming Joint Editor, since, by his own account, 'there were complaints that the news service in English of *RRG* was making itself ridiculous and that it should be better edited'.[24] In May 1940, he succeeded Walter Dittmar as acting head of the English section and was thereafter responsible for all English language broadcasts to the UK. Dietze formally became editor-in-chief of the English services of the *RRG* in the spring of 1942. He remained in this post until the autumn of 1943 when he assumed the duties of *Landegruppen Leiter Nordwest*, controlling broadcasts directed to Britain, Ireland and Holland.

The process by which each day's propaganda lines or *Themen* were drawn up and disseminated to the writers and editors who actually produced the material, is a microcosm of the confused and arbitrary way in which the entire executive and administrative system of the Third Reich functioned. As assistant to Winkelnkemper, Dietze accompanied his superior to Goebbels' daily Ministerial Conference, a meeting which never operated as a forum for the exchange of views and ideas, but as one in which the Minister would sound off to his assembled functionaries on the issues of the day, arbitrarily doling out directives, criticism and occasionally praise of their efforts. Thereafter, Winkelnkemper would hold his own conference at the *Funkhaus*, attended by all section leaders and most editors and chief commentators (but not, interestingly enough, William Joyce), and an account of Goebbels' instructions would be given, normally by Dietze. Again though, the *AA* demanded its right to influence overseas propaganda policy, not only through the participation of its representative at the Goebbels conference and regular weekly liaison meetings with the *RMVP*, but also through the establishment of standing committees, responsible directly to von Ribbentrop. The England Committee, chaired by Dr Fritz Hesse, Radio Advisor to Ribbentrop, attempted to exercise control over policy for the UK, while Professor Reinhard Haferkorn, head of the English-language section of the Foreign Ministry's broadcasting department (*Rundfunkpolitische Abteilung*), and his subordinate Dr Friedrich Schöberth acted as liaison officers between the *AA* and the *RRG*, exercising, among other things, *AA* control over *Concordia*.[25] This proliferation of authorities and agencies, in the *RMVP*, the *AA* and the *RRG* itself, staffed by armies of self-appointed experts on propaganda, on broadcasting, on foreign policy and on each of the individual target countries, would inevitably mean confusion and a lack of co-ordination in strategy and tactics in propaganda policy.

So, while it was William Joyce who would become infamous in Britain, Ireland and the United States as 'Lord Haw-Haw', and true that he became in time the most senior and trusted of the English-language broadcasters – he was formally appointed 'Chief Commentator' in 1942 – Joyce was only a part of a fairly large organisation directing material in English to the UK and beyond. Moreover, it is important to appreciate the distance between the propagandists and those with real knowledge of military and even propaganda tactics and strategy. Joyce and his colleagues received their instructions via their immediate superiors in the *RRG*, who were themselves instructed on policy by officials from the *RMVP* and the *AA*. And while Goebbels might have liked to believe that his propaganda was 'scientific', the reality was that the material was often produced on an ad hoc and impromptu fashion, based on little more than guesswork about conditions in Britain and the jaundiced cynicism of German and British Nazis about the nature of British society. General themes and directives were issued from time to time by the various official and semi-official organisations with an interest in propaganda, but scripts for specific talks and features were also written by individual commentators and freelancers working on their own ideas. Scripts would then be submitted to the chief editor for clearance, amendment and, occasionally, rejection. Complete talks would from time to time be written up by *AA* staff on specific issues, which would normally be read by professional *RRG* broadcasters. Again, disputes over content, enflamed by personal and petty jealousies, were not uncommon. News material was produced by the *RRG*'s Wireless News Agency and then, from the spring of 1941, a centralised *Nachrichten und Informationszentrale* (*NIZ*), which had the unenviable task of gathering news from the armed services, the *AA*, and the various news agencies. This organisation too would have to cope daily with directives, orders and interference from Hans Fritzsche, chief domestic radio commetator, or from Goebbels' office or the *AA*, sometimes demanding the rescinding or cancellation of items issued under the direction of other, competitor agencies. It was assumed that news material obtained from *AA* or military sources had already been censored, although a clutch of military censors were on hand at the *Funkhaus* to whom material could be submitted at short notice. Political censorship was supposed to fall within the ambit of the Foreign Division of the *RMVP*, but in practice Winkelnkemper encouraged his staff to take responsibility for their own material.[26] So, in consequence of the influence of the number of competing agencies at play, the process by which Nazi overseas propaganda was produced was often less scientific than chaotic.

Moreover, while Haw-Haw enjoyed a reputation in Britain for the most detailed knowledge of the goings-on of the British people at war, the propagandists for the UK were actually quite badly informed about conditions there. Unlike their counterparts in the British Ministry of Information (MoI), the German propagandists were unable to rely upon an organisation like the BBC, which had a monopoly of monitoring enemy and neutral broadcasting services. Instead, valuable resources were wasted through the duplication of this essential task by the *RRG*, the *AA*, the *Reichspost*, the *OKW*, the *Luftwaffe*, and the *Sicherheitsdienst* (*SD*) of the *SS*. No monitoring service was devoted solely to determining conditions in the UK. Such material as was available was picked up from the most banal of sources, from the official news agency, the *Deutsche Nachrichten Büro* (*DNB*) and from Reuters from all countries. The British newspapers were received via Lisbon. There was no network of spies or Fifth Columnists in the UK.

Moreover, as Alexander George points out, Goebbels was not beyond distorting and withholding information even from his closest confidants and subordinates. He considered it important to manipulate the body of factual information available to them in an effort to direct their attitudes and morale in order to improve their performance as propagandists.[27] It is worth bearing in mind therefore not only the physical distance between the Nazi elite who were making tactical and strategic decisions on propaganda policy at the pinnacle of a chaotic organisation and the scriptwriters and broadcasters at the bottom, but also the information gulf which separated them. William Joyce never even met the man he described as 'my old chief', although on one occasion he did receive a signed box of cigars from the *Reichsminister*.[28]

It needs to be stressed too that the number and quality of English-language broadcasters available to the Germans was less than ideal. When Joyce received his first contract of employment with the *RRG* in September 1939, he joined a small group of Anglo-Germans under Eduard Dietze, and the ad hoc way in which the group was brought together suggests a degree of disorganisation and lack of planning. The most senior of the broadcasters for Britain was Norman Baillie-Stewart. Baillie-Stewart had already achieved notoriety in Britain as 'the officer in the Tower', having been sentenced by a court martial in 1933 to five years' imprisonment for selling military secrets to the Germans.[29] The combination in his story of espionage, sex and farce, as well as his incarceration in the Tower of London, made him for a time a celebrity in Britain, if something of a laughing-stock. He abandoned his homeland upon his release and made his way to Austria. Suspected there of pro-Nazi activities, he was expelled by the Austrian authorities shortly before the *Anschluss*. In September

1938, he applied for German nationality (an act which probably saved his life in 1946) and in April 1939 approached the Propaganda Ministry with a list of complaints about the poor quality of the *RRG*'s English-language broadcasts. The result was an invitation to him to test as an *RRG* announcer. He passed and began his broadcasting career in August 1939. Baillie-Stewart continued to work on broadcasts and translations until the end of 1939, when he joined the *AA*. Thereafter his work consisted of translation and occasional writing of talks for broadcast. Two years later he recommenced broadcasting work, using the *nom de guerre* of *Lancer*. Baillie-Stewart would later claim that much of the work he did was under duress, and that his broadcasts could not be compared with Joyce's: 'I did not make any hateful attacks against England and stuck to what I believed to be constructive criticism based on facts and British propaganda.'[30] Nevertheless, in January 1946, Baillie-Stewart was again in the dock, this time charged with high treason and offences against the Defence Regulations. He was then still aged only thirty-six years. The former charge was dropped when it became plain that he had abjured his Britain citizenship before the war. Even so, he received a sentence of five years' penal servitude on the latter charge.[31]

Baillie-Stewart had taken over as chief broadcaster from Wolff Mittler, a blond Polish-German Anglophile playboy, described by Baillie-Stewart as having 'both snobbish manners and an aristocratic voice . . . he sounded almost like a caricature of an Englishman with his tone of light mockery and the affectation of his accent. He ended all his announcements with a ridiculous, "Hearty Cheerios".'[32] Mittler's near flawless English he had learned from his mother, who had been born of German parents in Ireland. He took up the offer of a position with the *RRG* in 1937 working, among other tasks, on a programme promoting tourism in the Reich. Finding political work distasteful, he was relieved at the arrival of Baillie-Stewart and later William Joyce, and thereafter Mittler was to be heard mostly on the services for Asia and Africa.

The other main broadcasters in the early days were Dr Erich Hetzler, later head of the *Concordia* outfit, a British actor by the name of Jack Trevor, a seventeen-year-old youth called James Royston Clark, and his mother Mrs Frances Eckersley, ex-wife of one-time Chief Engineer of the BBC and Mosley supporter, Peter Eckersley. Mrs Eckersley was well-known to the British authorities before the war as 'a strongly pro-German fascist and a fanatical admirer of Hitler'.[33] She was also a friend of William Joyce and of Unity Mitford, and a former member of Arnold Leese's Imperial Fascist League. In July 1939, she left England for Germany to attend the Salzburg festival, and also to attend the Nazi party rally in Nuremberg, as she had done in 1937 and 1938. Mrs Eckersley remained in Germany on the outbreak of the war and, short of cash, took up an offer of work with the *RRG* on 15 December 1939. From December 1939 to October 1941 she worked as a daily announcer, the greater part of the programmes she announced being musical items, the news in English and talks in English. 'All were propaganda', she later said, 'directed against England, and some of the commentaries were ghastly and frightful in their subject matters'.[34] From October 1941 until January 1943, Mrs Eckersley was employed in a variety of minor administrative capacities, although she also broadcast as '*Jeanette*' in a bi-monthly programme of playlets, called *Women to Women*. This little series was written by a former British actress, married to an Austrian and known as *Ann Thomas*, but whose real name was Jeanne Lange. In October 1945, Dorothy Eckersley was found guilty of assisting the enemy by broadcasting and was sentenced to twelve months' imprisonment.[35]

Dorothy Eckersley's son, James Clark, had been sent by his mother in July 1939 to Germany to continue his education at school at Berlin-Tegel. He was with his mother in Berlin in September 1939 when war broke out, and would later admit to having gained 'a very favourable impression of Germany under Nazi rule'.[36] Clark was allowed to continue to attend school until November 1939, at which point, at the suggestion of friends in Berlin, namely Dr Erica Schirmer of the *AA* and Herr Eisenbrown of the *RRG*, he took up employment at the *RRG* a few days after his mother. After interviews with Dr Harald Diettrich and *Sendleiter* Hetzler he was engaged as a newsreader at a salary of RM100 per week, replacing Baillie-Stewart.[37] Very shortly thereafter, on 31 December, Clark himself was replaced by Jack Trevor. In mid-February 1940, he was directed to report to Kamm at the Villa *Concordia* and was there given a voice test in the presence of Kamm and Hetzler. At the end, he was threatened by Kamm to the effect that, if he talked about what he had seen at *Concordia*, he should be executed. Shortly afterwards Clark was directed again to see Diettrich at the *Rundfunk* and was re-employed as a newsreader. He continued work thereafter until July 1942, engaged on the night transmissions in news reading, including occasional commentaries. He never wrote his own scripts, but merely read those presented to him. He would later claim that he remained in a somewhat 'hysterical state of mind' until the summer of 1940, when German air raids on London and other cities induced in him a certain pride in being an Englishman, 'although in my circumstances I was unable to say so'. Determined with his mother to sever their connections with the *RRG*, Clark exaggerated and feigned illness and nervous exhaustion, his mother and sympathetic Germans pleading his case to the authorities. His last broadcast was on 19 July 1942, Dr Richard Kupsch by then being also available to take over some of his duties. Clark and Mrs Eckersley were arrested at Christmas 1944, being taken together to the prison of the *Polizeipradisium*, and he thereafter was taken to Ilag XVIII at Spittal in Austria, where he remained until the liberation. At his trial in December 1945, when along with his mother Clark was charged with having aided the enemy by broadcasting propaganda, his judge took James Clark at his word, that he had been hypnotised when a callow youth by the trappings and tricks of Nazi propaganda. He was bound over for two years.[38]

Jack Trevor's real name was Anthony Cedric Sebastian Steane, a British actor who had made a reasonable living for himself playing stereotypical British upper-class figures in the German film industry of the interwar period. Interned in Germany at the outbreak of war Steane was allowed to leave his camp in January 1940, on the recommendation of a German actor, to begin a new career in broadcasting propaganda to Britain. He also featured in minor roles in a number of anti-British propaganda films, including Max W. Kimmich's 1941 piece *Mein Leben für Irland*, and Hans Steinhoff's anti-British epic, *Ohm Krüger*. He received a sentence of three years' imprisonment at the end of his trial at the Old Bailey in January 1947, of which in the end he served only three months.[39]

Margaret Bothamley was a long-term acquaintance of Dorothy Eckersley and was the individual who had first interested her in Nazi ideology. A Londoner, Bothamley was at one stage married to a German officer and her fanatical anti-communism took her to Germany in 1937.[40] She broadcast on the *Bremen Mirror* programme as '*The Lady in the Mirror*'. At the end of her trial in March 1946, for having assisted the enemy by broadcasting, Bothamley was sentenced to twelve months' imprisonment. She was described by one of her former colleagues as 'a rather old lady . . . quite helpless'.[41]

Best known of the British women who worked on the German wireless was William Joyce's wife, Margaret. Mrs Joyce had been an active member of the BUF in Carlyle in the 1930s and was subsequently Assistant Treasurer of her husband's National Socialist League. Vehemently sharing his political opinions, she left Britain with him for Germany in August 1939 and began her own broadcasting career early in 1940, although it was not until 9 December 1942 that she was announced using her own name.[42] Until May 1942, she gave weekly talks to women, dealing mainly with economic problems, contrasting the British system unfavourably with that of Germany. Thereafter she participated in the *Back Numbers* feature, which was aimed at demonstrating British propaganda lies by the use of selective quotation from the British press. No action was taken by the British authorities against Margaret Joyce, on the dubious grounds that at the time of her first broadcast she was a German rather than a British subject.[43] There was, however, anxiety that she should become the focus of a nascent fascist martyrology surrounding the Joyce name, and Mrs Joyce was removed in March 1946 to Germany.[44] Many years later she returned to England and died in London in 1972.[45]

It seems clear now that the notoriety and opprobrium attracted in Britain by her husband William was a major factor in the determination of the postwar Labour government to hang him for treason. Like his colleagues, William Joyce began his broadcasting career in anonymity, but in time he came to personify 'Lord Haw-Haw', the catch-all nickname invented by the British press which was applied willy-nilly by members of the public to any English voice heard on the Axis wireless.[46] The upper-crust accents heard in Britain in the first days of the war were probably those of Mittler, Baillie-Stewart and Eduard Dietze, and indeed in February 1940 the BBC noted that 'Lord Haw-Haw of the early war days' was most probably a German, vaguely believed by some people to be Dietze, but who now only rarely appeared. The BBC described the main speaker as

the one who spoke in the early days of the war from Podebrady. This man's presentations dominate the field: he has a firm grip on his audience with his sardonic almost mephistophelean voice. A slight Scottish accent has been observed in it. In order to simplify identification, our monitors have christened him *Sinister Sam*, owing to the sinister fascination which he breathes. Humour, it may be mentioned, is lacking in the range of his histrionic resources. Other announcers have less marked traits. They are Germans whose command of English is sometimes rather limited. No variation, however, occurs in the scripts; the standard remains on a high level.[47]

It seems likely that the BBC's 'Lord Haw-Haw of the early war days' was Wolf Mittler, and 'Sinister Sam' was Baillie-Stewart. Joyce, throughout 1939 very much still a background figure, did not even warrant a mention. As time went on though, and Joyce played an increasingly important role in reading news scripts and writing talks, the 'Haw-Haw' persona came to be applied exclusively to him. The Germans indeed came to capitalise on the publicity generated in Britain about Haw-Haw, and began announcing Joyce's talks as by 'William Joyce, otherwise known as Lord Haw-Haw'.

William Joyce was born in New York of Irish Catholic parents in 1906, his father having taken US citizenship some years earlier. In 1909 the family returned to Ireland, settling in Galway. Despite their Catholic background, the Joyce family were renowned locally as staunch supporters of the British in Ireland, the boy William claiming later to have spied on his neighbours for the Black and Tans. After partition the family took flight and settled in England. William took a first-class honours degree in English from Birkbeck College, having been thrown out of the army in which he had enlisted while under age. After graduating, he pursued a career as a freelance tutor.

Joyce, however, was involved from his early youth in radical right-wing politics. In 1923, he joined the extremist group, the British Fascisti, moving in 1928 to the Conservative Party, and then in 1933 to Oswald Mosley's British Union of Fascists, rising through the ranks to become Mosley's Director of Propaganda and finally Deputy Leader. Joyce's fanaticism, his gift for public speaking and his personal charisma rapidly established him as one of the figures in the movement best-known to the British public. His caustic performances at public meetings and the violence which often accompanied them kept his name regularly in the public prints.[48] Joyce became disillusioned with Mosley, since to his way of thinking, his erstwhile leader was insufficiently anti-Semitic. Joyce himself was a hopeless anti-Semite, who held the Jews responsible for everything from the rise of Bolshevism and the collapse of the capitalist economies in the interwar period to his own personal disfigurement. Certainly, his face bore vivid testimony to the violent nature of extremist politics in interwar Britain, sporting a savage razor scar from below his right ear to the corner of his mouth, inflicted, he claimed, by a 'Jewish-Bolshevik' in the attempt to cut his throat after a Conservative Party meeting at Lambeth Baths in 1924. Mosley dismissed him from the BUF in 1937, whereupon he founded his own National Socialist League, a blatantly pro-Nazi and anti-Semitic organisation which attracted only a small number of cranks and fanatics. As Britain and Germany moved closer to war in August 1939, Joyce and his wife fled to Berlin. 'England', he wrote later, 'was going to war. I felt that if, for perfect reasons of conscience, I could not fight for her, I must give her up for ever . . . in this great conflict, I wanted to play a clear and definite part.'[49] What that part was to be, however, he was not at all clear, and it was only after casting around rather aimlessly in Berlin for several days that Joyce managed to land himself a job as a newsreader in the English section of the *RRG*. His first broadcast was the reading of a news bulletin on 9 September, and a week later, on 18 September, he was given a contract.[50] Gradually, Joyce's superior intellect, his skills as writer and broadcaster, and above all his ferocious appetite for hard work shone through, and in time he established himself as the main broadcaster, writer and commentator on the German English service – the 'kingpin of the whole show' as one of his subordinates rightly called him.[51]

It is not necessary here to rehearse the well-known details of Joyce's capture, trial for treason, his two unsuccessful appeals and his execution. Suffice it to say that no trouble was spared by the British authorities in their determination to execute him. The prosecution case was presented by no less a character than Sir William Hartley Shawcross, the newly appointed Attorney-General and chief prosecutor for the United Kingdom at the trial of major war criminals at Nuremberg. At one point, when it seemed that Joyce might escape the vengeance of British justice because of his US citizenship, the authorities seriously considered handing him over the Americans for trial, until it became clear that as a naturalised German he owed no allegiance to the US government upon the outbreak of the German-American war in 1941.[52] It was then decided to proceed with a charge of treason on three counts, the third of which was so worded that it was only necessary to prove that Joyce had broadcast from Germany, 'while owing allegiance to the King', that is while in possession of a British passport, even though he was not entitled to such a passport and had actually obtained it fraudulently.[53] It being accepted by the judge at Joyce's trial in September 1945, in a ruling subsequently upheld at appeal, that he did indeed owe allegiance, Joyce was doomed, since he made no effort to deny that he had indeed broadcast, and had done so willingly.[54] He was hanged in Wandsworth Prison on 3 January 1946, when he was aged thirty-nine years. Joyce was described, probably accurately, by one of the smaller fry who worked with him as 'a clever man, in fact probably a genius, who worked for the Germans actuated solely by political convictions. A fanatic who saw no wrong in the Nazi system though it was before his eyes.'[55]

The other celebrity broadcaster on the Nazi wireless, if only by familial connection, was John Amery, dissolute son of Leopold Amery MP. Amery senior held high office in Britain from May 1940 as Secretary of State for India, having previously been the most outspoken critic of the Chamberlain government from the Conservative backbenches. To have the eldest son of such a prominent British politician as a member of their broadcasting team, should for the Nazis have been quite a propaganda coup, in spite of the now-forgotten fact that Leo Amery had been contemptuously dismissed in a German broadcast in May 1940 as a 'half-Jew'.[56] John Amery had inherited his father's imperialist views, but little of his learning or of his humanity. Always a wayward and troublesome child, Amery grew into a convinced fascist whose personal judgement was as skewed as his political. He left England in 1935, never to return until after the end of the war. He was in Spain during the Civil War, and spent time in Abyssinia. He went to Austria in 1938 to witness the *Anschluss* and accompanied the German Panzers to Vienna. In 1939, he hurried to Prague to witness the entry there of the German Army. Upon the outbreak of war, Amery was living in France and made no attempt to make his way back to England. He had no difficulties with the authorities until November 1941, at which time he was arrested.[57] Released early in 1942, he began his career as an Axis propagandist with a letter in the newspaper *Petit Dauphinois*, in which he protested against RAF bombing raids; he also wrote a series of articles for the *Éclaireur de Nice*. When he heard of the Anglo-American landings in Algiers and Morocco, 'he decided to approach the Wilhelmstrasse with a request to be permitted to address his compatriots at home over the German wireless'.[58]

Convinced he could do a better job than Joyce in bringing the British people to their senses about the evils of Jewish-Bolshevism, Amery was allowed to broadcast to Britain several times in late 1942, and again in 1944. He was, however, a poor broadcaster, and is likely to have caused little grief to anyone but his parents.[59] Amery also involved himself in abortive attempts to form a 'Legion of St George' of British anti-Bolsheviks, as well as acting as a roving propagandist throughout occupied Europe for both Germany and Italy. He pleaded guilty to a charge of high treason on 28 November 1945 and was hanged on 19 December at the age of thirty-three years.[60]

The English novelist, P. G. Wodehouse could, one supposes, be described as a third 'celebrity broadcaster', since following his release from German internment in June 1941 he made a total of five broadcasts to the United States on the German wireless, the series being repeated for British listeners in August. These broadcasts amounted to no more than humorous accounts of his time in internment, the propaganda impact being limited to the fact that Wodehouse, although English, was evidently being treated with humanity by his German captors. The Director of Public Prosecutions, Theobald Mathew, wrote of Wodehouse, 'whatever view one may take of the antics of this vain and silly man, I am satisfied that, on the present material, there is no evidence upon which a prosecution can be justified.' Nevertheless, given the treatment meted out to some other broadcasters and even more minor figures, Wodehouse was lucky to escape prosecution, perhaps because he wisely made his home in New York and never returned to the UK. In 1975, he was awarded a knighthood, only months before his death.[61]

A number of lesser known British broadcasters on the overt or 'white' propaganda stations are also worth remarking upon, if only because of the disparity between their treatment after the war and the severe penalties applied to Joyce and Amery. For some of these smaller-fry only sketchy details are available. Little is known, for example, of Lewis Barrington Payne ('Barry') Jones. Originally from Birmingham Jones was a Nazi sympathiser who left the UK for Germany in May 1939, taking up employment as a teacher of English at the Berlitz School in Cologne. He was not interned, and began his broadcasting career on the English language services for Europe sometime in 1940.[62] Fuller details are available on Edward Salvin Bowlby, who featured regularly on the Nazi wireless in the latter stages of the war, and whose fate is remarkable when contrasted with that of William Joyce. Edward Bowlby was born in Ireland in 1911 and came to England in 1922, remaining there until April 1939. He was a member of the British Union of Fascists and had acquired at some stage a criminal record. On the outbreak of war, Bowlby was living in Budapest, left there in 1941 to go to Turkey, but was arrested by the Germans at Belgrade and interned at Tost in Silesia. During his internment he claimed Irish nationality, and was indeed visited by the Irish Consul. Bowlby's intense anti-Jewish feelings were brought to the attention of the German authorities, and in October 1943 he was released and took up residence in Berlin. He undertook there for a time translation work for the *Sprachendienst* in the *AA*, but in January 1944 was interviewed by none other than Norman Baillie-Stewart, who recommended him for a position in the broadcasting services.[63] In March 1944, he began his broadcasting career over the German radio, using his own name in regular broadcasts to the British public and the armed services, broadcasts in which his obsession with Jews – he was described by Dietze as 'violently and sincerely anti-Jewish' – was given its full head. Following his capture there was a good deal of debate in British official circles as to whether it was worth acting against Bowlby, considering in particular the embarrassment likely to arise in prosecuting for treason a man with a claim to Eire citizenship. Like Joyce, however, Bowlby had travelled on a British passport, which – unlike Joyce – he had acquired quite legally, on 17 April 1939. Like Joyce therefore, Bowlby had placed himself under the protection of the crown, which, as was made clear in the Joyce case, demanded allegiance in return. Moreover, although Bowlby applied for an Irish passport in Berlin in January 1944, the application was refused. He then applied for registration as an Irish citizen to the Eire Minister for Justice. This application was also turned down in August 1945. On the face of it, therefore, Edward Bowlby had a much more valid case to answer as a traitor than Joyce ever did. Significantly, though, the case for a prosecution of Bowlby was regarded as less compelling than for either Joyce or Amery, since, as was one official noted, Bowlby was 'scarcely a public figure like Haw-Haw'.[64] In February 1946, the DPP decided that Bowlby should be permitted to go to Eire.[65]

Ralph Powell, a nephew of Lord Baden-Powell, was born in London in 1910. In 1938 he married a German woman and became a teacher at the Berlitz School in Haarlem, Holland, where he remained until the German occupation in 1940. Shortly afterwards he was interned by the Germans in Ilag VIII but was released in August 1941 on condition that he co-operate with the authorities. For about ten months he worked as a translator in the *Sprachen-*

dienst of the *AA*, and later, from May 1942 until April 1945, as a regular broadcaster for the German European Service. Powell himself never wrote any of the scripts which he read, but his voice was to be heard regularly from Luxembourg and Calais, on, for instance, the *Matters of Moment* broadcasts, as well as on the regular news bulletins. Powell later claimed in his defence that he was forced to work for the Germans by threats of reprisals against his wife's family, although MI5 took a sceptical view of his claim. In the opinion of that organisation, Powell seemed to be nothing other than a good worker from the German point of view, and one whose talks 'are perhaps less outspoken than those usually given by William Joyce but the difference is simply one of degree.'[66] Powell, however, seems to have been fortunate in that the prosecuting authorities took at face value the Germans' assessment of him that he was a weak, non-political character, much influenced by his domineering wife, whose 'submission to pressure as an alternative to internment, however reprehensible, is not difficult to understand.'[67] The DPP in the end decided not to take proceedings against Powell.

Equally fortunate was John Alexander Ward. Ward, a British subject born in Birmingham in 1885, had resided in Germany continuously since 1921, where he worked as a translator. On the outbreak of war in 1939, he was left at liberty but obliged to report twice a week to the police, until he was interned in July 1940. From then until June 1943 he remained in civilian internment camps, where he was regarded as pro-Nazi. During the summer of 1943, Ward was released, seemingly on account of his pro-German sympathies, and from that point until March 1945, he was employed in various sections of the German broadcasting services, including *Interradio* (an *AA* broadcasting outfit), the German European Service and the German Overseas Service. Despite his long residence in Germany, and the fact that he seemed to have become German in outlook, Ward had never made any attempt to take up German nationality, and indeed applied in 1945 to return to the UK with his wife and child. During his time at *Interradio*, that is until July 1944, Ward had worked almost exclusively on the entertainment side of *Radio Metropole*, a station run by Dr Harald Diettrich, claiming to be neutral, but aimed at propagandising Allied troops and civilians, and actually based at Semlin, Croatia. The station, which was first monitored by the BBC in December 1941 under the name *Teleradio*, specialised in news bulletins, commentaries, political and other sketches, and light musical entertainment presented in English, French, Polish and Persian.[68] However, while Ward was with the European and Overseas Services, his work was of a purely propagandistic nature. From December 1944, Ward also broadcast once a week under the name of '*Private Donald Hodgson*', late of the 3rd Gloucestershire Regiment, on the African programme of the *Übersee-sender*. The talks, which Ward wrote as well as delivered, consisted of defeatist, anti-Semitic and anti-Russian diatribes, at which time he was receiving from the Germans a monthly salary of RM600.[69] No action was taken by the British authorities against Ward.

Another British subject employed on *Radio Metropole* was Baer Joseph

Kospoth, born out of wedlock at Weymouth in 1881 of a American father and a Polish mother. Educated in America, he spent most of his working life in Europe, employed by one or other American newspaper. During the Great War, Kospoth had been in Germany, and to avoid internment as an enemy alien, had claimed German citizenship on account of his mother's nationality. He was excused service with the German armed forces on health grounds, made his way to Geneva, where, on production of his British birth certificate, he was issued with a British passport and secured employment with the Military Intelligence office there. The card about him in the department concerned was later found to bear the remark, 'bad man'. He resumed a journalistic career in the interwar period and was in Paris when the Germans arrived. Interned as a British subject, Kospoth claimed again to be German, was released and with the assistance of an Irishman named James Blair was given employment with *Radio Metropole*. He worked first on the French section, playing, he claimed, in non-political sketches, and afterwards as a scriptwriter and news broadcaster. Kospoth read the news in English about six times a week, from July 1943 until February 1945, for a monthly salary of RM600. He would later claim that he knew that the object of the English broadcasts in which he was involved was 'to undermine the morale of Allied troops, but I did not think they were calculated to achieve this purpose'.[70] At the end of the war, Kospoth decided again that he was British, managed somehow to make his way to the UK and secured employment once more, this time in Fleet Street, with the *Chicago Tribune*. Major C.M. Hughes of MI5 described Baer Kospoth as 'a renegade with no loyalty to anyone but himself [who] hastens to go wherever he can find an easy life'.[71] The DPP decided, however, to take no action against him.

Suzanne Louise Provost-Booth was born in the French Embassy in London in 1890, the daughter of a French diplomat. Although technically British – she acquired British citizenship through marriage into the gin dynasty – she was to all intents and purposes French, living continuously in France after the dissolution of her marriage in 1924. Her daughter Claudine was married to a brother-in-law of R. A. Butler. Provost-Booth was employed by the Gestapo as an agent in Paris throughout the time of the German occupation, and retreated with the Germans to Berlin in 1944, whereupon she began her career as a broadcasting propagandist, masquerading as the genteel Englishwoman, '*Mrs Evans*'.[72] She later described herself as

> quite harmless of course . . . I used to read the Japanese news in English every afternoon. Then I took part in dear Margaret Bothamley's sketches – poor dear Margaret, such a dear, but a silly old thing, quite harmless, too . . . I had to say in this sketch, "I do hate Adolf Hitler, my dear', and Margaret would explain how good Hitler was, and then I'd say, 'Now I'm beginning to understand. I think England should side with Adolf Hitler.' That's all.[73]

The long-term employment of individuals like Margaret Bothamley and Suzanne Provost-Booth was indicative of one of the most serious problems which afflicted the English service of the *RRG*, namely, the lack of enough able and willing native-born English speakers to write for and broadcast on the increasing number of transmissions. The situation was aggravated from February 1940 by the launch of the *Concordia* 'freedom' stations. Not only was William Joyce employed as chief writer for the stations, but also the pretended network of clandestine broadcasters demanded a cast of character actors to play the parts. Germans were used on the 'white' stations in some numbers, but could not of course appear on stations which were supposedly based in the UK. For the same reason, speakers could not be heard on the *Concordia* stations whose voices might be familiar to listeners to the official stations. Understaffed as they already were with competent English speakers, the Nazis had to recruit broadcasters and scriptwriters from among the small community of Britons who found themselves in Germany upon the outbreak of war, and from among those British prisoners of war who were willing to co-operate in return for their freedom. The difficulties experienced by the Germans though, and the types of individuals on whom they had to rely, are amply illustrated in the short biographical details of some of the broadcasters given below.

Once again, it is noteworthy that the *RMVP* did not have exclusive control over *Concordia*, but had to share it with the *AA*. Indeed, the head of the unit, Dr Erich Hetzler, had been transferred from the English Department of Ribbentrop's private office. Hetzler was a notoriously hard taskmaster who seems to have been feared and hated in equal measure by the renegade Britishers who ended up in his employ.[74] He was assisted at *Concordia* by Walter Hohman, Dr Joachim Schwalbe and Heinz Thorlichen, reporting directly to Winkelnkemper but liaising closely with the *AA*.[75]

The establishment of secret stations aimed at Britain and France had been suggested at Goebbels' daily conference as early as 30 October 1939.[76] The first and most important secret station for Britain was the *New British Broadcasting Station* (NBBS), known also as *Büro N*, which first appeared on 25 February 1940 and continued almost daily until 9 April 1945. Its original wavelength was 50.63m (which was outside the range of most domestic British receivers) but it later also used 16.9m and 25.08m, which in June 1941 were altered to 25.08m, 30.77m and 41.07m. Later still 25.08m was changed to 47.83m. These later wavelengths were capable of reception on ordinary shortwave domestic sets. The quality of reception in Britain was variable, suffering from the beginning from interference caused by Soviet stations operating on the same frequency. At the time of the station's very first broadcast, however, intelligibility was described as 'nearly a hundred per cent'.[77] The number of daily transmissions varied, but there were initially four per day, at 20.30, 21.30, 22.30 and 23.30 (on Sundays at 17.30, 20.30, 21.30 and 22.20); all broadcast times were altered when Double British Summer Time was in force in the UK. Broadcasts were introduced by 'Loch Lomond' or 'Annie Laurie' and sometimes ended with a playing of the national anthem.[78] The NBBS presented itself as the focal point for a group of patriotic dissidents, horrified at the disastrous course of action into which the government had dragged the British people by becoming involved in war with Germany. The message was not dissimilar to that propagated before the war by Mosley's British Union of Fascists, although no link was claimed with that organisation. Broadcasts consisted of an *Uncensored News Review*, and *Between Ourselves* talks for the station's 'collaborators'. As one senior official of the BBC would later put it: 'The activities of this station caused considerable concern to the authorities in this country and questions about it were asked and answered in Parliament.' The same official also described the NBBS talks as 'rather clever broadcasts to begin with and rather above the average . . . their best effort really'.[79]

The original speaker and scriptwriter on the NBBS was Kenneth Vincent Lander, an Englishman who had lived and worked in Germany as a teacher of English since 1933. He there became attracted to National Socialism, and after a short visit to Britain in August 1939, decided to return to Germany despite the imminence of war with a view to obtaining German naturalisation. His application was refused in January 1940. Lander was left unmolested when war broke out, but in February 1940 he was contacted by *RRG* staff at his school in Bieberstein and invited to Berlin, where he was interviewed by a number of unidentified individuals at the *Rundfunkhaus*. His interviewers told him that they were planning a secret radio transmitter in Berlin, the idea of which was that it should appear to the listeners that it was coming from England. They wanted, they said, to change the attitude of the English people and thus avoid a clash of arms between Britain and Germany. He agreed to work for them upon that basis. Lander's comments on the construction of talks are informative:

> The material which I broadcast consisted partly of notes from the German News Service which I was given to construct a small talk from in criticism, from a British point of view, of the British Government's policy, the idea being that they were not acting in British interests, and speeches already prepared which I was given to broadcast. I was told by Hetzler that some of these were by Joyce . . . Somewhere about the end of May 1940 Hetzler gave me the job of composing my own news service from the German News Agency. The reason was, so Hetzler said, to get news into England which he thought might be censored in England, although the greater part of my work lay in transmitting already completed speeches by others.[80]

Lander seems to have been quickly overshadowed on the NBBS by Leonard Banning (see below) and he left *Concordia* under a cloud in July 1940, whereupon he was interned, not because he was politically unreliable, but as he was a *Geheimnisträger* (bearer of state secrets). He was released in March 1943 and allowed to return to his school, after both his reapplication for naturalisation and an application to join the German army were refused. He himself, however, refused in May 1944 an approach to join the British Free Corps, again apparently without penalty, and his treatment by the Germans throughout the war was described by MI5 as 'exceptional . . . he appears to have been regarded as politically reliable . . . and to have been placed where the

Germans thought him most useful'.[81] No charge, however, was brought against Kenneth Lander by the British authorities after the war.[82]

The *Between Ourselves* talks were written and spoken by Leonard Banning, who operated under the aliases '*John Brown*' or '*William Brown*'. A language teacher at Dusseldorf, Banning was a former BUF member and one-time Conservative Party organiser. Allowed to live openly and freely as a civilian in Berlin, Banning was described by one of his erstwhile colleagues as the 'driving force' behind the NBBS.[83] He himself would later claim that he had worked for *Concordia* on the strength of a promise from Hetzler that no-one should put ideas into his head as to what he should say. Gradually, however, subtle pressure was put upon him by Hetzler who bullied and argued with him.[84] Towards the end of his career with *Concordia*, Banning appeared to one of his colleagues as 'disillusioned, in fear of his life, half mad and wasted away.'[85] At his trial for offences against the Defence Regulations in January 1946, Banning was found guilty on five of seven counts of assisting the enemy. Mr Justice Oliver told him, 'I am satisfied, while you did not desire to betray your country, you were so weak and so strongly determined to look after yourself, that you sold yourself to do this disgraceful thing.' He then sentenced Banning to ten years' penal servitude.[86]

Banning was joined at the NBBS by Kenneth James Gilbert at the end of 1940. Gilbert had travelled from England to Jersey in May 1940 ostensibly to work on the harvest, but in truth, as a professed pacifist, to escape military service or internment under Defence Regulation 18b. He registered as a conscientious objector in December 1939, and was apparently well-known to the police in Kent as 'outspoken in his Fascist sympathies', and to the police in Devon as a man of 'violent disposition' and a heavy drinker.[87] After the occupation of the island by the Germans, Gilbert approached a German interpreter and offered to do anything he could 'to help bring about peace'. He accepted an offer to go to Germany and arrived in Berlin in December 1940, where after interviews at the *RMVP* and the *RRG* with, amongst others, William Joyce, he began work on the NBBS using the alias '*Kenneth James*'. Gilbert was sent to a labour camp for five months early in 1943, following his attempted resignation from *Concordia* for the more congenial surroundings of *Interradio*. Along with Banning, he had been involved in a punch-up with a number of SS guards in October of the previous year, an episode now used as the pretext for his incarceration. He was released only when he agreed to return to *Concordia*, and it seems that his battered and sickly appearance was used as an unsubtle warning to his colleagues to remain in line. A colleague described him as 'a broken man', adding, 'we had all worked under the shadow of the threat of the concentration camp but now seeing James, everyone was terrified.'[88] Gilbert described his work for the NBBS as the broadcasting of news items and of articles written by Joyce, and he claimed to have been the chief writer of an item called *Last Words*. In addition, he wrote scripts about three times a week for the *Workers' Challenge* station, and also in 1942, 'entertainment' scripts for the *Interradio* organisation. For his work for the NBBS and *Workers' Challenge*, Gilbert received RM600 a month.[89] At his trial in September 1946, he was sentenced to nine months' imprisonment.[90] Like Gilbert, Douglas George Kene Johnston had travelled from England to Jersey early in the war. He too was a self-proclaimed conscientious objector and was interned by the Germans upon their occupation of the island. In 1943 he volunteered to work for Germany, arriving in Berlin in August 1943, whereupon he began broadcasting work on the NBBS. Johnston it seems was later sent to a concentration camp for some sexual offence.[91]

Unlike Gilbert or Johnston, Pearl Joyce Vardon was a native of Jersey, having been born there in 1915. Following the occupation, she formed a liaison with a German officer, and in August 1941 she volunteered to act as interpreter for a German building firm operating on the island. At the end of 1943, Vardon decided to go to Germany, so that even if Germany lost the war, she should not be separated from her friend. She accepted the offer for her passage to be arranged on condition that she agreed to work as an announcer on the German radio. She went via Paris and Stuttgart to the DES station at Luxembourg, where she was employed as an announcer of musical programmes and a speaker on *For the Forces and their Kin*, which consisted of readings of letters by British prisoners of war to friends and relatives in Britain. She also took part in the *Matters of Moment* programme with Margaret Bothamley. Vardon seemed to have been limited in her work only by her lack of competence. She was described by various of her German colleagues as 'very pro-Nazi' and 'a very fanatical Nazi', or as a woman who 'simply hated all things English and loved all things German and everything to do with Germany'. At the Central Criminal Court in February 1946, Pearl Joyce Vardon pleaded guilty to six counts of assisting the enemy by broadcasting propaganda, and received a sentence of nine months' imprisonment.

There also worked at the NBBS between 1943 and 1945 Rifleman Ronald Spillman of the King's Royal Rifle Corps, who had been captured at Crete in June 1941, and had begun his captivity by currying favour with his captors by spying on his fellow prisoners. He later claimed that he was recruited into broadcasting in February 1943 by *Sonderführer* Schlegl of the *Abwehr*, who had convinced him that continued conflict between Britain and Germany was immoral. In April he began work at *Concordia* as an assistant to Banning on the NBBS. His particular job was as reader of the *Uncensored News Review*, for which he would write about four news items each day during the two years he worked at the station. Hetzler, said Spillman, 'used to have a conference with the Germans and then he would see us and give us the points of our talks. All our talks were checked and altered by Hetzler before they were read. After about six weeks I realised that the station was working for peace but for a peace with the Germans on top.' Spillman would later claim that in time he came to realise the errors of his ways, but had meanwhile fallen for a half-Jewish girlfriend:

At the beginning, I was sincere and really believed I was doing right from the humanitarian angle. Later on, when I did come to my senses it was too late to back out. I know I should have backed out. I fully realised it, whatever the consequences would have been. I stopped on because for one reason I didn't think the station was having any effect on the English public, another reason was that I was engaged to the girl I met.

After a court martial at Chelsea on 2 November 1945, Spillman was sentenced at the age of only twenty-four years to seven years' penal servitude.[92]

Signalman William Alfred Colledge, alias '*Winter*' also worked for the NBBS between 1942 and 1945 as well as on *Workers' Challenge*. Originally from Matlock, Derbyshire, Colledge was captured in the fall of Crete in June 1941. A vain, egotistical and self-pitying individual, Colledge worked without scruple – or much success – for the Germans, engaged among other things in spying on wounded British prisoners in order to report back on their activities. Sometime in 1942 Colledge received a visit in Berlin from Hetzler and Joyce, who had been told that he was willing to work with them – given his recent past, he claimed to have little choice but to co-operate. He was then taken to *Büro Concordia*, by then at the *Reichssportfeld*, where he was coached in radio technique by Margaret Joyce with a view to his talking on *Workers' Challenge*. It seems, however, that Colledge was not up to the job, and instead was employed in editing and punctuating war reports dictated by Hetzler for the NBBS. He did, however, stand in on broadcasts on the *Workers' Challenge* station in 1944 when its regular broadcaster fell ill, and continued working on the station until its demise. At his court martial at York in April 1946, Colledge, like many others accused of collaborating with the Germans, tried to excuse his behaviour on the grounds that he was really a patriotic Briton, acting only in the hope of thwarting the Nazis, whereas his counsel tried to convince the court that he was merely 'a gibbering coward' and fantasist who acted as he did out of fear of the concentration camp. In the event, Colledge was found guilty, and sentenced to be discharged with ignominy and to penal servitude for life, a sentence later mitigated by the Army Council to one of seven years' penal servitude. He was then aged twenty-five years.[93]

The second secret station to come on the air was *Workers' Challenge*, known as *Büro S*. It commenced broadcasting on 7 July 1940 and continued until 26 January 1945. At first there were three transmissions a day at 20.10, 21.10 and 22.10, but they were later reduced to one at 18:10. *Workers' Challenge* broadcast on 213m on the medium waveband and in general reception in the UK was good, the station being readily receivable on ordinary household wireless sets.[94] As its name implied, *Workers' Challenge* purported to represent the downtrodden British working class who were being sacrificed in an unwinnable war in the interests of capitalism, and called upon them to stop the war immediately by withdrawing their labour from the service of the state. The broadcasts attracted a good deal of attention in Britain primarily because of the shockingly rude language which they employed. A representative of the

BBC gave evidence on the station's material at the court martial of one of its broadcasters in 1946 in these terms: 'It was foul language here and there, foul words particularly when speaking of personalities . . . The word "bugger" was one of the most frequent, with "bastard" and "sod" and things like that.'[95] After the entry of the USSR into the war in June 1941, *Workers' Challenge* agitated for the creation of a second front in support of Russia, while using this ploy to continue and expand upon the claim that the British government was secretly hoping for the destruction of the Soviet state. Again, Joyce seems to have been the main scriptwriter, while two British soldiers were the chief speakers. The first was William Henry Humphrey ('Bill') Griffiths, a Welsh Guardsman who at the age of thirty-four was sentenced by a court martial at Chelsea to seven years' penal servitude on 31 October 1945 for voluntarily aiding the enemy while a prisoner by broadcasting.[96] Captured at Boulogne in May 1940, Griffiths was taken to a POW camp at Thorn in the so-called Wartegau where he volunteered for work. After an interview with William Joyce, Griffiths was taken to Berlin, along with eleven other prisoners. The group was divided in two, and Griffiths was taken to Villa Concordia, where Hetzler told them they were to speak on the wireless. All initially refused to co-operate whereupon, according to Griffiths, Hetzler spoke of sending them to a 'special camp'. Shortly afterwards, they were visited by William Joyce who explained to them that the Jews were responsible for the war and that England would be a better place without them. He also told them that a lot of British prisoners were already doing propaganda work, and warned that if they refused to co-operate, they would be sent to a concentration camp. Two weeks later, Griffiths did his first broadcast on *Workers' Challenge*, reading a prepared talk and having to repeat it three or four times until Hetzler was satisfied with the recording. The talks were recorded at 16.00 and broadcast at 20.10. According to Griffiths, Joyce did all of the writing for *Workers' Challenge*, while he did the speaking. If a dialogue was called for, he was assisted by Sergeant MacDonald. For Griffiths, the message of *Workers' Challenge* was a simple one: 'We dealt with the air raids on London and the workers' point of view in regard to the war, saying we [meaning the workers in England], should pack it in and all that, and not fight any more.'[97] *Worker's Challenge* was also staffed at various times by Kenneth Gilbert, William Colledge, Sergeant MacDonald between June and October 1940 and in 1943, Donald Alexander Fraser Grant.[98]

Grant, alias '*Jock Palmer*,' an ex-civilian internee and one-time BUF member, was also the leading light on *Radio Caledonia* (*Büro NW*), first monitored in Britain on 19 July 1940, which he ran more or less single-handedly, both writing the scripts and reading them on the air. The station, designed to appeal to Scottish nationalist sentiment, broadcast daily at 19.20 on 42.55m, and reception in Britain was invariably poor. Transmission ceased on 31 October 1940 and recommenced on 8 February 1941, when the station started daily transmissions at 18:00. Subsequently these took place at 19.45 and 21.15. *Caledonia* used *Auld Lang Syne* as a signature tune and Grant, described as having a 'pseudo-Scots accent', appealed to the Scots to make a separate peace from England, by whom, he said, their native land had been too long exploited.[99] Grant continued to run *Caledonia* as a one-man band until it shut down late in 1943. Described by Griffiths as 'very anti-Jewish', Grant was very fortunate in his trial judge. Mr Justice Atkinson told him that, 'if you had really broadcast something offensive and really harmful I would have taken a different view, but I am given to assume you were activated by no feeling of hostility to this country and had no desire to help Germany, but that you genuinely believed it was your duty to help peace.' He received a sentence of six months' imprisonment.[100]

The fourth *Concordia* station styled itself the *Christian Peace Movement* (*CPM*), and was known to the Germans as *Büro P*. The scripts were written by Private Cyril Charles Hoskins and spoken by Corporal Jones, both members of the original Thorn group. Hoskins had been captured in France, but had visited Germany before the war and was a fluent German speaker. Colledge described him as a 'well-educated, religious young man. Quiet, reserved and spoke perfect German.'[101] The life of this station was comparatively short; it began broadcasting on 15 August 1940 and closed down in April 1942. The *Christian Peace Movement* directed extreme pacifist, religious propaganda to Britain, aimed at an audience of the Peace Pledge Union type. Hoskins in time became chief of *Concordia*'s listening post. The *CPM* broadcast twice daily at 19.45 and 20.45 on 31.76m. Reception in Britain was always poor.

The last of the *Concordia* stations, *Radio National*, known as *Büro F*, commenced operations in the summer of 1943 and lasted for about a year. *Radio National* was run by Peter Adami, a former *AA* official who appears to have been released from the Army to take on the job. As a *Concordia* station it came formally under the control of Hetzler, but whereas Hetzler personally supervised closely the other four, Adami appears to have been given a good deal of latitude in respect of *Radio National*. The station was sharply anti-Jewish in tone and, according to one of its broadcasters, it had as its main function 'to be a Fascist station run on the same lines as the BUF in Britain'.[102]

The two main broadcasters on *Radio National* were Gunner Francis Paul Maton of the Royal Artillery,[103] and Walter 'Roy' Purdy of the Royal Navy.[104] Roy Purdy, alias '*Ronald Wallace*', alias '*Pointer*', was born at Barking, Essex. At the age of sixteen he joined the Ilford branch of the BUF but by his own account did not remain a member for more than a few weeks. His vessel was sunk by enemy action off Narvik on 10 June 1940 and Purdy was taken prisoner. He seems to have passed his time in various POW camps without incident, until in early 1943 he made up his mind to assist the Germans by broadcasting. In June 1943, he was taken to Berlin, where he had a meeting with Joyce, a copy of whose book, *Twilight Over England* Purdy had acquired while in captivity and had had autographed by its author. It seems that Joyce promised him that if he made ten broadcasts over a period of five weeks, he would be allowed to escape to a neutral country, whereupon he began his broadcasting career which lasted until early 1944. At the Central Criminal Court on 18 December 1945, proceedings began against Purdy for treason, it being charged that he broadcast on behalf of the enemy between August 1943 and May 1944, that he had given information to the enemy while a prisoner, and third that he had served the German Secret Service by assisting them to prepare pamphlets and leaflets for distribution as propaganda. He was described by Griffiths as 'an energetic worker for the Germans'.[105] In his defence, Purdy claimed only to have broadcast to help the British war effort, claiming that he wished by these means to convey messages to the British authorities at home about the weather over Berlin and that he had sent home a code for the purposes. He also alleged that he had been forced to work for the Germans, as he had been sentenced to death by a German court martial for sabotage and other anti-German activities, including an attempt on the life of William Joyce. Although he was acquitted on the second charge, the jury disbelieved Purdy's story, and like Joyce and Amery he received the death sentence. He was then aged twenty-seven years. In February 1946, his sentence was commuted to one of life imprisonment.[106] Purdy's prison chaplain at Dartmoor described him as 'disdainful of his fellow man and the country that tolerates their existence' and as having 'a particular contempt for the Jew'.[107] He was released on licence in December 1954, the Home Secretary having decided that it was unnecessary to detain him longer than nine years.[108]

Gunner Maton was tried at Chelsea on 26 November 1945 on a charge of having voluntarily aided the enemy by carrying out work in connection with wireless propaganda and by joining the British Free Corps. He was then aged only twenty-four years, and received a sentence of ten years' penal servitude. A former member of the BUF, Maton was wounded and captured by the Germans in Crete in 1941. Through his friend Arthur Chapple, he met Peter Adami, who asked the two of them to broadcast on a station which he was forming. Both agreed and in September 1943 were taken from Stalag III D, given civilian clothes and taken daily to the *Reichssportfeld* to broadcast. Thereafter they were given false names, German passports and allowed to live as civilians in Berlin. The work consisted of reading the British newspapers in the mornings and doing a ten minute broadcast at 14.30, each man being on the air for only two to three minutes. Maton went under the alias '*Pat McCarthy*', while he actually broadcast under the name '*Manxman*'. He claimed to have joined the British Free Corps only to sabotage it, and to have befriended William Joyce so as to gain access to the *Funkhaus* in order to find out as much as possible about the German service for Britain. Spillman described Maton as '100% pro-Fascist, pro-German and pro-National Socialist'.

Maton and Purdy were assisted on *Radio National* by Reginald Arthur Humphries, alias '*Father Donovan*', Sergeant Arthur Chapple, alias '*Arthur Lang*', and for a short while Arthur William Gordon Perry and Raymond Davies Hughes. Sergeant Arthur Chapple of the Royal Army Service Corps was captured by the Germans in May 1940 at Doullens in France. Chapple would later claim that he was a lifelong socialist and anti-fascist, but that his 'unusual' political views had marked him out from the regular soldiers – he was a NAAFI employee – with whom he shared internment at the POW camp at Thorn. He would also claim that he was falsely suspected by his comrades of being pro-German and of having given away the location of a hidden wireless receiver. In September 1941, he accepted an offer of employment on the Germans' POW propaganda paper, *The Camp*, and with Maton, accepted Adami's offer of radio work in September 1943, on the grounds that Adami told him that someone of 'anti-fascist views' was required for a 'British Free Radio Station'. He later admitted to broadcasting what he claimed was revolutionary socialist and never anti-British propaganda, under the *nom de guerre* of '*Freeman*'. Adami also told him that *Radio National* was under his jurisdiction as an employee of the *AA*, and warned him to have nothing to do with Hetzler.

Chapple claimed that he realised that *Radio National* was not a good propaganda weapon as the majority of the broadcasts were really ridiculous. Adami, he said, explained to him that the people did not want to hear the truth, but at that stage of the war preferred to be entertained. The broadcasts made by Purdy were especially funny, he said, and were always broadcast to the accompaniment of laughter by Adami and the others in the adjoining room. Broadcasts by Humphries, as the Roman Catholic cleric '*Father Donovan*', also made quite ridiculous listening, while the daily news service was obviously concocted from the most absurd and contradictory statements. At his court martial in Brussels in April 1946, when he was aged twenty-eight years, Chapple was found guilty of having voluntarily aided the enemy while a prisoner, and received a sentence of fifteen years' penal servitude, of which sentence eight years were later remitted by the Army Council.[109]

Other scriptwriters on *Radio National*, included Norman Baillie-Stewart and William Joyce, an individual called V. N. Q. Vernon, and yet another former BUF member Pilot Officer Freeman, alias '*Royston*'. Benson Railton Metcalf Freeman, an obsessive anti-communist, had been shot down over France in 1940, and having made no secret of his extreme political views while in captivity, was approached by Hetzler with a view to joining *Concordia*. Although he initially refused – he described the other broadcasters as 'the finest collection of poor-type Englishmen one could hope to meet' – he was eventually persuaded to co-operate. For his pains, as well as for membership of the *Waffen SS* in which he held the rank of *Untersturmführer*, Freeman was sentenced to be cashiered and to serve ten years' penal servitude at his court martial at Uxbridge in August 1945.[110]

Gunner Maton claimed to be the most poorly paid of the British broadcasters in Berlin, receiving a wage of RM300 a month. Banning, Spillman, Gilbert, Freeman, Vernon and Baillie-Stewart he reckoned to receive RM400 marks a month, while Joyce earned RM4,000 a month. The rest earned between 400 and 600 a month. By comparison, the young German women secretaries, working ten hours a day and all of whom spoke fluently at least two languages, received only RM198 a month.[111]

However, it is unlikely that money alone is enough to explain why it was that this group of individuals took as drastic a step as to abandon their homelands and take up the cudgels for the enemy in wartime. Of course, the point here is that the Britishers who worked for the English services of the *RRG* were not 'a group' at all, but a ragbag of individuals operating from a mixed bag of motivations. Of the forty-one British persons which it has been possible to identify here with certainty who worked for the English services of the *RRG*, eleven had at one time or another belonged to a British fascist movement – either the British Union, the Imperial Fascist League, or Joyce's National Socialist League. However, it would really only be fair to say that eight of them had expressly abandoned their homelands with the intention of working for National Socialism, that is William and Margaret Joyce, John Amery, Kenneth Gilbert, Douglas Johnston, Kenneth Lander, Leonard Banning and Pearl Vardon, the latter probably having acted more from romantic than from political motives. Margaret Joyce was as much of a pro-Nazi as her husband, but it seems unlikely that she would have travelled alone to Germany in the summer of 1939. Mrs Eckersley and Mrs Bothamley were out-and-out fascists it is true, but both took to broadcasting out of necessity rather than for the love it. James Clark was in 1939 still a schoolboy, albeit one wholly mesmerised by National Socialism. Vincent Lander seems to have been a reluctant broadcaster, although he did abandon Britain for Germany at a point when war must have seemed inevitable, and was always treated most reasonably by the Germans. In retrospect, the decision not to prosecute him after the war seems extraordinary. Banning was a much more important figure in the long run, but one whose relationship with his employers was not always cordial. His sentence of ten years' imprisonment seems harsh in contrast to Lander's treatment but was lenient indeed when compared with the fate of William Joyce. Of the active servicemen, only three, Purdy, Freeman and Maton, had fascist pasts, and certainly Purdy and Maton were enthusiastic broadcasters, although paradoxically Purdy's death sentence was the result of a charge of which he was acquitted rather than of the charges of which he was convicted.[112] For the other prisoners, working for the Germans on the wireless must have seemed like an easy way out of a very long period of incarceration, especially for the group who signed up at the first meeting with Joyce in 1940. Britain's position after the debacle of Dunkirk would have seemed more or less hopeless, and when viewed in the wider context of the many prisoners who collaborated in one way or another with the Germans for the sake of an easier time of it, the actions of the Thorn group and their successors are at least understandable. The surprising thing perhaps is that so few could be persuaded to take advantage of the German offer.

The same would apply to the civilians who in 1940 or 1941 must have been looking ahead to a long and bleak period of internment. For those who had made Germany their long-time home, men like John Ward or Ralph Powell, the temptation to take up the offer of release and a reasonable salary must have been great. This would have been especially true for those individuals whose beliefs were in tune with National Socialism, and who could convince themselves that by broadcasting to Britain they were helping bring about the end of what must have seemed like a pointless war. Nevertheless, men like Edward Bowlby and Donald Grant were British subjects, British fascists indeed, who travelled on British passports and worked with enthusiasm for the downfall of their country. The leniency of their treatment at the end of the war is comprehensible only in the light of the political rather than judicial considerations of British decision-makers.

In February 1940, the BBC produced a detailed report on the aims and effectiveness of the Nazi wireless campaign in English.[113] The BBC analysts discerned, roughly speaking, three phases of broadcasts to Britain. The aims of the pre-war period were connected with the German attempts to win the confidence and sympathy of the British people, and to justify the actions of the German government before the British public. The second phase lasted up to the end of the campaign in Poland. The intention was then to achieve peace before real warfare developed. Even if the broadcasts were aggressive and spiteful, there were so only within well-defined limits. In the third phase, however, German propaganda became a method of warfare, its purpose being the destruction of the enemy. The next chapter will consider the style and content of Nazi propaganda in these latter two phases.

Notes

1 Jones, *Workers at Play*, p. 37.
2 Davies in Johnson (ed.), *20th Century Britain*, p. 267.
3 Balfour, *Propaganda in War*, p. 18.
4 Banse, *Raum und Volk im Weltkriege*, pp. 82–3.
5 Cited in Rolo, *Radio Goes to War*, p. 18.
6 Balfour, *Propaganda in War*, p. 17.
7 Sington and Weidenfeld, *The Goebbels Experiment*, p. 138.
8 P[ublic] R[ecord] O[ffice] WO 208/4466.
9 Wolf, *Presse und Funk im Dritten Reich*, p. 299.
10 Cited in Wolf, *Presse und Funk im Dritten Reich*, p. 319.
11 Quoted in Rolo, *Radio Goes to War*, p. 19.
12 Heiber (ed.), *Goebbels Reden*, vol. 1, pp. 82–107. The text is from Goebbels' speech to the Controllers of German Radio on 25 March 1933.
13 Warlaumont in *Journal of Broadcasting and Electronic Media*, p. 43.
14 Short-wave broadcasts with a frequency of 10–100m are designed to bounce back to ground level against the reflecting surface of the ionosphere known as the Kennelley-Heaviside layer. Short-wave transmissions therefore have an immense range, the distance which the beams traverse before returning to earth being known as the 'skip distance'. By the 1930s, engineers were able to calculate the 'skip distance' and adjust their equipment so that transmissions could be targeted at specific geographical regions. In addition, the technique known as 'beam transmission' meant that broadcasters could focus short-waves on a specific point of the compass, rather than allowing them to radiate over 360°, thereby greatly boosting the range and power of a given transmitter. German engineers were making use of both techniques at the short-wave station at Zeesen from 1937. See *Life*, 14 February 1938.

15 Balfour, *Propaganda in War*, p. 37.

16 Hitler, *Mein Kampf*, pp. 554–6, 581.

17 In addition, the British were running from the time of the Munich crisis a
clandestine operation from Luxembourg, broadcasting in German to Germany,
with the aim of dividing German popular opinion from Hitler. See Pronay and
Taylor, *Journal of Contemporary History*.

18 COLOG & HAM IGFG 22.00 1.9.39. This system for references to particular
broadcasts is used throughout this book. Abbreviations are used to signify the
station broadcasting, the language in which the broadcast was given, and its time
and date. Unless otherwise stated, the source is the BBC's *Daily Digest of Foreign
Broadcasts*.

19 Cited in Wulf, *Presse und Funk im Dritten Reich*, p. 350.

20 Bergmeier and Lotz, *Hitler's Airwaves*, p. 42.

21 PRO FO 371/24393, *The Voice of Hamburg*, 14 Feburary 1940.

22 Balfour, *Propaganda in War*, p. 133 and p. 136.

23 Cole, *Lord Haw-Haw*, pp. 111–12.

24 PRO HO 45/25794, Dietze's statement, 29 May 1945. A recording of his voice may
be heard on the CD at Track 13.

25 PRO WO 71/1117 and PRO HO 45/25794, Schöberth's statement 28 May 1945.

26 Bergmeier and Lotz, *Hitler's Airwaves*, pp. 27–34.

27 George, *Propaganda Analysis*, p. 74. It is not clear either, of course, that Goebbels
himself was all that well informed about military tactics and strategy at any stage of
the war.

28 Boelcke, *Secret Conferences*, p. 80.

29 *The Times*, 15 April 1933.

30 *The Manchester Guardian*, 3 November 1945.

31 *The Times*, 11 January 1946. Baillie-Stewart's voice can be heard on the CD at
Tracks 15 and 16.

32 Baillie-Stewart, *Officer in the Tower*, pp. 147–9.

33 PRO HO 45/25776.

34 PRO HO 45/25776, Eckersley's statement, 2 July 1945.

35 *The Manchester Guardian*, 11 December 1945.

36 PRO HO 45/25776, Clark's statement, 18 June 1945.

37 One British newspaper christened Clark 'Smith Minor', suggesting that he 'speaks
prim English in a voice of light, almost juvenile, calibre. He usually sounds as
though he is reading a prize essay from the platform at the annual speech day.' See
The Yorkshire Observer, 30 December 1939.

38 *The Manchester Guardian*, 11 December 1945. James Clark is now retired and lives
in England.

39 See the *Daily Express*, 16 January 1947. The leniency of Steane's treatment was
particularly galling to Baillie-Stewart, then serving his sentence in Wakefield
prison. He wrote to his solicitor, 'Be it noted in passing that his salary was higher
than mine – he was not taxed as a German, like I was, and had none of the
obligations of a German citizen. He was, in fact, in a far more advantageous
position, and, in comparison to myself, was a 100% volunteer.' See PRO HO 45/
25689.

40 *The Times*, 28 March 1946.

41 PRO HO 45/25813, Stoettner's statement, 30 June 1945.

42 A various times in 1940, a female speaker was announced as 'Lady Haw-Haw', and
although the speaker may have been Margaret Joyce, the nickname may also have
been applied to other broadcasters.

43 PRO HO 45/25779, *Newsam to Wilberforce*, 25 February 1946.
44 PRO HO 45/25779, *Newsam to Wilberforce*, 22 March 1946.
45 Her voice may be heard on the CD at Track 14.
46 The nickname originated in an article by Jonah Barrington in the *Daily Express* on 14 September 1939. Barrington had written: 'A gent I'd like to meet is moaning periodically from Zeesen. He speaks English of the haw-haw, damit-get-out-of-my-way variety, and his strong suit is gentlemanly indignation.' A few days later he extended this image: 'From his accent and personality I imagine him with a receding chin, a questing nose, thin, yellow hair brushed back, a monocle, a vacant eye, a gardenia in his button-hole. Rather like P. G. Wodehouse's Bertie Wooster.'
47 PRO FO 371/24393, *The Voice of Hamburg*, 14 February 1940.
48 See, for example, ' "Don't Bark at Me": Fascist's Rejoinder to Interrupters', *Bath Chronicle and Herald*, 4 April 1935; 'Fight at Fascist Meeting', *The Times*, 23 October 1936; 'Women Thrown Out by Fascists', *News Chronicle*, 23 October 1936; ' "Jews Responsible for Crisis": Joyce's Slanders at Hackney Meeting', *The Jewish Chronicle*, 13 December 1936.
49 Joyce, *Twilight Over England*, p. 11.
50 Joyce's voice may be heard on the CD at Tracks 1–5, 7–12 and 22–24. His final drunken talk (Track 24), although recorded, was never broadcast.
51 PRO WO 71/1117, Maton's statement, 9 September 1944.
52 PRO FO 369/3174 K16213/925/250.
53 PRO HO 45/22406. Deportation papers for Joyce were drawn up for the signature of the Home Secretary so that he could be immediatly expelled to Germany upon his expected acquital.
54 PRO HO 45/25780; PCOM 9/2122.
55 PRO WO 71/1131, Colledge's statement, 21 July 1945.
56 BREM IEFE 22:15 12.5.40. It has now been discovered that Leopold Amery's mother was indeed Jewish, although her son had taken great pains to keep the matter a secret. It seems highly unlikely that the Nazi propagandists were aware of this fact, and probably made up the 'half-Jew' remark merely for effect. See Rubinstein, *History Today*.
57 PRO HO 45/25773.
58 The circumstances of Amery's arrival in Berlin were transmitted by the German Transocean wireless service on 19 November 1942.
59 A recording of one of Amery's talks from September 1944 is included on the CD at Track 19.
60 *The Times*, 29 November 1945.
61 Orr, *CPS Journal*, May/June 1994, p. 16.
62 PRO FO 369/3174 K15809/925/250.
63 PRO HO 45/25789, Bowlby's statement, 29 May 1945.
64 PRO HO 45/25789, *Home Office Minute* (undated).
65 Bowlby's voice may be heard on the CD at Tracks 17 and 20.
66 PRO HO 45/25794, *MI5 Report*, 25 September 1945.
67 PRO HO 45/25794, *Home Office Minute*.
68 PRO HO 45/25826. The BBC in 1944 had described the entertainment material on *Radio Metropole* as 'lively and amusing. The speakers are well trained and have an excellent command of their respective languages. Sketches are well produced, humorous, and should appeal to the average listener.'
69 PRO HO 45/25826. Ward had actually served with the 3rd Bttn Gloucester Regiment from July 1918 until January 1919.
70 PRO HO 45/25802, Kosposh's statement, 19 June 1945.

71 PRO HO 45/25802, *Hughes to Mathew*, 12 January 1946.

72 PRO HO 45/25806.

73 *Daily Express*, 12 July 1945.

74 PRO HO 45/25827, *Hughes to DPP*, 15 January 1946. See also statements by Colledge and Griffiths at PRO WO 71/1131.

75 MI5 report on the *Concordia* outfit at PRO HO 45/25798.

76 See Boelcke, *Secret Conferences*, p. 3 The original suggestion was for an 'Irish' station aimed at Britain, although in the event no station of an Irish character ever appeared.

77 BBC, *Notes on Daily Digest of Foreign Broadcasts*, No. 223, 26 February 1940.

78 PRO FO 898 52.

79 PRO WO 71/1112, Lushington's statement, 21 July 1945.

80 PRO HO 45/25827, Lander's statement. Lander's voice can be heard on an NBBS broadcast from March 1940 on the CD at Track 6.

81 PRO HO 45/25827, *Hughes to DPP*, 15 January 1946.

82 Lander was probably the broadcaster known to BBC Monitors as '*Sunny Jim*', although the nickname was still being applied to speakers on the NBBS after he had left the station.

83 PRO WO 71/1112. Banning was the announcer known to the BBC monitors as '*The Professor*'.

84 PRO HO 45/25827 and PRO HO 45/25833.

85 PRO WO 71/1131, Colledge's statement, 21 July 1945.

86 *News Chronicle*, 23 January 1946. Banning is the character referred to in Rebecca West's *The Meaning of Treason* as 'Leonard Black'.

87 PRO HO 45/25833.

88 PRO WO 71/1131, Colledge's statement.

89 PRO HO 45/25833.

90 *The Times*, 12 September 1946.

91 PRO WO 71/1133.

92 PRO WO 71/1112.

93 PRO WO 71/1131.

94 PRO FO 898 52, Lushington's statement.

95 PRO WO 71/1131.

96 *The Evening News*, 31 October 1945.

97 PRO WO 71/1120.

98 A recording of a *Workers' Challenge* broadcast may be heard on the CD at Track 21.

99 PRO FO 898 52.

100 *Daily Worker*, 6 February 1945.

101 PRO WO 71/1131.

102 PRO WO 71/1117.

103 PRO WO 71/1117.

104 PRO HO 45/25798.

105 PRO HO 45/25798. Purdy appears in Rebecca West's *The Meaning of Treason* as 'Walter Putney'.

106 The second charge had determined Purdy's prosecution for treason, in the absence of which he would have been charged for offences against the Defence Regulations, which were not punishable by death but by a maximum term of penal servitude for life. The fact that Purdy had relinquished his naval rank upon the sinking of his vessel determined the fact that he was tried by a criminal court and not by court martial. Had he been court-martialled, it is highly unlikely that he would have been sentenced to death, since in none of the other cases of servicemen charged with

similar offences was a capital sentence imposed. See *Graham-Harrison to Hancock*, 2 June 1954, in PRO PCOM 2124.

107 PRO PCOM 9 2124.

108 PRO PCOM 9 2124, *Sir Hugh Lucas-Tooth MP to Anthony Nutting, MP*, 24 May 1954.

109 PRO WO 71/1133.

110 *Daily Mirror*, 3 November 1945.

111 PRO WO 71/1117.

112 See above, footnote 106.

113 PRO FO 371/24393, *The Voice of Hamburg*, 14 February 1940.

2

Nazi Wireless Propaganda in the 'Phoney War'

The pretext for the German attack on Poland was a fabricated Polish attack on the German radio station at Gleiwitz on 31 August. For some weeks before this episode the German press and radio had been running an anti-Polish campaign, designed to convince the world that Poland had launched a pogrom against her German population. On 31 August for example, the morning news in English from Zeesen reported that hundreds of Germans at Lodz, Katowitz and other Polish towns had been arrested and tortured by the Polish police. Polish neighbours were begging the police to stop since 'they cannot bear the screams.'[1] Hitler himself constantly repeated this atrocity propaganda in his negotiations with the British in the days immediately before the outbreak of war. At a stormy meeting with the British ambassador Sir Neville Henderson at Berchtesgaden on 23 August, Hitler furiously berated the British ambassador with details of Polish excesses, including castration, against Germans. So great was the persecution, alleged Hitler, that Germany was expecting 100,000 German refugees from Poland.[2]

The 'attack' on the radio station at Gleiwitz was widely reported on the morning of 1 September. Zeesen at 08.00 reported in English that the station had been attacked by Polish bandits and was the signal for an organised campaign of attacks upon other German stations. Polish irregulars supported by troops raided the German stations in West Prussia and after a fierce encounter the Poles retreated. One German was killed and one wounded.[3] Significantly, though, the same broadcast went on to quote the German morning papers to the effect that it was up to England to see that Poland 'did her share' in avoiding a generalised conflict. England had failed to bring a Polish negotiator to Berlin, and since the German proposals had been made known, Britain and Poland had made no sign of movement. Three hours later, at 11.40 BST, all German transmitters carried the War Ministry High Command announcement, that that morning German troops had made a 'counter-attack' into Poland.

The allegation on the very first day of the war that the British government was to blame for the outbreak set the tone, and throughout the first weeks and months of the conflict the German propagandists maintained the all-out effort to blame the Poles for the immediate commencement of hostilities, but to pinpoint the British as the real warmonger nation, the sinister manipulator, the ultimate guilty party. As was pointed out in the first *Survey of German Propaganda* prepared in September by the MoI for the War Cabinet, 'the main trend of German propaganda since the beginning of war has unquestionably been anti-British. From the very first day its fire has been concentrated upon us'.[4] And indeed, in the numerous accounts given in German broadcasts throughout early September of the sequence of events immediately preceding the outbreak of war, the essential thrust was that while negotiations for peace were proceeding in Berlin, London was secretly encouraging the belligerency of the Poles. On the afternoon of the invasion of Poland, an account was given of the events since the British note to Germany of 28 August, offering mediation between Germany and Poland. The speaker then spelled out the subsequent reactions in Berlin and Warsaw: the sixteen proposals made by Germany, as opposed to the silence of Poland and the absence from Berlin of a Polish plenipotentiary.[5] At 15.00 on the same day, this story was repeated, with the addition of a statement that, while negotiations for peace were proceeding in Berlin, London was giving Poland the signal for war by mobilisation, an angle corroborated by an account from the London *Daily Telegraph*.[6] Similar encouragement, it was further alleged, had been given by Britain to the Benes government in September 1938 while Chamberlain was at Godesberg.[7] Britain was guilty, however, not merely by actively encouraging Polish aggression, but by removing any chance of Polish 'compromise', by presenting Poland with an open ended guarantee back in March 1939. Cologne in English reported at 22.00 on 1 September that Italian and Spanish newspapers were entirely in agreement with the action taken by Germany against Poland. Comment in Berlin was to the effect that the English (sic) themselves were to blame for the present hostilities, which would not have broken out but for the blank cheque given by them to the Poles. For many weeks the Führer had emphasised the peaceful nature of his desires. Chamberlain had forgotten this and had made no attempt to prevent Polish aggression.

A special short talk was then given under the heading 'Why was the Führer kept waiting?' Henderson, it was stated, was given proposals by the Führer on 25 August, which included the suggestion of a conference of Great Powers. Consideration of the proposals, however, was delayed in London till the 28th. Meanwhile, the Führer waited, receiving every day reports of Polish atrocities. In this period no less than forty-one Germans were murdered by Poles. The British then sent counter-suggestions which were accepted by the Führer, who nevertheless emphasised that conditions in the East were becoming increasingly urgent. After accepting these proposals from the British government, the Führer was kept waiting for a further thirty hours, during which he learnt that seven more Germans had been murdered by the Poles. This action of the Poles was aggravated by their general mobilisation on 30 August. On the same day, Sir Neville Henderson gave the German government British proposals repeating those previously made, and adding only a request that the German government should refrain from the use of force. The German proposals, which were subsequently published over the wireless, were communicated to Henderson verbally on Wednesday. On Thursday, the Poles attacked the Gleiwitz radio station and other towns in Germany. They had in the meantime sent no reply to the German proposals, and their ambassador, when summoned to

Hitler, stated that he had no plenipotentiary powers. 'The sum of the matter', said Cologne, 'is that the Poles have, throughout, been unwilling to negotiate, and the British have made no effort to persuade them to negotiate.' The talk ended with the remark, 'Now perhaps you know who kept the Führer waiting, and why.'[8]

Of course this German version of events was fanciful to say the least. Henderson did indeed meet with von Ribbentrop on the evening of 30 August with the reply of the British government. The note consisted of a plea that while arrangements for negotiations got under way, no aggressive military movements should take place, and pointed out that it was impracticable to establish contact so early as Germany had demanded. Henderson suggested that von Ribbentrop should adopt normal contact with the Poles, but von Ribbentrop's reply was to produce a long list of demands which he read out in German at top speed. When Henderson asked for a copy of the text he was told it was now 'too late' as the Polish plenipotentiary had not arrived in Berlin. Henderson's view of von Ribbentrop's behaviour during 'an unpleasant interview' was that he had been 'aping Herr Hitler at his worst'.[9] The Polish ambassador, M. Lipski, had indeed been instructed by his government to establish contact with the Germans, and he finally managed to see von Ribbentrop at 6.30 p.m. The latter asked Lipski if he had come as plenipotentiary. When he replied that he had come in his capacity as ambassador only, the meeting ended. In any case the order for war had already been confirmed by Hitler at 4 pm. At 4.45 a.m. the following morning, 1 September, the attack on Poland began.

After 3 September, when Britain and France most reluctantly declared war on Germany, the German broadcasting stations continued and extended the notion that Germany was in fact the victim of Polish and British aggression. The work of the BBC monitors was interrupted by an air raid alarm that afternoon, and they were able at 13.35 to catch only the closing paragraphs of a broadcast reading from Zeesen of von Ribbentrop's reply to the ultimatum delivered that morning by the British government.[10] What von Ribbentrop had delivered was a robust, even contemptuous rejection of Britain's ultimatum, which the German government, he said, refused to receive or accept, let alone fulfil. For many months, he said, a state of war had existed on Germany's eastern frontier. Germany had been 'raped' and 'torn to pieces' by the Versailles Treaty at the end of the Great War. Successive German governments had tried to revise the treaty by peaceful means, but had been frustrated. The British had been consistently to the fore in thwarting Germany's peaceful plans, and Britain had again exercised her baneful influence over the Polish crisis. 'Without the intervention of the British Government – of this the German Government and German people are fully conscious – a reasonable solution doing justice to both sides would certainly have been found.' Britain had encouraged the Polish government to continue in their criminal attitude and behaviour which was threatening the peace of Europe. 'The British Government, therefore, bear the responsibility for all the unhappiness and misery which have now overtaken and are about to overtake many peoples.'

Germany would not tolerate Polish abuses any longer and therefore refused to withdraw her forces from Poland. For years the German people had said they wished to have peace between their country and England; it was not the fault of Germany if now the English had taken to threatening them with hostilities. The Germans, unlike the British, did not aim at world domination, but were determined to defend themselves and their independence and, above all, life itself. The German government noted the intention of the British government of carrying the destruction of the German people even further than was done through the Versailles Treaty. 'We shall therefore answer any aggressive action on the part of England with the same weapons, and in the same form.'[11]

Right from the outset therefore, Germany was portrayed as the victim and Britain the aggressor. Germany was a peace-loving nation, defending herself against the machinations of the British pluto-Imperialists, and their puppets, the Poles. Noteworthy too is the connection which is frequently made with the continuity of struggle from the Great War, through the Diktat of Versailles, and on to the present struggle for Germany's freedom. For example, some two weeks into the conflict, British listeners were treated to a talk in English on Zeesen by the Indian exile in Germany, Dr Nirogi. The root causes of the current conflict, he said, were to be found in the 'so-called Treaty of Versailles'. Peace could have been secured on 2 September if England had agreed to accept a conference of the interested nations. But England placed her desire for world supremacy above 'the dearest wishes of mankind'. Hitler, 'a thoroughly peace-loving man', had offered a non-aggression pact to the Poles some months previously, but his offer had been rejected 'because England had poisoned the Polish people against the Germans'. England had also tried to spin her net around Russia and Turkey, but failed because Stalin had more at heart the interests of the Russian nation than the hegemony of the British Empire. The result, he went on, was the signing of the Russian-German Pact which ensured the peace of the world more effectively than a hundred British promises.[12]

The continuity of struggle from 1914 to 1939 was the subject of a long talk in English for African listeners, broadcast on the morning of 15 September. As the BBC monitors noted, Britain was attacked by a great mass of material, which certainly showed much industry and research 'in past history and present economics'.[13] Just as in 1914, England was Germany's number one enemy. Then as now a pretext had been found to start a war against Germany. Then as now London wanted to crush the hated nation which successfully claimed the position as first power on the European continent. Even the methods of fighting were the same – blockade and starvation. But Germany had learned from past mistakes and had taken good care that they should not be repeated.[14] A similar point was made a day or so earlier on 14 September, in a talk in Spanish for Latin America. Zeesen argued that British tactics were not military, but consisted of the use of lies, calumny and the basest and most hypocritical intrigues, aimed at securing above all other people to fight on Britain's behalf, whether this help was to be gained by gold or the offer of territory. When the Great War was stopped by the German revolution, said Zeesen, it was interrupted only. On 1 September, the Great War began anew, and Britain alone was responsible.[15]

By the end of the month, the line was that England's war against Germany had been long in the planning:

> You have probably been confronted recently with German arguments that England's declaration of war was premeditated planning against the German Reich over some considerable period of time. As you may be inclined to reject this accusation we feel bound to mention some of our reasons . . .

The 'evidence' for British planning for war presented in this talk was, it has to be said, slim. It was claimed that between 1918 and 1933 there had been a 'noticeable diminution of British authority in the Empire'; that pacifism had been the order of the day in England 'until 1933'; that England began by disarmament but changed suddenly on the rise of Hitlerism to 'frantic rearmament'; that there had been 'deliberate distortion of the German political and economic system in English books of all sorts', to say nothing of the activities of the press; that Baldwin and Duff Cooper had declared the British frontier to be on the Rhine. The speaker concluded:

> You know as well as I do that for several years an immense propaganda force has been employed inciting you to war against Germany, though Germany was always ready to accept your friendship. Who paid for this propaganda? Settle that question and you will find your real enemies. Meanwhile, do not be surprised if we accuse your Government of plunging you into war with malice aforethought.[16]

This short extract provides an interesting example of what E. H. Gombrich, himself a former BBC Monitor, described as characteristic of Nazi propaganda, namely the imposition of 'a paranoiac pattern on world events'.[17] Gombrich's formula, summarising both the style and contact of Nazi radio broadcasts, was that whatever was reported of the home front should be represented as a symbol of German strength and heroism, while anything that was reported from the enemy camp was to be interpreted as a symptom of his depravity and basic weakness. Gombrich is correct, but the whole National Socialist movement in Germany might well be described as a form of politicised paranoia, arising at it did from deep-rooted complexes of national and personal inferiority, persecution, shame and frustration. The outward manifestation of these inner frustrations was a propaganda which had to portray every historical and contemporary event or phenomenon – however innocuous – within a world-view in which Germany was always the innocent, noble victim of lesser enemies, resentful and jealous of her nobility and her strength. This paranoia too resolves the paradox which allowed Nazi propaganda to be at one and the same time boastful and whining, bombastically declaiming Germany's might and the weakness of the decadent enemies she would face down, but also bemoaning the unfairness of a world in which such powerful enemies should be ranged against her.

The military campaign in Poland provided ample opportunities for Germany's paranoid propaganda to be given its head. Material for home consumption in particular concentrated upon the successes of the German armies in Poland, and the propagandists repeatedly insisted that while her own troops were models of restraint and forbearance, the Poles acted with the vilest barbarity against the German minorities. *Deutschlandsender* for Germany reported on 13 September that of a total of 600 native Germans living in Northern Silesia, 400 had been found murdered. Throughout Poland, bodies of Germans were found individually and in heaps bearing signs of terrible torture. Official reports allegedly proved that this was all due to English encouragement. It was estimated, said *Deutschlandsender*, that more than one-quarter of all the Germans in Poland had been killed. Again, neutrals were employed for backup: 'The *Amsterdam Telegraaf* confirms these stories and contrasts them with German discipline . . .'[18]

Zeesen in German for the Far East reported that, according to Lithuanian sources, Germans who were tortured and murdered by Poles on the orders of British agents were nailed to the doors of the houses in which they lived. A Pole who crossed the border declared: 'I left my country because I could not bear the awful deeds that are being committed there.'[19] *Deutschlandsender* told its home audience on 18 September that terrible atrocities were being committed against everything German in Warsaw:

> Two little German children were thrown from a fourth floor window into the street. Polish refugees from Pruzana say that a German was nailed to the door of his house by the Poles, and his wife and daughter were forced to stand by and watch. In another town Germans were driven naked from their homes into the streets, and eventually done to death.[20]

Stories of German atrocities on the other hand were dismissed as British propaganda. Hamburg in English on 11 September launched a vituperative attack on the British press. Ever since the beginning of hostilities, it argued, the British press had given news of German atrocities. Pathetic stories were flashed all over the world of women and children being bombed and machine gunned by German planes. In fact, it was argued, civilian casualties in Warsaw had been caused by the Poles themselves. The German army command had decided to withdraw into the suburbs the troops who had entered the centre of Warsaw because the Polish artillery bombarded the city centre without taking into consideration women and children.[21] By the second week of the campaign, however, this line was amended. Now it was alleged that Polish radio stations were encouraging resistance among the civil population of the occupied districts, including among women and children. This was the justification for a new policy, announced on 13 September, of bombing and shelling towns, villages and hamlets. *Deutschlandsender* broadcast an announcement to this effect in Polish at 7.30 BST:

> Owing to the defence of Warsaw by the civil population and to the bombing of Warsaw by Polish artillery, German GHQ has issued the following order:

'From this moment the German Air Force and German artillery has received orders not to spare any civil town or open village if the circumstances prove the necessity of bombing. We are determined to break Polish resistance by all means and as Polish artillery bombed the town of Warsaw, we find that we have the right to do likewise.'[22]

Here again one sees the emergence of a familiar pattern. As Germany embarked upon some act of adventurism or outright criminality, her actions were justified in terms of Germany's victimhood. Since her enemies had broken international law or committed atrocities, Germany was justified in taking whatever action was necessary to protect herself. These tactics were used again with regard to Warsaw, from 16 September, when Germany presented an ultimatum to the population of the city to surrender within twelve hours, failing which the capital would be completely destroyed. Hamburg, for Germany, in the evening carried a special announcement from the High Command of the *Wehrmacht*:

A company of German pioneers while crossing a bridge near Jaslo on 8 September had been attacked by Poles, many being killed or injured in an explosion. Some soldiers, it was alleged, died of acute bronchial pneumonia. A special commission of doctors and chemists which flew from Berlin was able to state that the deaths and wounds were caused by poison gas. Thus, the Poles have violated the international convention of Geneva of 1925.[23]

By 17 September the explosion, it was simply asserted, was caused by a mine filled with mustard gas.[24] Although in the end the Germans did not use poison gas during the Polish campaign, interesting again is the extent to which they tried to justify such policies as air attacks on civilian habitations by pointing out that the British had made use of similar tactics in the past. British complaints about German attacks on open Polish towns – denied by Germany as far as civilians as opposed to guerrillas were concerned – were denounced as examples of Britain's towering hypocrisy. Hamburg in English on 24 September quoted three instances upon which British statesmen – including Thompson, Eden and Amery – had recommended the bombing of civilians in open towns.[25] Indeed, it was regularly claimed, Warsaw continued to resist only because of Germany's humanitarian reticence in the hope of avoiding unnecessary civilian casualties, in spite of insupportable provocation by the Poles.

And of course, behind the crazy and suicidal continuation of Warsaw's resistance were to be found the British. Zeesen told listeners in South Africa on 22 September that by inciting the citizens of Warsaw to resist, Britain was responsible for the deaths of women and children.[26] And following the fall of the besieged city, which held out heroically until 27 September, Stuttgart for France again pointed the finger:

See also how much English promises are worth. These facts show once again the treachery of the English . . . Moscicki and Smigly-Rydz declared after two days of war that Poland was ready to negotiate with Germany, but England encouraged the Poles to continue the struggle, telling them that 1,500 British planes had left for Warsaw.[27]

Within days too of the outbreak of war there appeared another theme which was to be constantly reiterated over the coming years. On 8 September at 03.00 BST a Zeesen broadcast for Latin America contained the now familiar attacks upon Britain. The speaker, however, went on to spell out three 'fundamental facts': firstly, Britain's lying campaign had the objective of dominating the world; secondly, Poland had been encouraged by Britain to reject Hitler's 'generous settlement proposals'; thirdly, Germany was 'not only fighting to repair a wrong while others fight to preserve it, she is fighting against British lies and for the establishment of a new Europe.'[28] Indeed this latter notion had appeared as early as 5 September in a *Deutschlandsender* talk entitled '*German Workers – who are your friends?*' 'The young nations of Germany and Russia', said the speaker, 'will bring a new dawn to Europe'.[29] And while rarely if ever did the Nazi propagandists link their version of 'national' socialism with the socialism of the Soviet Union, a great deal of propaganda material from this period of the war was overtly left-wing, even communistic, at least to the extent that it was anti-capitalist and anti-plutocratic. A talk from Hamburg in English at the end of September, which seems barbed and vitriolic enough to have been written by William Joyce, was typical:

> It is a waste of time to try to analyse very deeply the thought processes of Palaeolithic crustaceans who feebly move now and then in nice easy chairs in the Carlton Club . . . [But] what is the Socialist party doing? Beyond the fact that its leader is paid to oppose the Government it seems to have very little significance. Socialists seem to have shelved attempts to introduce social revolution, and to be defending capitalism . . . Gone now are all dreams of Socialism in England. They now dream of crushing Socialism in Germany. The time will come when British workers will ask what they are going to get from this capitalist war. Our Socialism in Germany is real Socialism. Just as England hinders all reform in world politics, so she also hinders social reform in her own country . . . Will someone in England ever wonder whether materialism is everything in the world?[30]

The fact of the matter was of course, that Nazi Germany and Stalinist Russia were the most bitter of ideological, and for the Nazis at any rate, racial enemies. The Molotov-Ribbentrop Pact of August 1939 was an act of cynicism almost without parallel in a cynical age. However, what is interesting here is the early appearance of a characteristic of Nazi propaganda, which is its operation on numerous different and often contradictory levels at the same time. At one moment, Germany claimed to be involved only in a limited defensive operation to protect German nationals in Poland. At the next, she was embarked with 'the young nations of Europe' to rebuild the continent. And of course it was in their joint action against Poland that Nazi and Soviet co-operation was at its most cynical, a cynicism reflected in their joint anti-Polish propaganda. Just as the Germans had done a month or so earlier, Soviet radio and *Pravda* had begun displaying considerable anxiety about the fate of their kinsmen in Poland. On 14 September, Hamburg for the UK approvingly quoted a *Pravda* article entitled '*Real Reasons for Polish Defeat*', to the effect that the three million White Russians and eight million Ukrainians in Poland were subjected to 'continuous terror'.[31] On the following day, 15 September, Hamburg for Germany reported that the Poles were forcing Ukrainians and White Russians to burn their villages before the Germans could enter them. 'This is commented upon by the neutral press as another example of brutal treatment meted out by the Poles to their minority subjects.' Hamburg went on that: 'The calling up of reserves continues in Russia as the USSR must be fully prepared with war at her frontiers.'[32]

Following the Russian invasion of Poland on 17 September, Cologne on the long-wave band, Hamburg on medium-wave, and Zeesen on the short-wave, broadcast in English a joint Nazi-Soviet declaration:

> The German and Russian Governments have declared that in accordance with the spirit of the Russian-German pact, the action of their armies consists in the restoration of law and order in Poland which has been destroyed by the disintegration of the Polish state.
>
> Numerous meetings in the Soviet Union have passed resolutions endorsing the policy of the Government. The White Russians and Ukrainian minorities regard themselves as coming back into the fold of the Russian family. The *Pravda* says that in accordance with Soviet ideals, Russia is remaining neutral and has only liberated brethren from Polish oppression.[33]

The issuing of a joint declaration, of course, was designed to give the impression of co-operative and responsible internationalist behaviour by two reasonable and responsible sovereign states. Note too the use of language in this short extract. Germany and Russia had acted benevolently in intervening jointly in Poland 'to restore law and order', thus giving the impression that their act of joint piracy was an act of joint policing. Note too that the intervention was necessary because of the 'disintegration' of the Polish state. A very different impression would have been given had the more accurate term 'destruction' been employed instead. That the Germans and the Russians co-operated so closely in the dismemberment of Poland is often overlooked, given the course of subsequent events, but what is of particular interest here is the extent to which both Germany and Russia felt the need to disguise their cynical actions in a flimsy cloak of moral rectitude, and the appeal to an international conscience. In the age of propaganda, the Communists and National Socialists could do no better than resort to the traditional apologia of the land-grabber and the imperialist – the 'protection of minorities' and the 'restoration of law and order'.

On the same day, 18 September, the Germans and Russians issued a six-point agreement on the partition of Poland. The Polish state, it was claimed, from the moment of its creation lacked 'the element of life', and had collapsed through its own incompetence. Germany and Russia now faced the task of establishing a new settlement of their respective spheres of influence and of dealing with nationalities within them. The Anglo-French claim that they should assist Poland had proved groundless, and those two countries were now confronted with the question: 'What is the object of fighting Germany?'[34]

The defeat of Poland meant that by the end of September 1939, the Nazi propagandists were in as strong a position as their comrades in the Armed Forces. Following the publication on 28 September of a joint communiqué in Moscow by von Ribbentrop and Molotov calling for a peace settlement between Germany and the Western Powers, the Nazi propagandists clearly attempted to take the moral high-ground, and much prominence was given to the Russo-German peace offer, building up to Hitler's speech to the Reichstag on 6 October. Zeesen, in an English talk for Europe on 30 September, made the point that Britain played the lead in 'the anti-German campaign' and would be responsible for the acceptance or rejection of the peace offer. Note the friendly, almost sorrowful tone in the following short extract. Even Chamberlain is almost absolved from blame for beginning the war, a terrible act instead ascribed to a (presumably) small group of warmongering politicians:

> Lack of confidence in German intentions has already lead the English people into an undesirable position. Why has Chamberlain allowed anti-German politicians to make him break faith with the spirit of Munich? Why did the British Government not listen to the German complaints about Polish brutality instead of giving Poland that unfortunate guarantee? Hitler has insisted that Germany has no territorial claims in Western Europe and as Eastern Europe is now safeguarded by the Soviet-German agreement a lasting peace can be established for the benefit of civilisation.
>
> My dear listeners, if you were in Germany now you would see how little antagonism there is against the British people. The Germans know that the British people are not in favour of permanent hostilities; perhaps their politicians think it might be difficult to change their anti-German policy.[35]

The German government too, though, it was claimed, was in favour of a reasonable peace. Germany's case as expounded by Hitler was that she had no quarrel with France, and had for years made every effort to come to an understanding with Britain. It is likely of course, that Hitler had already made up his mind for military action against Britain and France, and that his speech was as much aimed at convincing the German people that if this unpopular war were to continue, it was through no fault of their Führer. Three days after this speech, Hitler drew up a memorandum for his commanders-in-chief in which he wrote:

> the German war aim is a final military settlement with the West, that is, the destruction of the power and ability of the Western Powers ever again to oppose the State Consolidation and further development of the German

people in Europe. As far as the outside world is concerned, this aim will have to undergo various propaganda adjustments, necessary from a psychological point of view. This does not alter the war aim. That is and remains the destruction of our western enemies.[36]

Certainly, the propaganda value of the peace offer was clear, for the overseas as well as the domestic audience. The Germans were convinced that a sizeable peace party existed in Britain and in France and well-argued and apparently reasonable offers to bury the hatchet, whether sincerely meant or not, were an obvious means of encouraging pacifist tendencies. Goebbels for instance saw such evidence in Lloyd George's urging of the consideration of Hitler's offer. 'He would not be able to do this', noted the Minister in his diary, 'if the right mood did not exist in England. Above all, the neutrals are gradually seeing the light. We must make sure that we press the message home.'[37]

The news in English from Hamburg at 10.30 on 7 October reported that the Führer's speech had been very favourably received in neutral and in particular in Italian circles. The reply of the Western democracies was awaited with much interest there. In Germany, the press was quoted as saying that Hitler had presented a complete programme for permanent peace and it fell to the democracies to give a straightforward answer if they were willing to co-operate or preferred to wage a terrible war:

> Hitler proposes to replace the Treaty of Versailles by conditions which would bring peace to Europe. He is prepared to forget the past. The peoples of Europe want peace and Hitler appealed to the logic and commonsense of the Nations. Europe stands at the cross-roads and Hitler desires to create order and construct a solid foundation for peace. The Democracies have for days, by press and radio, been telling people that Hitler would menace, threaten and then destroy whereas in reality he has come with outstretched hands ready to conclude a sane peace. All the peoples of Europe now await the reply to the Führer. If the peace of Europe is to become a reality then the co-operation of all responsible statesmen of Europe is required. If this great chance is missed, then arms would have to decide the problem. Germany's armies would march under the banner of Hitler's words: 'I do not doubt for one second that Germany will be victorious'. History will decide.[38]

We consider later the extent to which there was really ever any mileage in 'peace offers' propaganda in terms of its reception in Britain. However, just as his successors would reject subsequent offers, Chamberlain rejected this offer on 12 October. Other tactics were utilised as well, however, to fill the gap left by the absence in this period of the war of any real fighting. One propagandistic technique was to seize upon events which were in themselves not particularly significant and manipulate them into set-pieces, which conformed with and confirmed the chosen picture of the enemy. The earliest and one of the longest-running of these set-pieces originated in the sinking on 3 September of the Cunard liner *Athenia* off the coast of Ireland, en route from Glasgow to

Montreal, with the loss of 112 lives. Twenty-eight of the dead were American citizens. It would later emerge that the *Athenia* had been torpedoed without warning by a German U-boat, the commander claiming to have mistaken the liner for an armed vessel.

Now, it was a commonplace of radical right discourse in Germany after the Great War that British anti-German atrocity propaganda had enjoyed considerable success in encouraging support among neutral states for the Allies. In this new war, Germany was much keener to use atrocity stories than were the British, whose own propagandists feared to make use of a weapon which the experience of the Great War had discredited in the eyes of the British public. The Germans had fewer scruples, and immediately the news broke of *Athenia*'s fate, the Nazis denied any involvement. On 4 September, Cologne in German vehemently denied the allegations of the British press that a German torpedo had sunk the liner. The Führer had ordered German warships to observe international maritime regulations for shipping during wartime. Therefore the *Athenia* must have been sunk in error by a British warship, or else have struck a floating mine of English origin.[39] It is extremely unlikely that at this stage the Nazi propagandists could have known the true cause of the liner's fate, since not until U-30 reached Wilhemshaven on 27 September was the truth made known even to Hitler himself. Very rapidly, however, the Nazi line on the *Athenia* story became an open declaration that the vessel had been deliberately targeted by Britain on Churchill's personal order, and this story would become a stalwart to be trotted out on a regular basis.[40] Hamburg in English at 14.30 on 6 September continued the story. It was proved, it claimed, that no German warships or mines were in the area of the *Athenia*, and that the sinking was carefully planned by the Admiralty to compromise Germany. It would be stupid of Germany to sink the *Athenia*, and Hamburg quoted an unnamed American paper to the effect that it was not incredible that the *Athenia* had in fact struck a British mine.[41] It would indeed have been stupid for Germany to have sunk her, given the need so early in the war to avoid outright confrontation with the USA; it takes no great leap of the imagination to conclude that the wisest propaganda ploy was simply to assert that Britain had been responsible, especially bearing in mind the American public's residual suspicion about Britain's past skill at manipulating them. Indeed, it is the view of one historian that for the first months of the war, Britain was on the defensive in neutral Europe with regard to the *Athenia* and other stories.[42]

Certainly, the fact that Germany was often so outrageously brass-necked in her propaganda did allow her at times to make some telling points against Britain, especially given British claims to moral superiority over the Third Reich. That Chamberlain and his colleagues had for so long appeased Hitler, had so cravenly submitted to his blackmail at Munich before providing an open-ended guarantee to Poland, could be and frequently was used against Britain in the propaganda war. As Poland crashed to defeat, Chamberlain, unable to render his ally any meaningful assistance, found himself declaring that his aim now was the destruction of Hitlerism, leaving himself open to charges from Germany of traditional British arrogance, expansionism and of course hypocrisy. Chamberlain's claim to moral superiority was merely another example of Britain's lying propaganda against which the Nazi wireless kept up a persistent tirade in the early months. A broadcast from Hamburg in English on 11 September drew parallels with Lord Macmillan's Ministry of Information and Lord Northcliffe's 'notorious department' from the Great War. Hamburg denounced the BBC's story that German troops had destroyed the monastery of Chestochowa and the image of the Black Virgin, an object of veneration for Polish Roman Catholics. This story, said Hamburg, had an equally fictitious parallel in 1914 when Germans were accused of destroying the famous altar of Louvain. In 1939, Hamburg continued, 'the world knows too much about the methods of British propaganda and it does not take so long to refute a lie.'[43]

British hypocrisy too could be easily enough illustrated by her blockade of mainland Europe, at a time when constraints of geography and Hitler's concern for the sensitivities of neutrals confined the U-boat fleets to the waters immediately around the British Isles. The blockade – invariably referred to as the 'starvation blockade' – was consistently used to demonstrate Britain's cruelty and high-handed lack of concern for the well-being of non-belligerent nations. For example, a bulletin in English from Hamburg on 14 September consisted almost entirely of an attack on the blockade. The list of contraband goods drawn up by Britain was said to be an unscrupulous violation of international law and evidence of the cruelty of British warfare. Contrary to the generally accepted rules, Britain was trying to starve the women and children of all European countries. She assumed the right to control foodstuffs and cattle fodder that Europe must import from abroad. She assumed the right to prescribe to Italy, Spain, Yugoslavia, Greece, Holland, the Scandinavian and Baltic countries what they should be allowed to eat, what clothes they might wear and how many head of cattle they might keep. These measures, said Hamburg, would especially affect women and children and the aged. Britain threatened starvation to the young of Europe and early death to old people. But the blockade was only a blow against the weak. Germany, with access to Poland and other eastern countries, would not be affected. The trade of neutrals would be destroyed and their economic life throttled:

> Will neutral states and great powers put up with this British impertinence? Germany will not: she is ready to fight these measures. She had intended to adhere to international law, but since Britain does not she will retaliate. Neutral countries will know that Germany did not desire this development for which Britain must bear the sole responsibility.[44]

The attack was continued in a talk from Hamburg, late on the evening of the 14–15th:

> The starvation blockade will affect mothers and children in countries adjacent to Germany that have nothing to do with the war. All this is done in the name of freedom, independence and humanity. The British Govern-

ment has even issued a decree regulating the way in which the prize money shall be distributed – 75% goes to the Exchequer, 25% to the officers and crew of the capturing vessel. The Elizabethan buccaneers have come back.[45]

We assess in more detail in later chapters the impact and effectiveness of propaganda broadcasts, but it is worth posing a question here on what exactly it was that broadcasts such as these were supposed to achieve. It may be one thing to lambaste the British blockade for a neutral audience in mainland Europe, but what was to be gained in denigrating the British to the British themselves as hypocrites and pirates? Goebbels seemed to believe that by lashing and haranguing the British in this way, by 'exposing' them, he could help force them to come to terms with Germany. He noted in a highly significant entry in his diary as the war moved into a new phase: 'England must be exposed and completely discredited. Only then shall we be able to negotiate with her.'[46]

Numerous other opportunities for 'exposing and discrediting' the British presented themselves in the 'phoney' period of the war. For example, in the conspiracy-strewn world imagined by the Nazi propagandists, it was self-evident that the British should be behind the attempt on Hitler's life at the Bürgerbräukeller in Munich on 8 November. As Goebbels told his conference on 11 November, the moral responsibility of the Western democracies, in particular of Britain, was proved by her continuous murder propaganda; Britain therefore was to be pilloried and exposed. Sure enough, the story that the assassination attempt had been organised by the British appeared regularly over the next few days.[47] Some of these attacks on the British were more successful than others. For instance, the question 'Where is the *Ark Royal*?' was repeatedly asked on the German wireless from the end of September 1939 onwards, with the obvious implication that the aircraft carrier had been sunk, until that is, the vessel turned up at Cape Town in December. The Germans were on much firmer ground with the spectacular and irrefutable sinkings of the aircraft carrier *Courageous* off the Hebrides in September and the *Royal Oak* at Scapa Flow in October. At the end of the year, the *Admiral Graf Spee* held centre stage, the incident in which one of Germany's finest modern ships was scuttled off Montevideo being treated as a victorious page in the history of the German navy.

In the 'phoney' months of 1940, however, it was the attack on the German auxiliary naval vessel *Altmark* in Norway's Jössingford by the destroyer HMS *Cossack*, which was the key propaganda set-piece. The *Altmark* was the supply ship for the *Admiral Graf Spee*, and was on route for home through Norwegian territorial waters with some 300 British prisoners aboard from captured merchant vessels. Chased into the fjord – in violation of Norway's neutrality – the *Altmark* was boarded on 16 February 1940 by sailors from the *Cossack* and after a skirmish in which four German crewmen were killed the prisoners were released. The British version of events was the first by several hours to be released, the German version somewhat delayed due to differences between the *AA* and the *RMVP*. Hitler himself was reported to have voiced his displeasure at this loss of the propaganda initiative, and perhaps as a result Goebbels ordered at his conference on 19 February that 'all propaganda must be focused on this single incident'.[48] The Minister's demand was certainly complied with, and the *Altmark* incident was given greater publicity in Nazi propaganda than any other single issue since the end of the war in Poland, practically monopolising all German propaganda for the next four or five days.[49] Hamburg in English on 20 February drew lessons from the episode not just about the specific British involvement, but for Britain's wider relationships with neutrals. Note the reference to Finland – then involved in a war inconvenient for Nazi propaganda with the Soviet Union – as a small nation shaping its policy under British influence:

> The attack on the *Altmark* has not only revealed to the whole world the cruelty and brutality of British naval warfare, but is also an important object lesson to all neutrals of the value which can be placed on Britain's guarantees, pledges, and promises of protection. Neutrals should note that the *Daily Mail*, in commenting on the *Cossack*'s action, said it hoped that the whole world would be convinced that Great Britain, in similar circumstances, would act again in the same manner. The British paper observes cynically that the result of this exchange of Notes with Norway is a matter of indifference. The fate of Poland and Czechoslovakia, ought to provide other European countries with important information about the sincerity of British pledges, and the value of British support politically. Finland is now the third victim of British offers to protect all small nations who, at the instigations of British ministers, may by dragged or pushed into conflicts with their neighbours.[50]

So, while these various episodes were used in a tactical fashion in the attempt to discredit the British, the attack was also mounted at a more strategic level, and the inhumanity and hypocrisy of the British could be so easily illustrated for the Nazis by the existence of the British Empire. It was a simple enough matter to accuse the British of hypocrisy in attacking Germany as an expansionist nation, when the British themselves were holding down the largest empire in world history. In a simple but effective talk from Zeesen in English on 11 September, listeners were told that the leaders of the British Empire were having difficulty in explaining to its citizens why they must fight Germany. There followed a long list of dates of the numerous annexations and conquests by which the Empire had been acquired.[51] Another clever talk from Hamburg in December made simple and effective use of the gift which the Empire represented to any anti-British propagandist:

> It would be interesting to know what single work or act of Germany's could be construed by any unbiased mind as a belief in her right or destiny to rule the world. On the contrary, the amassing of the British Empire, and the wars of conquest that have been fought to gain it, are a standing monument to this

very same belief on England's part. The comparative smallness of Germany's colonial possessions before the last war, and the very fact that, through the centuries, Germany has not even been a united nation are sufficient refutations of this baseless accusation of German claims to world hegemony.[52]

An Empire so acquired, of course, had to be maintained by force, and Britain's long history of cruelty towards native peoples would often be the subject of German propaganda broadcasts. Given the tenets of Nazi racial ideologies and their own plans for the enslavement of peoples of supposedly lower racial standing, such broadcasts, telling as they may have been, perhaps as well as any other illustrate the utter cynicism of the Nazi system and its propagandists. But as well as the strategic attempt to use the Empire as a stick with which to beat the British in the eyes of world opinion, attempts were frequently made to stir up animosity towards Britain on the part of the numerous more or less disaffected groups within it. As one might expect, the content, while sticking in general terms to the central themes of Nazi propaganda, varied depending upon the intended recipient. Propaganda for South Africa for example stressed the potential and real divergence of views between British South Africans and the Boers. A broadcast from Zeesen for South Africa in English on 9 September emphasised the political differences between Herzog and Smuts. Herzog, the so-called 'Hindenburg of the Boers', had camouflaged his feelings during the Great War, but his hatred of England was always smouldering. As for Smuts, 'one need only say that he threw his lot in with the British invader.' The real feeling of the Boers, it was argued, was expressed by the member of the South African Parliament who said that the war was started not by Germany, but by a hypocritical Britain, a country which had built its Empire by robbery and blackmail. The Boers wanted peace, in the face of oppression by a power abrogating to itself the title of advocate of freedom.[53]

But the Nazis were also capable of producing material not just for groups like the Boers with whom they may well have felt some racial sympathy, but for groups for whom normally they would have had little or nothing but racial contempt. On 14 September Zeesen broadcast in English for African listeners a report of a meeting of the Islam Association in Berlin, the Arab Club in Berlin and the Moslem Defence Committee of Palestine in Germany, which addressed the following appeal to the Moslems of the world:

> Whereas England and France have foisted another war on the world in which they intend to involve Indians and other Moslems with quarrels of other nations and England and France [are the] greatest enemies of Islam, as has been proved by the history of last two centuries, and whereas they have instituted a reign of terror in Palestine and the British Empire, this general meeting of Islam Association in Berlin, Arab Club in Berlin and Moslem Defence Committee of Palestine in Germany have passed the following resolution unanimously: All Moslems of the world, especially Indian Moslems, should at this critical juncture refrain from giving money or support to

the British, but Moslems of India and whole world should utilise this opportunity to the fullest extent and make themselves free from the yoke of British Imperialism which presses so heavily upon them.[54]

But the Germans were also at pains to show that they were just as concerned with the oppression of the masses in Britain by the plutocrats against whom Germany was battling in revolutionary conflict. The notion that the Third Reich represented a dynamic indeed a revolutionary force, pitched against the atavistic forces of British capitalism, would become with time a staple of Nazi propaganda, despite the fact that there was little which was revolutionary about this essentially reactionary and backward-looking regime. Even so, the 'plutocracy' argument was a favourite of Goebbels; he told his conference just before Christmas 1939 that 'the propaganda against plutocracy in Britain is attracting notice and is beginning to be effective.'[55] He noted in his diary early in the New Year that 'growing defeatism [is] in evidence in England. Particularly so far as social questions are concerned. We exploit this weakness.'[56] Certainly a good deal of time and effort was expended in telling the British how badly they were exploited by their masters and in contrasting the pathetic social conditions in the UK with the great advances made in Germany under National Socialism. *Deutschlandsender*, for example, on 13 September interrupted a musical programme for '*A Trip to London*'. This programme included heartrending descriptions of endless streets of miserable houses swathed in heavy fog, emaciated children playing and hopeless unemployed youths smoking cigarettes at street corners. This picture, it was claimed, was repeated in hundreds of thousands of streets, especially in the distressed areas.[57] On 19 September Zeesen gave a graphic account of life in British slums for the edification of its African listeners; British children and dogs were resigned, said Zeesen, to living with vermin. 'If English people must kill, why don't they kill their own cockroaches before sacrificing the lives of their French friends?'[58]

Rather different in tone was a talk for the British themselves in early December, which used a speech by Stanley Baldwin to make a number of telling points about Britain's own social set-up. No note was made of the identity of the speaker, but the measured, moderate and not unreasonable style and content, suggests that the broadcaster was perhaps Eduard Dietze:

> With all deference to the hospitality which I once enjoyed in Dudley – where the speech was delivered – I am not at all surprised that this place rivalling others in grime, soot and blackness, should have set Baldwin dreaming about the new world to be created. It is a most extraordinary thing for a professedly democratic government like yours to acquiesce in a state of social affairs which the National Socialist Government in Germany would not tolerate for a single minute. In fact, when I told two friends, who are foremen in big works near my home town about the way in which the English working class population is looked after, or rather neglected, by those in power, they would not believe me. I told them about the march of the unemployed in 1936 from

Jarrow to London. The marchers met with a friendly reception everywhere except in Whitehall, where they were not allowed to present their petition and had to return home, hardly gratified by the veiled promise that their case would be considered . . .

But what is the new world going to be like? I should not be surprised if the conception of simple British workmen from Jarrow or Dudley is not quite the same as that held by Baldwin. I have a shrewd suspicion that the latter had in mind a world made safe for democracy through British initiative in fighting Hitlerism – a world which enjoys its freedom and independence under the protection of the British Fleet. The British workers on the other hand, might be of the opinion that democracy begins at home, and that the foundations of the new world must be laid on a basis of social justice and government efficiency in dealing with the vital problems of the good old country itself. I sometimes wonder whether the British Government is aware that insufficient knowledge and lack of judgement might have fatal consequences for the future of the country. Well, sometimes they must be wondering themselves.

Of all of Britain's social problems, however, the issue which had been most starkly to the fore throughout the interwar period was unemployment, and astonishingly for a nation supposedly at total war, Britain still had over a million unemployed in the spring of 1940. Here again was a too-easy target for the Nazi propagandists, the more so since the eradication of unemployment in Germany was one of the Hitler regime's most spectacular domestic achievements. In December 1939, a speaker on Hamburg, introduced as 'Lord Haw-Haw', made good use of Britain's sorry social record, which was particularly marked when contrasted with the achievements of Germany's National Socialism:

903,000 men, 418,000 women, 109,000 boys and girls. That makes the total 1,430,000 altogether. That is the mighty army of the British unemployed. It is substantially larger than the British Army in the field. It is utterly unproductive. It is demoralising the nation and it is a tremendous drain on Britain's purse . . . What interest do you suppose these people who need work, whose first necessity is the opportunity to earn a few pounds and get back the self-respect long unemployment has taken from them – what interest have they in a war for democracy, freedom and human rights? What concern have they in Poles and Czechs, or any other European people when British people are allowed to walk the streets without bread and clothes? . . .

You know there is nothing to be afraid of in that word socialism, which has been well defined in the following words – to replace competition with co-operation and to apportion equitably the opportunities of life and the rewards of labour. That has been the aim and the achievement of National Socialism in Germany, where we have no slums, no unemployment problems and no social degradation and decay such as haunt your cities and industrial centres . . . In spite of this, the talk about unlimited expenditure goes on when, in fact, millions are being spent in your attempt to destroy a country which is decades ahead of you socially. Germany has solved problems you have not even started to tackle and some day your 1,430,000 unemployed men and women, boys and girls will call your government and you to account for this.[59]

These ghastly social conditions, of course, arose as a direct result of Britain's degenerate Judeo-plutocratic system, and the hack politicians who ran that system in the interests of international Jewry. The favourite target was Churchill but a long cast-list of other British public figures was to be regularly abused and vilified over the coming years. In the early months of the war, Chamberlain was an obvious target. He was not only senile, but a warmonger with a lifetime's experience of oppressing the British masses.[60] A clever and sophisticated pillorying of Chamberlain was conducted on Bremen after the Prime Minister's speech at the end of November, the sarcastic tone again strongly redolent of William Joyce:

I am well acquainted with the bankrupt mentality of British politicians, but unless I had heard it with my own ears I should never have believed it possible that any of them, however lacking in imagination, would dare to come before the British people once again and tell them that they were engaged in war to end war. What reaction must this hypocritical claim arouse in the minds of heroes of Mons or the Marne who have for so many years been waiting for justice outside your Labour Exchanges?[61]

And of course while Chamberlain was roundly abused, it was Churchill who headed the Nazis' British hate-list, having long since been identified by Goebbels as Hitler's chief antagonist. *Deutschlandsender* interrupted a musical programme on 18 September for what the BBC monitors called 'the most scurrilous attack on Mr Winston Churchill which has been made since the outbreak of the war.' The First Lord was described sitting in the House of Commons eating a beefsteak, the red blood flowing over his lips. It was explained that throughout his whole life this man had sought one thing – blood. As a young military correspondent, 'coarse and red-haired', he was found to have his pocket filled with cartridges – that is he was a *franc-tireur* not a journalist. Later in his inglorious career he earned from the Turks the sobriquet 'Satan's Knight'.[62] 'Why are we at war again?' asked Hamburg in October:

Because Churchill longed for the glory of a dictator or the second Napoleon. Churchill is the chief of the warmongers. The world is wondering why among British statesmen there are warmongers like Churchill.[63]

The answer to this conundrum, in the paranoid world-view of the Nazi propagandists, was revealed in the talk on Chamberlain cited above, in which the 'charitable' view of Chamberlain's behaviour was that he had been 'misled and gulled by wily Jews who relied on his unswerving devotion to orthodox finance to make him their tool.'[64] If any one feature distinguished National Socialism from the ragbag of other central European fascisms, it was the centrality within its ideology of the hate figure of the Jew. Indeed, so central

was anti-Semitism to National Socialism that it was the bedrock upon which all
Nazi propaganda – for internal and external consumption – was founded.
Propaganda for the UK was no exception and anti-Semitism was a consistent
and persistent feature of broadcast material. Even those talks and items which
did not deal explicitly with the Jews were informed, coloured and given
meaning by the anti-Jewish obsession at the heart of National Socialism. Early
in October 1939, Hamburg carried a stinging talk on Jewish control of the
British press:

> A certain Mr Abraham Abrahams also of non-British origin is one of the
> largest shareholders of the *Daily Herald*. The *Sunday Pictorial* and the *Daily
> Mirror* whose wallowing in obscenity has long been disgusting the British
> public, are partly owned by Sir John Ellerman, whose father the unscru-
> pulous shipping magnate came from Hamburg, but was not of German
> origin. He is a multi-millionaire. His wife De Sola is also of non-British
> origin . . . Another person who makes a profit out of pornography and anti-
> German propaganda is Mr Israel Sieff, chief proprietor of Marks and
> Spencer. What has become of Mr Spencer, the British partner, seems to
> be unknown. This Mr Israel Moses Sieff is reported to have acquired a
> predominant interest in the *Daily Mail*, which changed its attitude towards
> Germany a few months before the war . . .
>
> The *Daily Express* is largely controlled by Lord Beaverbrook, formerly
> Aitken, an adventurer of Canadian origin who shows no urgent desire to visit
> Canada. The Managing Director is Mr R. D. Blumenfeld, who as you might
> judge by his old Chinese name, is not of British origin . . .
>
> Please reflect upon these facts. Do you propose to allow such people to
> make up your mind for you? They have already played a great part in landing
> you in your present predicament. People of England, you must either assert
> your independence of these corrupt forces, or serve their selfish purposes till
> the life of your culture is extinguished and the final chapter of your history is
> closed.[65]

As in this example, the anti-Semitic material broadcast was scarcely sophisticated, but merely dealt in the basest stereotypes, although of course it is in
the nature of propaganda that sophisticated argument is not required for
successful impact. Very often indeed, Nazi anti-Semitic propaganda for the
UK was mere abuse and unsupported assertion. Much mileage, for example,
was gained from the resignation from the Cabinet in early January 1940 of the
Secretary of State for War, Leslie Hore-Belisha, who had long been a favourite
Nazi target. Hamburg broadcast in English a talk on the evening of 18 January
which was typical. Note the way in which the sneering attack on Hore-Belisha is
used as a vehicle through which to blame the Jews in general for the entire war:

> In the War Office as in all other Whitehall departments there has been and
> still is hopeless muddle. Don't just take our word for it. Ask your fighting
> men. Ask them about all the comforts they were promised so glibly by these

Jews and friends of Jews in order to get them to fight. Ask your husbands, sons and brothers if they have even yet received wireless sets, games and sports equipment and warm clothing which have been subscribed so willingly by you all.

One cause of the ex-Jewish furniture salesman's dismissal was that he tried to dictate to a General who admittedly does know his job. And a secondary cause is that military leaders refused to be ordered about by a member of that race which is responsible for this ridiculous war . . .

Who is behind the mysterious organisation which puts the Belisha advertisement in some of your papers? Probably the British Committee for Jewish Refugees. Very significant is the remark printed in the *Mail* made by a member of the firm of advertising agents who offered the advertisement. This remark is: 'Advertiser has insisted that his name is not to be revealed. He is an English businessman, not a Jew'. Humph![66]

So, by early 1940 the main lines of Nazi propaganda about and to Britain had been clearly laid down, and while the attack upon Britain took place on a broad front, the various threads were variations on a single theme, a theme which Britain's own cloak-and-dagger propagandists at Electra House expressed in the phrase 'Britain the crumbling monster'.[67] She was 'the vampire of the continent of Europe' which throughout history had ruthlessly exploited the European nations for her own ends. Just as she had driven France and Poland into war with Germany, and Finland into war with Russia, she was now using the League of Nations in an attempt to set the rest of the world ablaze. Not content, however, with sucking the blood of Europe, she possessed in her Empire the greatest slave-realm in the world, an Empire won by cunning, treachery and violence, and maintained by cruelty and oppression. While the German soldier fought an honest fight for freedom and the righting of old wrongs, Britain's Secret Service fought against right and justice with poison and treacherous murder. Her time, however, had come. Far from strangling Germany and starving her women and children through blockade as she had in the Great War, Britain herself was under siege, struggling with inadequate naval resources to keep open the sea-lanes upon which her life depended. Her wretched plutocracy, in which the greedy few leeched upon the flesh of the hungry many, was incapable of meeting the stringent economic demands of modern warfare, in contrast to Germany's truly socialist, truly efficient people's community. In time, the British people would see the truth, would rid themselves of their oppressors and save themselves before disaster struck them. In short, Britain was being thrust aside by the onward march of destiny. The pathetic, weak, corrupt old men and political non-entities who ruled her were irredeemably of the past. The future belonged to the young nations of Europe. Russia and Germany had now formed a 'geographical unity from the Rhine to the Bering Straits'.[68]

The techniques used to promote this message were simple enough: the selection and distortion of suitable current events, each of which on its own may have been trivial enough, but which could take on a new significance in the mosaic of the decaying Empire. As the BBC had noted, a typical Hamburg broadcast could be easily composed from any day's issue of the British morning press: 'Thus, news of a divorce case could be represented as a sign of moral disruption, the delay of a train as a disorganisation of British transport . . .'[69] This selection and distortion was designed to provoke and manipulate psychological and emotional responses in the target audience. In these early days, the frequent harping on Britain's responsibility for the outbreak of the war, her wicked treatment of Germany and of her slave Empire were designed to stimulate feelings of guilt. The stress on the worsening economic situation was designed to foment anxiety. The incitement to class warfare played upon natural feelings of aggression, directing them away from Germany, and towards the nation's leaders. As war progressed, and objective circumstances altered and developed, the scope of this emotional and psychological stimulus and manipulation would broaden also.

The relative importance of various elements within this single concept – Britain 'the crumbling monster' – would and did change over time and in relation to circumstances, but 'the intensity of the whole theme', as Electra House put it, remained remarkably consistent. It was expressed with almost equal force in propaganda for Great Britain, the neutrals and for Germany herself, accounting, in fact, for over two-thirds of the entire output of the Nazi propaganda system in the 'phoney war' period.[70] The BBC also attempted in this period to summarise the goals and techniques of the Nazi wireless war. The aim, the Corporation reported, was to separate the public from their leaders, by the presentation to them of an image of their nation as an Empire in decay, and to replace in their minds the traditional views they held of themselves and of their place in the world. The material presented was varied and of varying quality but this central notion was a permanent fixture. Writing early in the new year, 1940, the BBC analysts summarised the image of Britain, thus:

That picture is of an England where the people are misled by corrupt and irresponsible leaders, where the small wealthy class leaves the masses to misery, unemployment, hunger and exploitation; of an Empire built on brutality and rapacity, now as decadent and as divided as its Mother Country; of an England hated by the world for her selfishness and ruthlessness. The picture in outline resembles the Roman Empire in the Fourth Century AD – itself decrepit and superannuated, but striving to hold its place in the world by playing off one neighbour against another. From such a portrait it follows that in the present war, Germany – a fresh new power – is fighting to free herself and the world from the tyrannous shackles of Britain; or, with greater accuracy, to free herself, the world, and the British masses, from the tyrannous fetters of the British ruling class. Rarely, if ever, do the Hamburg broadcasts make their picture so clear-cut as it has been made here, but every separate news item is selected or twisted, every talk is designed, to take its place as a facet in such a general picture. As in half-tone block the picture is composed dot by dot. If this picture is accepted by the British people, the German aim is achieved.[71]

To achieve this aim, the propagandists required an intimate knowledge of the target audience, since the message must be tailored and adjusted seemingly to conform with, but at the same time to manipulate and direct, existing prejudices. The extent to which the Germans were able to do this will be discussed later. For the moment, though, it is worth noting that the attempt was certainly made to identify target groups and to produce propaganda accordingly. For the working classes, material was produced which emphasised the socialist element within National Socialism. Britain was represented as a rotten society, run by and in the interests of a decadent, feudal aristocracy and bloodsucking Jewish capitalism. So, the extent of unemployment in Britain might be emphasised, the problems associated with evacuation, the delay and meanness of payments to soldiers' families, the extent of politicians' investments in the armaments industries, the iniquities of the rationing schemes and so on. For contrasting effect, the achievements of German socialism would be described, emphasising in particular Hitler's early eradication of unemployment.

For the middle classes, the message was less emotionally presented, but equally pernicious. The destructive effects would be emphasised of increased tax, the deleterious effects of war on British trade and finance, the shifting balance of world power in favour of the United States, the weakening of links with the Empire, and so on. The BBC, too, discerned a propaganda aimed at 'the Intellectual', who was approached in a totally different way, and the argument ran here on lines which could best be described as 'British home-made'. The view taken by the German government was now the same as that taken in the past by such papers as the *News Chronicle* and the *New Statesman*. The colonial problem, the failure of the League of Nations, the revival and history of imperialism, were all treated in this way. The arguments were chosen with such skill and presented in so familiar a phraseology that:

> the listener forgets these are actually Nazis who talk about the Concentration Camps in the Boer War, about suppression of self-determination in India, and on the consequences of D.O.R.A. for British life and habits. These arguments are not without effect. They appeal to the moral sense of the British listener. The implied idea is that Britain is not entitled to reproach Hitler, who is after all no worse than Warren Hastings; what Germany has done to the Czechs, Britain has done to the Irish; and in this war even the last difference will fade. Democratic institutions are bound to vanish and war against Fascism in Germany will create Fascism in England.[72]

We assess in later chapters the extent to which the German propagandists succeeded in achieving their objectives. In the meantime, though, it is necessary to continue the analysis of propaganda, as the war against Britain moved into its most dangerous phase.

Notes

1 ZEE IEFE 08.00 31.8.39. The extracts cited here from the earliest days of the conflict are necessarily brief, since few early *Digests* contain verbatim transcripts, but are in précis form only.
2 Blue Book (1939), document 57.
3 ZEE IEFE 08.00 1.9.39.
4 PRO CAB 68/1 WP (R) (39) 17.
5 ZEE IEFFE 13.45 1.9.39.
6 The technique of quoting selectively from enemy or neutral papers in support of some German accusation was one which would become familiar. In particular, much use would be made in time of quotations from 'neutral' papers which were in fact owned by the German Propaganda Ministry. See PRO FO 371/30946.
7 ZEE IEFE 15.00 1.9.39.
8 COLOG IEFE 22.00 1.9.39.
9 Blue Book (1939), documents 89 and 92.
10 ZEE IGFG 14.15 3.9.39.
11 Blue Book (1939), document 119.
12 ZEE IEFE 14.20 14.9.39.
13 BBC DD no. 35 – 16.9.39.
14 ZEE IEFA 08.30 15.9.39.
15 ZEE ISFLA 03.00 14.9.39.
16 PODE IEFE 20.52 29.9.39.
17 Gombrich, *Myth and Reality*, p. 14.
18 DEUT IGFG 14.00 13.9.39.
19 ZEE IGFFE 06.30 14.9.39.
20 DEUT IGFG 07.00 18.9.39.
21 HAM IEFE 02.00 11.9.39.
22 DEUT IPFP 07.30 13.9.39.
23 DEUT IGFG 23.40 16.9.39.
24 DEUT IPFP 10.30 17.9.39.
25 HAM IEFE 19.00 22.9.39.
26 ZEE IAFSA 20.00 22.9.39.
27 STUTT IFFF 00.15 30.9.39.
28 ZEE ISFLA 03.00 8.9.39.
29 DEUT IGFG 12.50 5.9.39.
30 HAM IEFE 23.20 28.9.39.
31 HAM IEFE 17.30 14.9.39.
32 HAM IGFG 14.10 15.9.39.
33 COLOG, HAM, ZEE IEFE 17.30 18.9.39.
34 WCBX (USA) IEFUSA 08.30 18.9.39.
35 ZEE IEFE 22.15 30.9.39.
36 Cited in Bullock, *Hitler*, pp. 555-7.
37 *Goebbels' Diaries*, Taylor (ed.), entry for 9 October 1939.
38 HAM IEFE 10.30 7.10.39.
39 COLOG IGFG 14.40 4.9.39.
40 Hans Fritzsche, *Deutschlandsender*'s leading radio commentator, claimed only to have discovered the truth in a conversation with Admiral Raeder while they awaited trial at Nuremberg in December 1945. See *Trial of German Major War Criminals*, p. 249.
41 HAM IEFE 14.30 6.9.39.

42 Cole, *Britain and the War of Words*, p. 9.

43 HAM IEFE 00.15 11.9.39.

44 HAM IEFE 02.00 14.9.39.

45 HAM 00.15 15.9.39.

46 *Goebbels' Diaries*, Taylor (ed.), entry for 29 April 1940.

47 Boelcke, *Secret Conferences*, pp. 4–5.

48 Boelcke, *Secret Conferences*, pp. 21–2.

49 PRO FO 371/24393, A[nalysis of]G[erman]P[ropaganda], 16–29 February 1940. A short extract from one of William Joyce's talks on the *Altmark* episode, may be heard on the CD at Track 4.

50 HAM IEFE: 20.15 20.2.40.

51 ZEE IEFE 15.40 11.9.39.

52 HAM IEFE 22.15 5.12.39.

53 ZEE IEFSA 13.22 8.9.39.

54 ZEE IEFA 22.15 14.9.39.

55 Boelcke, *Secret Conferences*, p. 10.

56 *Goebbels' Diaries*, Taylor (ed.), entry for 12 January 1940.

57 DEUT 08.50 13.9.39.

58 ZEE IEFA 07.36 15.9.39.

59 HAM IEFE 21.15 7.12.39.

60 FRANK IFFF 00.15 11.9.39.

61 HAM & BREM IEFE 22.20 29.11.39.

62 DEUT IGFG 15.15 18.9.39.

63 HAM IEFE 10.30 4.10.39.

64 HAM & BREM IEFE 22.20 29.11.39.

65 HAM IEFE 23.20 1.10.39.

66 HAM IEFE 22.15 18.1.40.

67 PRO CAB 68/4 WM (R.) 40 13, AGP, 1–15 December 1939.

68 DEUT IGFG 20.00 18.9.39.

69 PRO FO 371/24393, *The Voice of Hamburg*, 14 February 1940.

70 PRO CAB 68/4, AGP, *passim*.

71 PRO FO 371/24393, *The Voice of Hamburg*, 14 February 1940.

72 PRO FO 371/24393, *The Voice of Hamburg*, 14 February 1940.

3

Subversive Wireless Propaganda in Total War

Propaganda is likely to have its greatest impact when it appears to be in line with objective reality. This was true of Nazi propaganda for much of the 'phoney' period of the war. Germany had conquered Poland with little difficulty and the Allies' military response had been minimal. Whatever might be said about her ideological propaganda, it was difficult to refute Germany's claim to the military initiative. And it was also true in the period between the German conquest of the Low Countries and her invasion of the Soviet Union. This truth was well recognised in official British circles. Frank Roberts at the Foreign Office ruefully noted in April 1941 that 'German propaganda has been successful largely because the big battalions (or rather the tanks and aircraft) have been on the German side. It is only when the big battalions are on our side that our propaganda can be really effective.'[1] Unfortunately for the British, it would be some time before the 'big battalions' would be on their side, and from April 1940 the military situation rapidly went from bad to much worse. The succession of military disasters which the Germans inflicted on the Allies, from the rout in Scandinavia, through the invasion of the Low Countries to the fall of France, had gigantic implications for Britain's military position, for her home morale, and also for the role and content of German propaganda. Whether or not the propagandists planned it so in advance, it seemed by the summer of 1940 that propaganda in the phoney war had merely functioned to soften up British morale in the run-up to serious hostilities, while propaganda in the second half of 1940 aimed to foment out-and-out revolution in the UK, to undermine morale and to bring about social collapse in advance of the country's invasion. No one, of course, in 1939, could have predicted the astonishing sequence of events which unfolded in 1940, and there is no evidence that any master propaganda plan existed. Nevertheless, as events developed rapidly, so too did the propagandists try to keep pace with them. We consider here the content of that propaganda for the UK from the invasion of Scandinavia to the beginning of the Russo-German war.

With the outbreak of serious hostilities in the West, the pattern of Nazi propaganda shifted. The analysts at Electra House noted in April 1940 that hitherto Nazi propaganda had been dominated by the variegated theme of 'German Strength'. After 8 April, however, when Germany invaded Norway and Denmark, the invasion was naturally enough the dominating topic in propaganda, and the theme of 'Military Operations' moved to the fore.[2] Before the invasion, military propaganda had centred upon the destruction of Allied aircraft, German reconnaissance flights over France and Britain, and air attacks on British shipping. Now, however, that the war of words had been replaced by a real shooting war, the war propaganda machine could be given its head for the first time since the end of the war against Poland. By the end of April, 50 per cent of the total output for all countries of the German propaganda machine was concerned with military topics.[3]

At the start of the campaign, actually on 10 April, Goebbels had laid down at his Ministerial Conference his directives for the treatment of the Scandinavian campaign:

> Germany does not need to blow her own trumpet; for that our position is too strong. On the other hand, the world and above all the British people, must be made to see as clearly as possible the humiliating position into which Britain has manoeuvred herself . . . At all costs must the thesis be maintained and underlined that the operation was solely a reply to the British operations in Norwegian waters, and was only triggered off by these operations.[4]

Indeed, this was a technique which was frequently used afterwards: Germany would claim that she had successfully forestalled by her actions a planned threat by the Allies either upon herself or upon others, in this case forestalling Allied aggression against Norway by a mere ten hours. Here again was a shift in propaganda technique from that which accompanied the attack on Poland. In the latter case, it will be recalled, the assault was accompanied by repeated complaints of Polish brutality towards ethnic Germans, and with claims of Anglo-Polish machinations aimed at the destruction of Germany. Germany, in other words, wholly inaccurately, was portrayed as the victim of Anglo-Polish aggression. In the case of Norway however, the Nazis' armed assault was accompanied by claims that Germany was actually acting to save Norway from Allied aggression. It is worth pointing out that this material did have some basis in reality. As Alexander L. George has noted, this was no mere case of 'projection' – the technique of attributing intentions similar to your own to an opponent who does not have such intentions – since the Germans were correct in thinking that the Allies did indeed have aggressive intentions towards Norway, whose neutrality had already been compromised by Britain at the time of the *Altmark* incident.[5] At any event, Germany's first utterances on the invasion of Norway – the High Command communiqué issued on the morning of 9 April – made the point that the operation was entirely of a protective nature:

> The High Command of the German Defence Forces announces: To counter the British attack on the neutrality of Denmark and Norway, the German defence forces have taken over the armed protection of these countries. This morning strong German forces have entered or have been landed in these two countries. To cover these operations extensive mine barrages have been laid, it is authoritatively stated in Berlin. To resist hostile enterprises, minefields were laid last night in front of the important harbours of the Norwegian West Coast.[6]

On the same afternoon, Hamburg claimed again that the Allies were responsible for the extension of the war, and indeed that Germany was acting only in defence of international law. Note the way in which the link is made repeatedly with the *Altmark* incident to add credibility to Germany's claims:

For months Great Britain and France have tried to make Scandinavia a new theatre of war against Germany. The attempted intervention by the Western Plutocracies in the Russo-Finnish conflict aimed at seizing the iron ore mines of Scandinavia and preventing the export of iron ore via the Norwegian harbour of Narvik, through the occupation of Norway. The Russo-Finnish Peace Treaty, which was so deeply resented by Great Britain and France, encouraged the British warmongers to seek new ways and means of achieving their object. The German Government has carefully watched all these events. The number of provocative violations of Norwegian neutrality increased rapidly. The attack on the *Altmark* indicated that Norway was either not capable, or not willing to oppose these violations. After the attack on the *Altmark*, ships were torpedoed in Norwegian territorial waters. As a preparatory measure for the occupation of strategically important points in Norway, the British Government yesterday finally set itself Norwegian sovereign rights. The Norwegian Government has only answered with a feeble protest. The German Government on the other hand, is not prepared to restrict its activities to a mere protest against these British violations of international law. The German Government has therefore taken the necessary steps definitely to exclude the Northern part of Europe from the British plan to extend the theatre of war.[7]

The point here, though, is that, after allowance has been made for exaggeration and unsupported assertion, such broadcasts still carried credibility because their content – or at least the main thrust of it – was substantially true. The British had been illegally mining Norwegian waters since 8 April to divert ore-carrying German ships from them, and it is also true that the British were determined to occupy Norwegian ports if need be.

Moreover, it was undeniable too that not only were the British beaten in the race to occupy Norway, their forces there were soundly beaten by German troops, who forced their retreat from Scandinavia by the end of April. Hamburg, at the beginning of May, revelled in Germany's victory, and enjoyed Britain's humiliation:

The British War Office issued an official communiqué late this afternoon which has done very little to dispel the gloom cast over Britain by the heavy defeat suffered in Norway. The War Office has been forced to admit that British troops had to retreat in the face of the constantly increasing enemy force. It is now contended that the British Expeditionary Force only had the task of delaying the enemy. If that is really true, then one surely had been rather modest in London. But how then was it possible that the British Press was allowed to write such stories and splash such headlines about enormously

important military developments which were expected to take place, in the
area of Trondheim? Evidently, they have taken place, only perhaps in a
different sense from what British public opinion was misled to expect and to
hope. Besides, not even this modest task of delaying the German advance has
been fulfilled by British troops. Or could one have expected German troops
to have advanced still more rapidly than they did? The communiqué speaks
of British troops successfully embarked at Andalsnes and other harbours in
the vicinity. Surely this is a rather unique way of describing the wild flight of
British troops striving in vain to escape contact with the enemy following in
close pursuit and leaving huge supplies of arms, ammunition and all kinds of
equipment and rations behind? Surely no military enterprise has ever ended
in a more dismal defeat, and no dismal defeat has ever been more disgrace-
fully and shamelessly announced.[8]

As Goebbels had directed, the official German stations were attempting to
bring home to the British people the humiliating position into which their
Government had manoeuvred them. The first of the freedom stations, the *New
British Broadcasting Station*, also seized its opportunity:

> That fact that we are against war and are working to end it does not diminish
> our regard for the fighting Services, and we cannot help asking today what
> has happened to the 'Contemptible Little Army' of 1914. Ask yourselves
> whether you would have believed a fortnight ago that British troops could be
> beaten from Lillehammer to Andalsnes in a few days.
>
> At the beginning of the last war, a mere handful of British troops held up
> the great German Army and battled month by month for every inch of
> ground, but this time the story is different indeed. We don't want to think our
> men of 1940 are so inferior to the men of 1914. We should prefer to accept the
> explanation that they are badly commanded and wretchedly equipped. The
> Norwegian fiasco indicates, we hope, not that our rank and file are at fault,
> but that the highest command is incompetent.[9]

It will readily be apparent that these broadcasts were aimed at working a
particular form of psychological manipulation upon Germany's British listeners, associated with the engendering of a certain form of emotional turmoil. As
above, attempts were made to instil feelings of class antagonism and recrimination, to encourage the projection of feelings of shame and disappointment at
British defeats away from the listeners' own peer groups and onto the nation's
leaders, and to promote feelings of fear at the likely consequences for the British
themselves of the incompetence of those leaders. The attempt was made too at
the end of the campaign to encourage feelings of guilt and self-hatred, which
together produce depression. In early May, listeners were told that Norwegian
officers who were taken prisoner during the last encounters covering the British
retreat to Andalsnes had stated that they had not been informed of the intention
of the British to re-embark at Andalsnes on 2 May. Great indignation was
particularly expressed by these officers and men at the fact that the British

Command evidently intended to sacrifice them in order to cover the British retreat. British troops left Andalsnes 'without even pausing to consider for a moment what might be the fate of their gallant Allies.'[10]

That the Norwegian campaign was well-handled by the German propagandists seems clear enough, but since the aim was to humiliate the British, this was no very difficult task. The impact in Britain of events in Scandinavia was such that it brought about the collapse of a government with a secure majority at a time of national crisis. Moreover, no sooner had the public caught its breath than new disasters followed in rapid sequence.

The invasion of the Low Countries was preceded by a good deal of decoy propaganda and projection from Germany, centring on the allegation that the Allies were about to extend the war into south-eastern Europe or were themselves threatening the security of Holland and Belgium. Indeed, a directive that the German press was to concentrate on Britain's search for an extension of the war in the south-east and the Mediterranean area was issued, not by the Propaganda Ministry, but direct from the Führer's headquarters on 3 May.[11] The point was made in an NBBS broadcast that very evening:

> If the failures of the last three weeks which now emerge from behind the facade of lies and equivocations represent the best that our combined forces could do against Germany, the sooner we make peace the better. Peace, however, does not seem to be in the Government's mind at present. Mr Chamberlain actually indicated that he and his colleagues were now to fish in the troubled waters of the Mediterranean. He even suggested that the withdrawal of our forces from southern Norway would enable us to use the Navy elsewhere.[12]

The first suggestion of a threat to the Low Countries appeared on the evening of 8 May, but was given little prominence, the line being that British stories of a German threat to Holland were bogus, and in reality masked an only too real Allied threat to the Low Countries. After the launching of the German assault on 10 May – and the rapid collapse of Holland on the 14th – diversionary tactics could be dispensed with and the military campaigns against Belgium and Holland dominated the scene, accounting for 52 per cent of all propaganda to Britain.[13] The picture of Germany's military success presented by her propaganda was one of an uninterrupted and irresistible advance which the bravest resistance might delay for a few hours but could never check. Germany, having produced a revolution in everything else, had now brought about a revolution in the art of war. A good example of this type of material is contained in a broadcast in English from Hamburg on 16 May. Note the obvious attempt to terrify the British into believing that their turn was next:

> If you were seek to explain the miraculous success of German arms in terms of strategy, tactics, and organisation as so far known, you will never succeed. It would be infinitely easier to use Roman numerals for long multiplications.

We are using new and terrible weapons, the nature of which you may perhaps guess but cannot know – weapons which revolutionise the conditions of warfare, and in comparison with which old fashioned armaments are as bows and arrows. We are employing tactical and strategical methods which have no precedent. Whilst the politicians who have misled England are thinking in terms of Marlborough's campaign, all military experts worthy of the name are preparing to burn their text books after presenting a suitable number of copies to libraries and museums which may be interested. For what becomes of old concepts of frontal attack and out-flanking when it is possible to land from the air a dozen, a score, or if necessary a hundred expeditionary forces behind the enemy lines? This is the technique which Germany has brought to perfection and which her foes do not possess . . .

Perhaps you think that even the most conditional reference to the invasion of Britain is out of place. I can claim no special knowledge. I can only look at the map, as you can, and see the array of German power from the north of Norway right down to the Channel . . . Now look at the map, if you have one handy. Flushing is less than 90 miles from Dover; Rotterdam is about the same distance from important strategic points on the English coast as London is from Birmingham. The Hague is distant from Harwich by only 120 miles – let us say, twenty minutes' journey by a plane whose pilot has no need to hurry. He could comfortably get from Holland to Whitehall before you could get from Richmond to South Kensington, or from Earls Court to the Mansion House by Underground. This fact might be of less importance if the German Air Force had not proved its incontestable superiority. In view of the successes which it has achieved, it seems hardly worth while mentioning that well over 1,000 Allied planes have been destroyed in the last few days.[14]

Even so, it was not considered enough for Germany to terrify and browbeat her enemies with bombastic military propaganda. Goebbels insisted that the Allies be constantly reminded of their war guilt. He ordered at his conference on 11 May that:

Britain and France must be told again and again, before the whole world, that it was *they* who declared war on us and that they were now having to pay the price for it. It was *their own* war which was now bursting upon them. On no account must we allow ourselves to be manoeuvred once more into the role of aggressor.[15]

Certainly it is worth noting that the tone of Nazi propaganda during the attack in the West, and especially of that for home consumption, was more defensive than the objective military situation might lead one to expect. Writing as early as November 1941, Hans Speier made the important point in this regard that the 'situation' is defined not only by objective facts and events, such as the positions and accomplishments of the armed forces, the food supply and so on, but also by the predispositions of the publics to which the propaganda is directed. Thus, Speier argued, at the beginning of the campaign in the West, the social-psychological situation in Germany was less favourable that the 'objective' situation, because of apprehensions that the 'miracle of the Marne' might repeat itself.[16] Whatever its origins, Goebbels' demand was fulfilled, and in that same Hamburg broadcast on 16 May, the point was reiterated that the British and French were the masters of their own misfortune. They rejected Hitler's peace offer, and would need now to pay the price:

> Within six weeks after the British Government declared war on Germany, Hitler offered peace. His terms could have easily been accepted, and they would have left Germany far weaker than she is today. He did not make his offer abruptly and withdraw it before there was time for consideration. Night after night we broadcast his proposals until the whole world knew them by heart. When the warmongers of Downing Street intimated that there could be no terms of peace with the present German Government, we knew that the war must be fought out to the bitter end. Britain appealed from negotiation to force. Force then it had to be, and force it shall be until German victory is total.[17]

And German victory in the west was indeed total. By 14 May the German Panzers had broken through French lines at Sedan, and thereafter drove through northern France in a swooping motion towards the Channel coast. With victory after victory to report and analyse, Nazi propaganda became not surprisingly ever more dominated by military subjects, comprising the themes of German Military Strength, Military Operations and Allied Military Weakness, which together were occupying no less than 67 per cent of propaganda aimed at Britain by the end of May.[18] Events given especial prominence were: the piercing of the Maginot Line on a 100km front (announced on 17 May); the piercing of the Dyle Line (announced also on 17 May); the destruction of the French 9th Army, the capture of Arras, Amiens and Abbeville and the reaching of the Channel Coast (announced on 21 May); the fall of Calais (announced on 26 May); the surrender of the King of the Belgians and his 500,000 men (announced on 28 May).

Disaster followed disaster for the British and French in breathtaking sequence. News of the defeat and evacuation of the BEF from the beaches at Dunkirk was given by the German wireless in almost awestruck and apocalyptic tones, clearly designed to bring home to British listeners the immensity of the defeat their forces had suffered:

> Germany had now reached the goal which in 1914 she was unable to attain, the occupation of the Channel coast. *The Times* also warns its readers against undue optimism. Perspectives which had now been opened after the loss of the battle in northern France give no ray of optimism. On the contrary, all necessary preparations should be made to meet the German invasion of Britain which was now more than probable, concludes *The Times*.[19]

On 11 June, Paris was declared an open city, and on 14 June the city was taken by the Germans. That same evening, the Hamburg broadcasters made certain that the lesson of the fate of the French capital should not be lost on the British:

> It is surely time for the English people to reflect that if it is only Paris today, it can be London in the very near future . . . The day cannot be distant when the full force of Germany triumphant will be turned against Britain herself . . . To any Englishman, who still follows these politicians who have led him to the tragedy in which he finds himself, I can only say, 'Look thy last on all these lovely things every hour'.[20]

At 19.30 on 17 June, the Bremen News announced that Pétain's government had sued for peace, some six hours after the news was known in the UK. On the same day, Churchill made his 'finest hour' speech in the House of Commons, and the text was broadcast in the evening on the BBC. At 22.15, Bremen was ready with Germany's comment on the defeat of France, and with a series of rejoinders to Churchill:

> Mr Churchill said tonight that Britain now stands alone. Did he tell you that on 3rd September, 1939? On the contrary, then he said that Germany stood alone, to be throttled by the British blockade without even the sacrifice of a single British soldier. How many of the BEF, how many of the British Navy and the RAF have already been sacrificed only that your Prime Minister could tell you that you now stand alone? Was it worth it? Surely not. Surely the time has come to meet the bill, the bill that Mr Churchill and his accomplices ran up for you, and which you will be called upon to meet if you do not force your Government to meet it.[21]

Following the collapse of France there was naturally enough a shift of emphasis from direct reports of military operations to assertions of German military invincibility and the need to prepare for Germany's next military adventure. In addition, the theme of the 'European Revolution' or the 'New Order' had become by June 1940 one of the main threads of German propaganda, increasingly pervasive rather than being seen as a distinct line. Electra House noted that

> it has become what may be called an integrating principle of propaganda, giving unity, consistency and character to the whole . . . The consistent effort made in the past to build up a picture of the decay of Germany's enemies is now bearing fruit . . . Germany has shown an increasing tendency to claim, together with Italy, a monopoly of 'European consciousness'.[22]

On a foundation established by consistent work in the past a clear picture had been built up of a Germany irresistibly marching forward and inevitably destroying the anachronisms which stood in its path. 'France has been conquered not by numbers but by history.' And connected with the class-based nature of much of Nazi propaganda in this period was the wider notion that Germany was fighting for a New Order while Britain was desperately struggling to maintain the old one. The British plutocrats who had started the war were fighting against Germany's vision of a new social and political order. The Axis Powers would create a new Europe, a Europe of tomorrow without capitalism and bourgeois habits, a Europe freed from the tyranny of gold. The war, therefore, was no war merely between Britain and Germany but rather was the war of all Europe against the one state opposing the New Order, a war to free Europe from British tyranny. Germany and Italy were leaders of 'the modern revolutionary bloc, supported by powerful alliances and by a deep international solidarity'.[23] As Electra House put it, the social themes which formed such an important part of German propaganda up to February 1940 had now merged almost entirely into this more embracing conception.[24]

Only Britain now stood in the way of the implementation of the New Order in Europe, and Hitler's uncertainty about what to do about Britain is reflected in a perceptible lack of surefootedness in propaganda, particularly on the question of invasion. The propaganda set-pieces continued to arise, and most were confidently handled. The sinking by the Royal Navy of the French Fleet at Oran on 3 July, for instance, with the loss of nearly 1,300 French lives, provoked 'an explosion of indignation whose volume only fell below that which followed the *Altmark* incident.'[25] On 9 July, Hilversum, now of course in German hands, broadcast a particularly bitter account from a French newspaper on feelings there at the latest treachery from perfidious Albion:

> The sad events succeed one another so rapidly, and are so overwhelming our country, that they would not be so unbearable were not our will equal to the task of controlling our grief and suffering. First it was Germany, and now Great Britain, our old ally, whom we have supported for 25 years . . . Whatever the terrible damage, the fact remains: one must know the particulars of the drama at Oran in order to be able to estimate the significance of this event. At the first news of it we were dumbfounded and could only ask ourselves, helplessly, whether it were conceivably possible that Britain should want to cause our downfall at sea now that we have been broken and defeated at home. You who fought in Norway, under the flags of the Allies; all you who fought and hoped – now you see once again the traditional and treacherous Albion for whom you sacrificed so much and offered your life's blood . . . Churchill, heir of Marlborough! You could do this to us after we had admitted defeat, after we had given up a great part of our country. We sacrificed our country to save Britain and the alliance which we have paid for, so often, with the blood of our children . . . The world has watched many alliances collapse, but few have ended with such shame and disgrace as that in Oran.[26]

The British 'starvation blockade' of Europe, on the other hand, was not so clear-cut an issue. The blockade was given a new lease of life in the summer of 1940 thanks to speculation from former President Herbert Hoover that Europe faced serious food shortages in the coming winter. The issue was difficult for Britain as Edwin L. James pointed out in *The New York Times* in August 1940.

'She is depending to no little degree on supplies from this country and it is evident that if there grows up in the United States a movement, for example, to feed French babies in unoccupied France that a refusal by London risks creating an unfavourable impression over here.'[27] But if the presentation of the blockade caused problems for the British propagandists, it did so too for the Germans, and just as it had done in the Great War, the blockade presented challenges as well as opportunities. On the one hand, to attempt to use the blockade as an example of British brutality was to pay a back-handed compliment to the relative power and weakness of the British and German navies. On the other hand, to play down the effectiveness of the blockade was to throw away a potentially valuable weapon which could be used to discredit the British in the eyes of the world. The solution adopted to solve the dilemma was boldly to assert that Germany was well-fed, but that Britain was to blame if food shortages occurred in the occupied areas of Western Europe.

The war in the air presented similar difficulties. To admit too fully the extent of bomb damage in Germany was to undermine the notion that the RAF was on its last legs, and the German claim that the *Luftwaffe* could defend German cities. Air operations against England did become a consistent and important item after the 'beginning of reprisals' for British attacks on Germany on 20 June. Items on British brutality were dominated by bombing of non-military targets by the RAF. The names of places bombed and the number and type of bombs dropped were enumerated in detail. Bombed churches, hospitals and peaceful villages were listed, accompanied by the warning that these crimes had no excuse and that retaliation would follow. 'Threats of reprisals', noted Electra House in June, 'have become increasingly sharp'.[28]

In the meantime, on 19 July, Germany seized the propaganda initiative again when Hitler made another dramatic offer of peace to Britain. The attack upon the French vessels at Oran had underscored British determination to continue the fight alone, but even so, the Führer continued to hope that the British would see sense and come to terms with him, which explains the delay of the offer until the 19th.[29] As Bill Shirer recalled, Hitler's oratorical form was at its best:

> In this hour, I feel it to be my duty before my own conscience to appeal once more to reason and common sense in Great Britain as much as elsewhere. I consider myself in a position to make this appeal since I am not the vanquished begging favours, but the victor speaking in the name of reason. I can see no reason why this war must go on.[30]

Hitler had, however, given the order for the invasion of Britain three days before his Reichstag speech, and his offer is perhaps best seen as a propagandistic manoeuvre designed to rally German and world opinion behind him for the coming attack on Britain, since he could be seen to have behaved with creditable reasonableness and restraint from a position of overwhelming strength. However, if he did genuinely expect a positive response from Britain he was disappointed, and Nazi officials were infuriated by the short shrift given the Führer's offer by the British.[31]

For the remainder of the summer, the message from all German stations was that Britain was doomed. By mid-July 1940, almost a third of Nazi propaganda to Britain was concerned with British weakness, over two-fifths of it focused on military unpreparedness to face invasion. First, however, it was necessary for the Germans to win control of the skies over Britain, and throughout July and August by far the largest single theme in Nazi propaganda to Britain – addressed in something around 40 per cent of the total – remained that of British weakness, centring in particular upon Britain's weakness in the air.[32] The RAF, claimed the Nazis, was incapable of defending Britain from the enormous air onslaught which was always just about to begin. Indeed, a new chapter in the air war appeared to be opened with the large-scale attacks on 8 August, and the German airforce, it was claimed, was annihilating the RAF and Britain's air defences on the ground. Her naval bases were being pulverised and her aircraft factories destroyed. The RAF too was under-trained, under-equipped and under-manned, while morale within the service was cracking, German pilots often remarking on the unwillingness of their opponents to take to the air.

There was a considerable increase too at this time of propaganda on the theme of British mendacity. Since the outbreak of war, a great deal of Nazi propaganda on this theme had been concentrated on Britain's alleged habit of lying about the extent of her shipping losses. In May Goebbels had noted in his diary: 'I have Haw-Haw flay Churchill over the wireless about the as yet unacknowledged English shipping losses. London however refuses to make any statement. An admission!'[33] The increase in this type of material in August 1940, however, had much more to do with argument about the results of the air attacks. Reuters, it was claimed, was the greatest institution for aircraft destruction known in the world and Churchill ordered the number of planes to be destroyed from his desk. Germany's veracity, on the other hand, had been proven to the world in the campaigns in Poland, Norway and France. On 16 August, well over half of the output of the entire Nazi propaganda machine, including German press and telegraphic services, was concerned in one way or the other with the Nazi air attack on Britain.[34] On 17 August, British listeners were told that her fighters had already given up the struggle, and a few days later, Hamburg, in a searing retort to Churchill's speech in which he paid tribute to the 'few', told its British listeners that the end for them was clearly in sight:

Winston Churchill was one of those who did most to procure England's declaration of war last September. And we now have his admission that nearly a year later his country is neither properly equipped nor has it properly started. Surely the time to think of proper equipment was before the war was launched! One day the British people will have cause to remember this confession of the chief warmonger – that he drove them into this disastrous conflict well knowing, as he did, that they were not prepared to wage it. Out of his mouth, Churchill stands convicted as a traitor to England . . . But this much the people of England have failed to realise. It was, until very recently, [that] their war was fought by proxy. They had not heard the roar of those engines of destruction, which, thanks to Churchill, descended on their cities, towns, factories, docks and railways.

It will not be long before Britain has to yield to the invincible might of German arms, for Germany started when the war began, and was equipped before that. But this also I feel, that short as the time may be, every day will have the length of a year for the people whom Churchill has condemned to ruin . . . in his crazy and fantastic plan to blockade Europe, the dictator of this little island showed the depths of his immoral malice.[35]

Even so, by the end of August, accounts were still being given of how Britain's resistance was being worn down, and it was not until 26 August that it was announced that mastery of the air over Britain had been achieved, following air attacks on aerodromes in Kent and Essex and around Portsmouth. At this point, claimed the Nazis, the dividing line between 'armed reconnaissance' and 'systematic destruction' had been crossed, and thereafter reports of 'the heaviest raids so far' became commonplace as Germany's overwhelmingly superior strategic position allegedly allowed her bombers to attack Britain from all sides.[36]

The treatment of the air war against Britain was of course inextricably bound up with the coming 'decisive blow' for which the air war was merely a preparation – the invasion of Britain. For much of the summer of 1940, however, invasion had been treated in a very cautious manner, with few positive threats of invasion at least on the openly German or 'white' propaganda stations. Indeed, as Walter Ansel has pointed out, the initiative for the line of thought that Britain might actually face invasion came, following the Norwegian debacle, from the British rather than the Germans. Josiah Wedgwood MP, for example, wondered in the House of Commons as early as 7 May whether the Navy was capable of preventing invasion. If it could not thwart a landing in Norway, was it not conceivable that a German landing on Lincolnshire and the Wash was not preventable either? 'This ironic turn', writes Ansel, 'recurred not once but time after time, until it became the peculiar history of publicity about Invasion England 1940 to have British uneasiness take the lead.'[37] Certainly, invasion was widely anticipated in Britain, particularly in early September, but, it should be said, most people seemed confident enough that it would be a failure. Rumours too were widespread in many areas that invasion had already been attempted, but had been repulsed. A rumour was rife in Nottingham that hundreds of German bodies were floating in the Channel. In north Nottinghamshire the invasion was said to have been attempted on Lincolnshire and the south coast. In Northampton, it was said that the attack was launched on the west coast. Invasion rumours were also reported in the south-west and in Scotland.[38] However, the general tone on the white stations for most of the 'invasion summer' of 1940 was that Hitler was ready and able to produce the knock-out blow, but that he would do so in his own good time.

The covert or 'black' propaganda stations, *Workers' Challenge*, the NBBS, the *Christian Peace Movement* and *Radio Caledonia*, were, however, all much more active in trying to whip up fear and trepidation about invasion throughout this period. Listeners were told repeatedly that 'fear of invasion has reduced the British people to a condition of complete hysteria.' They were encouraged to abandon their homes forthwith and to flee to the North and to Wales, and, on *Workers' Challenge*, to rise up and kick out their government. The NBBS was especially adept at introducing material in its 'uncensored' news reports designed to encourage panic and rumour-mongering about the Fifth Column, saboteurs and parachutists. Invasion was definitely coming, and resistance was useless:

> I make no apology for saying again that invasion is certainly coming soon, but what I want to impress upon you is that while you must feverishly take every conceivable precaution, nothing that you or the government can do is really of the slightest use. Don't be deceived by this lull before the storm, because, although there is still the chance of peace, Hitler is aware of the political and economic confusion in England, and is only waiting for the right moment . . . Then, when his moment comes, he will strike, and strike hard.[39]

On 15 August, the station reported that parachutists had landed near Birmingham, Manchester and Glasgow.[40] On 1 September, it was announced that raiding of coastal towns nearest the French coast had been so heavy as to contradict the misguided rumours that invasion was not imminent:

> It is clear that landings must soon be attempted. Dover is already practically German territory. The civilian population has fled, chaos reigns; the only opposition the raiders meet from the ground is a little rifle shooting . . .[41]

Whether or not they were ever really serious about launching an invasion, much effort was expended by the Germans in attempting to convince the British that they were wholly incapable of resisting it. Particularly and repeatedly stressed was Britain's dire economic position. About three-quarters of this type of material was concerned with Germany's strangling blockade of Britain, and its increasing impact in shortages of food, aluminium and iron. Britain's sources of supply for the Continent had been cut off, and no shipping was available to carry substitutes from overseas, even if the air and sea blockade permitted these to pass. The long-term goal of course was to cause morale to crack, but both the short-term goal and the technique was to depress and terrify:

> When Paris was besieged by Germany in 1871, food became so scarce that one pound of dog's meat cost one shilling and eightpence and a cat was valued at 11 shillings and threepence. Animals in the Zoo were slaughtered for food and elephant meat cost 15 shillings per pound.
>
> Is England likely to see such days? That is the fearful question confronting English men and women at the moment. It is the anxiety which fills the hearts of English mothers as they put their children to bed . . .

In April, Mr Morton in the *Daily Herald* said that England could suffer in
the same way as Paris in 1871. Morton when he wrote these words must have
scarcely believed it possible that within three months the German counter-
blockade would reach from Narvik to Biarritz, and that in July England
would become a beleaguered fortress. It is hard to believe that today he would
write as he did then. Londoners will now know the taste of monkey or
alligator, and the Zoo will continue to be one of the few institutions in
London to keep to the old slogan 'Business as Usual'. Starvation now
threatens England. Who is to blame for this? No-one, but the small circle
of rich people which is indifferent as to whether the people starve or not.
These people have already got their children into safety. When things get bad
enough they will make a getaway as well. The British people will in the
meantime, starve. It is the wish of the British people?[42]

Just at the moment though – around 13 September – when invasion anxiety
and rumour-mongering was reaching a crescendo, the time devoted to invasion
propaganda on the German wireless began to drop away.[43] It is again probably
a significant indicator of the distance between the policy makers and the
propagandists that the major shift in military tactics at the beginning of
September was not reflected in propaganda until the middle of the month.
However, even before the heavy bombing of British cities began with the raid
on London on 7 September, the Germans had been keen to convince their own
population and the rest of the world that the British would be to blame for the
outbreak of a war of the cities, since they had already carried out numerous
murderous attacks on German civilians. As early as April 1940 it was charged
that British aircraft had bombed a railway station in Schleswig-Holstein.
Similar allegations were made at the same time about the alleged British
bombardment of the open town of Bergen. Britain had been warned that
'Germany would know how to draw the necessary conclusions from this
violation of the rules of aerial warfare.'[44] In mid-May, Britons were again
warned:

> The random dropping of bombs by British planes during their nightly flights
> over German territory continues in spite of our repeated warnings. Their
> shamelessness is only surpassed by their incompetence. An exact list is being
> kept of all civilians killed and damage done. Let England beware, we forget
> nothing. When the hour of reckoning comes, every bomb will be repaid many
> times. Reprisals will be sure and resolute.[45]

In early August, the 'wicked' bombing of the centre of Hanover by the RAF
was given much prominence, and by the end of the month, 11 per cent of radio
output for Britain was concerned with British brutality and unscrupulousness,
of which a third was concerned with the deliberate bombing by the RAF of
non-military targets in Germany.[46] The most prominent crime had been the
deliberate attacks on German national shrines, such as Goethe's house at
Weimar and Bismarck's mausoleum, both allegedly carried out on Churchill's

orders. As Electra House noted, 'it is quite clear that German propaganda took pains to convince the German people that Britain bombed Berlin before Germany bombed London.'[47]

And when the heavy bombing did begin in September, the purpose of the propaganda was to assist the terrorism from the air with terrorism on the wireless. As Goebbels noted in his diary on 11 September: 'We're re-orienting our radio service. The English-language and the Freedom stations to produce terror and panic. We're really stepping up the pressure. Lord Haw-Haw is brilliant.'[48] Certainly the air war overshadowed all other items in propaganda to the UK, and no less than two-thirds of propaganda aimed at Britain in the first half of September 1940 concerned this one issue. In the middle of the month it was said that the decisive battle of London was taking place, and considerable stress was placed on the fact that the defeat of London might mean the defeat of England. The emphasis, though, was continually laid on the systematic destruction of military objectives in London. Hitler, said Joyce on 9 September, had long-since warned England of the penalties for her continued attacks on German civilians, and pointed the finger at the real culprits. The British were making a pathetic attempt to represent the damage done to military objectives in London as having most affected the homes of the workers, with the transparent hope of evoking the sympathy of the world:

> Must we remind them of the fact that it was Britain who declared war on Germany, who started to wage it on women and children by preparing the hunger blockade? Must we remind them of the *Altmark* incident, when defenceless German seaman were murdered in cold blood? Must we recall to their memories the air raid on Freiburg when children were killed in an attack on an undefended town in broad daylight, with no military objective even in the vicinity? For months the German people and their Führer have suffered indiscriminate bombing of non-military objectives. Time and again the Führer has offered the hand of understanding and even friendship to the very nation which starved the German people after the peace was concluded in 1919. Time and again the Führer has warned Britain of the necessary consequences that these brutal attacks might have. Last week he uttered what was his last warning in no uncertain terms. Now just retribution has befallen Britain. If there are civilian casualties and destruction of homes in London, then these are such as cannot be avoided in any really large-scale attack on the main objectives of military and economic importance in the east of London. Misery thus caused is not to be laid at Germany's door. Those who refuse to listen to reason – those who drove their nation into a senseless war in order to perpetuate an injustice, just in order to save the interests of a small group of Jewish financiers and inveterate warmongers with Winston Churchill at their head – these men are responsible, not Germany.[49]

In this talk we see a typical example of German material on the war of the cities, and a good example too of the paranoid propaganda produced by the National Socialists. Even when operating from a position of overwhelming strength, the persecution complex and self-pity at the heart of National Socialism comes to the fore. After the parade of bitter complaints at the wrongs done to Germany comes the threat. This is baulked, however, because of a propaganda which must present the Germans as too noble to behave ignobly. The palpable lie about military objectives and the cowardly dodging of responsibility, however, are as likely to have generated contempt, as much as fear or panic. While propaganda in the Phoney War had often sought understanding from the British of Germany's position through its professed empathy in their suffering under plutocracy, in the Blitz it whined at them while raining bombs on them. An honest opponent might invoke respect as well as fear; the self-pitying bully elicits fear but also scorn.

The secret stations too gave great emphasis to the suffering of the British public and of Londoners in particular under the ceaseless onslaught from the air. Again though the point was consistently made that it was not Hitler who was responsible, but Churchill. *Workers' Challenge* made a special point of the compulsion on workers to carry on through air raid alarms, and much of the station's output in September was concerned with exactly this theme. Consider the following example, from a broadcast on 11 September, which included a short and typically stereotyped 'dialogue' between two supposed British workers. The speakers at this stage would have been Bill Griffiths and Sergeant MacDonald:

> *Worker A:* What about the raid the other day? They didn't sound the alarm until a quarter of an hour after the raid started.
>
> *Worker B:* That might have happened. Then again, there might have been a slip-up somewhere. Mistakes can happen you know Bill.
>
> *Worker A*: Mistakes be buggered. Do you call it a slip-up when my pal had his house blown to bits, and his wife and kiddies killed whilst he was at work? Now where the hell does the mistake come in there, thickhead? . . . The bosses have been hollering and whinging about the workers trooping down to the shelters when there's a raid, so the khaki buggers have the alarm delayed.
>
> *Worker B:* Strike me bloody pink. Things must be in a queer state when they start blocking the workers like that.
>
> *Worker A:* Why you bleedin' twerp, it's as simple as A.B.C. A delayed alarm means more production from the workers, and more profit for the bosses, and besides they don't care about Jerry dropping a few bombs on the factory, as long as they're out of the danger zone . . . I suppose they'll say, what's few thousand workers' homes or lives to us, when our democratic country's at stake.
>
> *Worker B:* Well, I'll be buggered.[50]

As will be seen later, a large part of such popularity as this station managed to generate stemmed from its salty language, in the days when 'cultured' accents only were permitted on the wireless. Nevertheless, the delivery by *Concordia*'s collection of amateur dramatists of 'working-class' dialogues in stilted accents with laboriously dropped aitches, must very often have produced only laughter and derision.[51] Nevertheless, the stations did work hard throughout the summer to whip up social unrest and panic in advance of the German invasion. Goebbels himself had laid down these particular themes for the secret stations at his ministerial conferences on 24 and 25 July. The freedom stations, he said, were to pick up and amplify the mistrust of the ruling caste and the fear at what was about to befall which were being encouraged by the official propaganda media, 'to make sure the very first blows against Britain fall on psychologically well-prepared ground.' Since the freedom stations had the task of arousing alarm and fear among the British people, and since this intention should at all costs not become apparent, 'they must wrap up their real intentions in moral tales and good advice. Among other things, they should now put out expertly prepared ARP classes of which all details must be so accurately described that the civilian population is seized with horror from the start.'[52] Sure enough, the NBBS began a campaign of ARP and first-aid advice on 28 July, the thrust of which may be gleaned from this extract:

> Tonight we will tell you what to do with fractures, simple ones, and the nasty kind where bones stick out through the skin. You ought to know, too, how to stop the flow of blood if one of your family gets a leg blown off and no doctor is available. These things sometimes even happen in shelters remember, and most often of all just as people are going into them. There is a horrible but apposite little story we might remind you of, which happened on the south coast, when a man and a woman were just dressing the baby to rush it to the shelter, and a piece of splinter came in at the window and literally tore the baby's arm out of its socket. No doctor was available and, in spite of desperate efforts, it died in their arms. It is very important to know how to cope with these everyday domestic occurrences, so don't miss our next installment . . .[53]

A few evenings later, the station was ready with more first-aid 'advice':

> Tonight I shall expand my talk on fractures by describing what patients look like with broken ribs, collar bones, shoulder blades, spines and skulls. I will try to give you some idea of what ought to be done [Monitor's comment – speaker made it sound as difficult as possible, but made no suggestions how to do it]. In all these cases there will be an unpleasant amount of blood lying about the home. Always get a doctor as soon as possible, and don't loose your nerve if you see any particularly repulsive sights – stomach wounds for example. When these are bad the patient is frequently in such agony that he tries to dash about the place. Well, you mustn't let him. Just do what you can and wait for the doctor. Tomorrow we will tell you what shock means . . .[54]

Although as Goebbels directed the attempt was frequently made to divide the British public from its political leaders, this effort should be seen in the context of a broader mass of propaganda material which was still vaguely socialist in nature, or which at least emphasised the sufferings of the workers, victims not of Nazism, but of their own plutocratic exploiters. Throughout the months of the air attacks upon Britain, the Nazis continued the phoney-war tactic of bombarding Britain with 'social propaganda' concerning her societal shortcomings, shortcomings heightened now by German air attacks. By the end of October 1940, the two themes of British political and social weakness together accounted for 10 per cent of all propaganda to Britain. There was the occasional mention of the 'incomprehensible stupidity' of the British people, but on the whole German broadcasts to Britain focused the attack on Britain's leaders, her plutocratic democracy and the Jews. As will be shown later, this type of material caused a good deal of anxiety among policy-makers in Britain about its likely effectiveness, and certainly one can discern from around the time of Dunkirk, a readiness among Britain's elites to pay at least lip-service, even in the grimmest days of 1940, to the idea of postwar reconstruction, of building a 'New Jerusalem', quite different from the old class-ridden and unemployed Britain of the 1930s.[55] For the Nazis, however, pious British promises of the 'New Jerusalem' type were no more than a sham, designed to delude the proletarian cannon-fodder into continued co-operation in the bosses' war. Such feeble efforts at social reform made by the British were pilloried as a partial death-bed repentance of the plutocrats and a sop to keep the workers quiet. Meanwhile vast profits continued to be made by the armament manufacturers.[56] The plutocrats, claimed the NBBS, indulged their nightly lusts while the workers suffered:

> We have learned with horror and disgust that while London was suffering all the nightmares of aerial bombardment a few nights ago, there was a contrast between the situation of the rich and the poor which we hardly know how to describe. There were two Londons that night. Down by the docks and in the poor districts and the suburbs, people lay dead, or dying in agony from their wounds; but, while their counterparts were suffering only a little distance away, the plutocrats and the favoured lords of creation were making the raid an excuse for their drunken orgies and debaucheries in the saloons of Piccadilly and in the Café de Paris. Spending on champagne in one night what they would consider enough for a soldier's wife for a month these monied fools shouted and sang in the streets, crying, as the son of a profiteer baron put it, 'They won't bomb this part of the town! They want the docks! Fill up boys!'[57]

Even the very pets of the plutocrats were better treated than workers: luxury air-raid shelters were built for their dogs; race-horses, greyhounds and even the Duke of Westminster's orchids had preference over workers' children where evacuation was concerned.[58] Clark Gable's home for evacuated dogs was contrasted with the lot of East End children. The rich smacked their lips over choice food in luxury shelters while the poor shivered in their death-traps of Anderson shelters or huddled sleeplessly in the disease-laden Tubes. The 'unspeakable horrors of London's mass shelters' was one of the major themes in propaganda during the early period of the mass bombing, and the freedom stations in particular pushed it without restraint. *Workers' Challenge*, as the station identifying itself most directly with the city-dwelling proletariat, specialised in little playlets which none too subtly conveyed the desired impression:

> *Worker A*: These blasted little tin huts ain't much good, especially for a bloke with a touch of rheumatics. Why, if I stay here very long, I shall catch my death of cold. Brrr! If it's like this now, what's it going to be like in the middle of winter?
>
> *Worker B*: It's a bit late in the day to start letting people go down in the Tubes, isn't it, after thousands have been killed because they haven't got a shelter to go to? And it's all the bloody Government's fault too. They never bothered to provide decent shelters for us, and wouldn't even let us go down to the Underground. The people wouldn't stand for it any longer, and I don't blame them. They can spend millions a day on their blasted capitalist war, but they can't spend a few paltry thousand providing proper protection for the workers. There's a government for yer – makes no attempt to save us from being bombed to smithereens, and then comes whining to us, and wanting us to do everything we can to keep the war going . . . Well, it's bleeding cold and draughty, I'll tell you that for a start. And it gets damned unpleasant after you've been down there for an hour or two. The place is usually packed like sardines, and the worst of it is, that people have got to stick there for hours without a bleeding drink, or anything to eat, unless they bring it with them. And as for sanitary arrangements, it doesn't bear talking about. If you haven't been, you can't imagine what it's like. People huddled together, trying to sleep, scared kids wandering about, mothers with squawking babies in their arms. Blimey Arthur, it's awful – there's no getting away from it. And rows – there's arguments and fights going on practically the whole time. You remember that long raid we had, the other night? Well, I was near Leicester Square when the bloody alarm went, so I dived down in the Tube. I practically had to fight my way in to start with, and that was only the beginning. What a sight! I shall never forget it. Talk about confusion, the place was simply crowded out, and the noise and the stink was bloody awful. Soon you could have cut the air with a knife. You know what it's like when there's a lot of people in a room, and there's no fresh air? . . . Everybody was fighting like mad to get out. Strike me bloody pink, talk about panic – why, one bloke said to me that he'd rather suffer hell up on top than go down in the Underground again. And I shall think twice before I go down there again myself.[59]

The NBBS painted the picture of the workers' suffering in the blackest colours, with the object of creating the panic which it described and of inciting its listeners against the government:

> All our daily social relationships are overthrown; people are deprived of sleep, and in many cases of food. Gas, electricity and water supplies are interrupted. We are being reduced to a primitive and nomad condition of subsistence. It is expected that pestilence and plague will break out. We have not seen nearly

the worst . . . if this continues, every one of our cities will be wiped out. Existence in this country is bound up with industry. The land cannot feed one quarter of the population. For better or worse, we are linked up with industrial production, and if that goes, we all come to grief. Our means of life are being literally destroyed every hour, and there will be left in this island nothing but a destitute population, unless the process is stopped. Do you intend to wait until our last machinery has been put out of action, before considering whether it would not be wiser to make peace, more especially as the Government will not tell us why we are supposed to be fighting? This great population of 50 millions will find itself without means of subsistence. People will starve by the million. Pestilence will creep through the land, and no means will remain of creating order out of chaos. Unless we want this to be the fate of our country, we must summon up both courage and common sense, dismiss from office the corrupt and incompetent politicians, and save ourselves by demanding peace, as a whole people, which has been governed too long by rulers without conscience.[60]

Now propaganda of this type, with references to plague and pestilence, famine and mass destitution, clearly has a limited lifespan. Only so many times can you tell a man that he's starving, since if he fails to expire he will soon cease to take you seriously. The point is though that the employment of this apocalyptic material demonstrates the extent to which the propagandists believed that the moment of Armageddon for Britain had arrived. These were, as Goebbels noted, 'dramatic hours'. And the great question of the hour was, 'will England endure it or not?'[61]

Anti-Semitism on other hand had a much longer lifespan, and continued to be a factor which informed so much of Nazi propaganda in the Blitz period. It was also a weapon which the Germans were prepared to use at many levels. The Jews were portrayed as directly responsible for the war and therefore for the bombing, but the Jews too were blamed for hardship and squalor suffered by Britons in the shelters. On the face of it, the figures produced by Electra House on themes in German propaganda seem to show that anti-Semitism played a much smaller role in Nazi propaganda than, say, 'British Weakness' or 'German Strength'.[62] This impression, however, is misleading, since, like the New Order, anti-Semitism was pervasive rather than representing a distinct, unmixed line of propaganda. Since the Jews were the root of all evil in the Nazi *Weltanschauung*, Britain's supposed enslavement to the Jews explained Britain's weakness, just as the liberation under National Socialism of the Reich from Jewish control explained German strength. So while the plurality or even a significant number of news broadcasts or talks at a given moment might not have been about the Jews *per se*, the issue was never far from the surface and could and did erupt into view at any moment. In early October *Workers' Challenge* featured another of its regular talks about conditions in the shelters, where, it was claimed, 'the racial question' had come up strongly. British workers were sick of 'stinking foreigners who can't speak the English language', pushing and jostling English women and children to get first place. The attack, however, quickly moved from foreigners to Jews and to the Jews' role in starting the war in the first place:

> If you really want the Government to get a move on with the air raid shelters, we can only think of one way of doing it and that is to pitch every Yid onto the street. When that happens their rich brethren in Government circles will begin to squeal – 'Oy, Oy, isn't it 'orrible?, Something must be done abaht it.' But so long as the Yids can dig themselves in and keep the British people out, the Government won't give a damn. I suppose you will call this racial prejudice, or anti-Semitism. Call it what you bloody well like. We know quite well it was the Jews who agitated for this war, and it was the big capitalist Jews that paid our lousy politicians to lead us into it. If the Government didn't build enough shelters, then it's simply too bloody bad for their Jewish pack.[63]

And while *Workers' Challenge* specialised in foul-mouthed abuse, the official stations too could fly into near hysteria when the Jewish question was featured. Zeesen broadcast a talk on the Jews in September 1940, shortly after the commencement of the raids on London. The tone was clearly more elevated and sophisticated than that of the *Workers' Challenge*, but the message is the same, and by the end of the talk, the moderately delivered lecture had been replaced by a violent anti-Jewish rant:

> Can a greater anomaly be imaged that a Jewish Colonel of HM Scots Guards? No. None the less, up to a few years ago, a Colonel Levy commanded a battalion of the Scots Guards. A glance down the Army List will reveal not only such names as Levy, but other more high-sounding names, such as Montefiore. Jewish owners of these names almost invariably choose crack regiments of the British Army. Thus for instance, no greater snobs can be found anywhere than in the Durham Light Infantry, a regiment which is crack on account of the polo-playing propensity of its officers. So the tale goes on. Jews in the Army! Jews in the Navy! Jews in the Air Force – or running the Air Force! Jews in the House of Commons! Jews in the House of Lords! Jews running Masonic Lodges! Jews at Court! Jews controlling the Press! Jews running the film industry! Jews owning all stage interests! Jews governing dominions! In fact, Jews! Jews! Jews! Yidds![64]

As the air raids on London continued, Hitler allowed himself to be convinced that the war was as good as won, invasion or not. Indeed, although on 17 September the invasion of the UK was postponed, Hitler confidently told Mussolini at their meeting at the Brenner Pass in early October that England was beaten. The propaganda stations too told the world, and British listeners in particular, the same story:

> To sum up your position, you cannot hold out. These words may come as a shock to you, but they are true. No amount of individual heroism or of

personal courage can save the situation for you. In the long run, further
resistance will become impossible. The war, as far as Britain is concerned, has
long since been lost. To prolong it at this point can only lead to further misery
and destruction throughout your country.[65]

On the face of it, therefore, the signing of the Three-Power Pact on 27
September 1940, which dominated propaganda at the end of that month,
might well have been trumpeted as another nail in Britain's coffin. Interestingly enough, however, Electra House noted, especially in propaganda for
German home consumption, indications that Germany realised that she had
failed to win the war in the air. There was a great fall in propaganda to all
regions on military subjects, particularly on British military weakness.
Simultaneously, there was a rise in propaganda on Germany's diplomatic
strength, of which the Three-Power Pact was given in evidence, and rapidly
growing attention to Germany's New Order. Neutral countries were given
the impression that Britain was at her last gasp, but at the very same moment
the home population was being warned – sometimes almost in terms of
eulogy – that Britain was a very tough opponent and had plenty of fight left
in her. It was noted that 'tributes to British courage and power of endurance,
which six weeks earlier would have seemed unthinkable, have appeared in
both the press and in home broadcasts.' Every indication in home propaganda fitted in with the assumption that the German people had to be
prepared for a long war and that Germany's defeat in the air was recognised
by her rulers.[66]

Certainly, this notion of the 'long war' was noticeable in all German press
and wireless output throughout October. Hans Fritzsche told his domestic
listeners on 22 October that: 'We know that a fight between two mighty
empires cannot be decided with the speed of a fight between two
boxers . . .'[67] Moreover, it was admitted that although the outcome of
the war was decided, it might be some time before the Führer gave the
word for the final blow. That blow would be prepared by the methodical and
steady strangulation of the British Empire. Britain would be starved by
blockade and her industry and armaments destroyed from the air. Certainly,
much the most important topic in propaganda was the damage done by
German air raids: on 7 October, it was claimed that Britain had lost 10,000
airmen and 50 per cent of her 130 air fields were destroyed or damaged.
Great prominence was given to the figures for losses in August and
September – it was claimed that 2,474 British planes had been downed,
as opposed to 706 German.[68] A month later, a quarter of propaganda both to
Germany and Britain still dealt with the war in the air, while there was a
very marked fall in stress on naval operations. The war at sea only occupied
about 8 per cent of the entire output of the Nazi propaganda machine.[69]
Much stress too continued to be given to Britain's economic weakness and
emphasis was divided between the difficulties of war finance, the cutting off
of imports by the blockade and the disorganisation caused by attacks on

British industry and ports. With the destruction of the key ports of London and Liverpool, England would starve.

The year 1940 had begun with a German propaganda spectacular set-piece in the *Altmark* episode. It ended in another very different one, with the destruction of Coventry. A spectacular raid of some sort was an attractive propaganda ploy for the Germans at this period, given the number of difficulties which they were experiencing, aside from the failure of the British to come to heel. To begin with, an overtly hostile President Roosevelt had been recently re-elected on a landslide in the USA. The Italians, despite Hitler's strongest opposition, had gone off on their own in a disastrous campaign in Greece, which was by now seriously bogged down, and to cap it all the balance of forces in the Mediterranean had been changed at a stroke in Britain's favour by the British naval successes at Taranto and in the Straits of Otranto. As Electra House noted, 'some sensational military stroke may have been felt to be an urgent propaganda necessity'.[70] To the British public, however, Coventry became immediately a monument to German barbarism and British stoicism.

In German domestic broadcasts, the raid on Coventry was given complete coverage, and its effects greatly exaggerated. Indeed, so great and so unrestrained was coverage for home audiences that Electra House noted that Germans must have been led to expect that the war could be soon ended, referring to 'remarkable lack of caution' in domestic wireless talks.[71] Of course, care was always taken to present these raids as 'reprisals' for the brutal attacks by the RAF on non-military targets in Germany. The raid on Coventry, said Fritzsche, was 'a decent and soldierly punishment for an unsoldierly deed.'[72] A similar line was spun on broadcasts for the UK, the point again being emphasised that Coventry was a military target, and that responsibility for the destruction caused lay with Britain's masters:

I know something about the romantic history of Coventry but, if links with the past were so valued, it was a great pity the rulers of Britain should have made it one of the main workshops in which weapons for the destruction of Germany were to be forged. From the British point of view, it was a pity that, when such a centre of war potential had been established, the Government should have done nothing to protect it. It must be assumed, either that Churchill had no interest in what happened to it, and that assumption is unlikely, or that Britain's means of defence against aerial bombardment have been exhausted. It may perhaps be pleaded that the bulk of the nation's AA artillery had to be moved to London for the protection of the capital, but the answer to this excuse is that such a measure, however detrimental to the provincial cities, has not saved the capital. Indeed, Londoners know for themselves, from the evidence of the last few nights, that Reichsmarschal Göring was perfectly right when he said on Sunday week that the attacks had not yet reached their climax. Whatever Air Marshal Joubert and his fellow propagandists may have said last week, it can surely be taken for granted now that the retaliatory raids on Britain are to continue and it could be wild folly to hope that they would, in any way, abate.[73]

Free, however, from the constraints of accuracy or realism, the secret stations could take the lessons of Coventry to extremes. The NBBS took a typically apocalyptic view:

By next spring the greater part of our transport and industry will be in ruins, making invasion a comparatively simple matter . . . If the RAF comes out in force, either now or in the spring, it will be faced with an opponent four times as strong and we are not forgetting that the Italian Air Force will also be against us. On the other hand, we know that the enemy will destroy whatever they choose if they are not met by the RAF. This dilemma cannot be blamed entirely on Hitler. It is also caused by those responsible for our air weakness before the war.

The bombing of Coventry has given us a terrible example of what night bombing can be. The only protection against night raids is air superiority which we lack. There is no solution to our predicament but peace, before the country is destroyed. The people must decide whether things are to continue as they are. They must act against the incompetent dictatorship which brings disaster on us for the sake of its own personal profit. It is officially stated today that the Coventry death toll exceeds 250 and that it is feared that more bodies may yet be found. The Government will probably never divulge the truth. It is well known to every Coventry survivor that many hundreds of workers were killed when aircraft factories were destroyed. The total number of killed is actually in the region of 1,500. The official statement is therefore true in saying that casualties exceed 250 . . .[74]

Zeesen provided a somewhat laboured justification for the raid on Coventry for listeners in the United States on 22 November. The piece took the form of a 'dialogue' between 'Jimmy' and 'Johnny', which, as was usual, began trivially but developed into a description of the raid. Jimmy asks Johnny how he would like to live in Coventry, and tells the 'real' story:

Coventry is, as you might know, the most important place in England for the manufacture of aeroplane motors and such like. One bright night about 500 German aeroplanes flew over Coventry. They dropped about 1,000,000 lbs. of bombs. If you have any imagination at all you can imagine what kind of a hell they let loose in Coventry that night. Swedish and American papers say that nothing has happened that can be used as a comparison. It was formidable, the worst hell that mankind can imagine. And that went on almost the whole night through. When dawn came there was nothing left but one pile of rubbish. The factories were gone altogether. Coventry will manufacture no more engines for months and months to come. It was the heaviest blow for British industry. Even Americans express their doubts after Coventry, as to whether England can last much longer.[75]

But as extensive air raids on the British population continued unabated throughout the winter and spring of 1941, the analysts at Electra House detected what they felt to be a sudden shift in propaganda broadcasts to Britain. Hitherto, it was argued, the paramount aim of German propaganda had seemed to be to undermine British morale during a period of 'indecisive military action'.[76] It seemed now that the attack on present morale was developing into 'preparation for a future and much greater attack on the British will to resist'. Since the middle of January 1941 broadcasts to Britain seemed to have been planned on the assumption that in the near future British morale would be subjected to a sudden and severe strain, either by military attack aimed at morale, or by the kind of military action whose success depends largely or wholly on the breaking of morale – the chief suspects for Electra House were gas attack or bacterial warfare. The attack on British propaganda, hitherto extremely strong in broadcasts to Britain, yielded to positive statements of British weakness and the hopelessness of the future. Electra House detected greatly increased emphasis on themes suggesting that everything which the British were fighting to preserve was already well on the road to destruction at the hands of Mr Churchill; that Britain's potential for peace production, already seriously damaged, might well be destroyed within a few months; whether Britain could avoid defeat by invasion or not, she was doomed anyhow by the German counter-blockade.

In fact, Electra House had drawn precisely the wrong inference from this material. The truth of the matter was that by the time these broadcasts were being given, Hitler had already admitted to himself and his subordinates that bombing of British cities had failed to bring Britain to her knees, just as the threat of invasion had failed before it. His *War Directive No. 23 – Directions for Operations against the English War Economy* stated in February 1941 that the bombing campaign, had had 'least effect of all, so far as we can see, on the morale and the will to resist of the English people. No decisive success can be expected from terror attacks on residential areas.' The bombing however was to be intensified on ports and shipping so as to inflict the maximum possible economic damage, but also 'to give the impression that an invasion is planned for this year.' As early as July 1940 Hitler had ordered preparations for an attack on Russia, and in December 1940 that decision had been officially confirmed by him, to be carried out whether the British had come to terms or not.[77] There were no plans for gas attacks or the launching upon Britain of bacteriological warfare. Propaganda to Britain, therefore, throughout the first half of 1941 was at best part of an elaborate bluff, designed – like the continued threat of invasion itself – to maintain political and military pressure upon Britain. The distance between the jobbing propagandists and the decision-makers of the Third Reich meant that the writers and broadcasters in the *Funkhaus* in Berlin were as much victims of that bluff as were their counterparts in Electra House in London.

So, attacks on British morale continued in much the same vein throughout the winter and into the spring of 1941. Electra House affirmed in February that their suspicions of a campaign preparing the way for a military attack on British morale were correct. There was the same type of propaganda as before, urging the British to 'reflect on the sense and nonsense of the present war and recognise that it is being prolonged only because the British Government is unwilling to retract the lies which it has published about Germany'.[78] Appeals to reason continued (involving the suggestion that peace was possible, but not holding out hopes of anything except escape from the consequences of continuing the war) and these were indirectly reinforced by greatly increased terror propaganda. It was useless for the Home Guard to fight the German Army – it was suicide for the British people to continue to resist.

By the spring of 1941, however, Hitler's victory was incomplete. The period of astonishing success one year previously had given way to a period of intense frustration. The British had obstinately refused to see sense, forcing the Führer to threaten them with invasion, and when that failed, to attempt to bomb them into reason. The Italians had refused to play second fiddle in accordance with Hitler's schemes and had gotten themselves into a fix in Greece. Neither Franco nor Pétain would act out the roles which Hitler had envisaged for them as junior partners in his war against the British. Nevertheless, writing the British off as a busted flush, Hitler had long since decided upon war with Russia in realisation of his lifelong dream. Chapter 5 will consider propaganda in the struggle which transformed Hitler's European war into a world war. First, though, it is necessary to consider the impact in Britain of Nazi propaganda from the outbreak of hostilities in 1939 to the beginning of the Russo-German war in 1941.

Notes

1 PRO FO 371/26352 C4836/154/18, *Minute*, 24 April 1941.
2 PRO FO 371/24394, AGP, 1–15 April 1940.
3 PRO FO 371/24394, AGP, 16–30 April 1940.
4 Boelcke, *Secret Conferences*, pp. 30–1.
5 George, *Propaganda Analysis*, p. 31.
6 HAM IEFE 10.55 9.4.40.
7 HAM IEFE 14.18 9.4.40.
8 HAM IEFE 23.15 2.5.40.
9 NBBS IEFE 21.30 3.5.40.
10 BREM IEFE 19.15 3.5.40.
11 Boelcke, *Secret Conferences*, p. 37.
12 NBBS IEFE 21.30 3.5.40.
13 PRO FO 371/24394, AGP, 1–16 May 1940.
14 HAM IEFE 22.15 16.5.40.
15 Boelcke, *Secret Conferences*, p. 40.
16 Speier in *Social Research*, p. 401.
17 HAM IEFE 22.15 16.5.40.
18 PRO FO 371/24394, AGP, 17–31 May 1940.
19 BREM IEFE 19.15 1.6.40.

20 HAM IEFE 23.15 14.6.40.

21 BREM IEFE 22.15 17.6.40.

22 PRO FO 371/24394, AGP, 1–15 June 1940.

23 BRUSS IEFE 16.10.40.

24 PRO FO 371/24394, AGP, 16–30 June 1940.

25 PRO FO 371/24939, AGP, 1–15 July 1940.

26 HILV IEFE 00.15 9.7.40.

27 *New York Times*, 11 August 1940.

28 PRO FO 371/24394, AGP, 16–30 June 1940.

29 Bullock, *Hitler*, p. 592.

30 Shirer, *Berlin Diary*, pp. 355–9. Bullock, *Hitler*, p. 592.

31 An almost immediate, unauthorised and scathing response to Hitler's speech was
broadcast on the BBC's German Service by the journalist Sefton Delmer, later the
man behind Britain's own black propaganda stations. See Delmer, *Black Boomerang*, pp. 16–19.

32 PRO FO 371/24395, AGP, 1–16 August 1940.

33 Goebbels, *Tagebücher*, entry for 6 May 1940.

34 PRO FO 371/24395, AGP, 17–31 August 1940.

35 HAM IEFE 21.30 21.8.40.

36 BREM IEFE 20.15 27.8.40.

37 Ansel, *Hitler Confronts England*, p. 63

38 PRO HO 199/436, *Daily Observations by Home Intelligence*, 16 September 1940.

39 NBBS IEFE 21.30 06.08.40.

40 NBBS IEFE 19.30 15.8.40.

41 NBBS IEFE 21.30 01.9.40.

42 HAM IEFE 21.30 25.7.40.

43 PRO FO 371/24395, AGP, 1–15 September 1940.

44 PRO FO 371/24394, AGP, 1–16 April 1940.

45 PRO FO 371/24394, AGP, 17–31 May 1940.

46 PRO FO 371/24395, AGP, 16–31 August 1940.

47 PRO FO 371/24935, AGP, 17–31 August 1940.

48 Goebbels, *Tagebücher*, entry for 11 September 1940.

49 ZEE IEFE 22.15 9.9.40.

50 WC IEFE 20.10 11.9.40.

51 BBC Monitors often made notes to this effect. See, for instance, BBC DD 523 22
December 1940.

52 Boelcke, *Secret Conferences*, p. 70.

53 NBBS 21.30 28.7.40.

54 NBBS 21.30 30.7.40.

55 See Addison, *The Road to 1945*, *passim* and Calder, *The People's War*, *passim*.

56 PRO FO 371/24395, D[evelopment of]G[erman]P[ropaganda], 1–16 December
1940.

57 NBBS IEFE 21.30 29.8.40.

58 The story of the Duke of Westminster's orchids provides a good example of the
way in which the German broadcasters relied upon and made use of the British
press for hooks upon which to hang their propaganda pieces. 'Cassandra' in the
Daily Mirror of 11 November 1940, had carried the story of the orchids being
shipped to Florida, while pointing out without comment that 643 children had been
killed in air raids in October. The Duke sued the *Mirror*, his counsel arguing that
'how widely such unfounded statements could be spread, and how damaging they
could be, was perhaps best shown by the fact that the announcer on the Bremen

radio, who was usually known as Lord Haw-Haw, repeated them for German propaganda purposes.' See *The Times*, 28 January 1941.
59 WC 21.10 10.10.40.
60 NBBS IEFE 21.30 17.10.40.
61 Goebbels, *Tagebücher*, entry for 12 September 1940.
62 PRO CAB 68/4, AGP, *passim*.
63 WC IEFE 21.10 5.10.40.
64 ZEE IEFE 22.15 9.9.40.
65 BRES IEFE 21.30 2.11.40.
66 PRO FO 371/24395, AGP, 16–30 September 1940.
67 DEUT IGFG 22.10.40.
68 PRO FO 371/24395, AGP, 1–16 October 1940.
69 PRO FO 371 24935, DGP, 16–30 November 1940
70 PRO FO 371/24395, AGP, 1–15 November 1940.
71 PRO FO 371/24935, DGP, 16–30 November 1940.
72 DEUT IGFG 16.11.40.
73 BRES IEFE 19.30 18.11.40.
74 NBBS IEFE 20.30 18.11.40.
75 ZEE IEFE 04.50 22.11.40.
76 PRO FO 371/26531, DGP, 15–28 January 1941.
77 Bullock, *Hitler*, p. 599.
78 PRO FO 371/26531, DGP, 29 January–11 February 1941.

4

Reactions in the UK
to Nazi Wireless Propaganda

The most difficult aspect of propaganda analysis, historical or otherwise, is the attempt to assess its impact. To the extent that the propagandist has clearly defined aims, these are normally easy enough to detect. Likewise, if the material is at all well constructed, the historian or analyst can identify the techniques used to transmit the themes, which together amount to the idea to be propagated. Impact or effectiveness is more difficult to assess. Propaganda deals in psychological manipulation to produce psychological effects upon a mass audience in the expectation of stimulating, reinforcing or altering attitudes, in the hope of producing some desired behaviour. Behaviour of course can be readily enough identified, while attitudes are more difficult. The real problem, however, lies in relating attitudes and behaviour to propaganda, or more exactly in establishing a causal relationship. In the summer of 1940, for instance, very many Britons would have agreed with the MoI view that 'the collapse of France was due as much to the disintegration of the French nation, as a result of powerful and persistent propaganda, as to the force of German arms.'[1] Establishing that this belief was rooted in reality, however, is extraordinarily difficult.

Nevertheless, since one of the purposes of analysing propaganda lies in drawing lessons about societies from its successes and its failures, making the attempt to assess its impact is essential and unavoidable. The case study of German wireless propaganda to the UK brings with it its own particular problems. We do have some apparently clear evidence about the extent of listening to German stations throughout the war years, although there are grounds for treating many of these statistics with a good deal of caution. Of course statistics on audience numbers alone tell us little about the psychological impact of the material. All that we can say for certain is that if no one listened, then the broadcasts had no impact, while a large and long-term audience at least implies interest and involvement on the part of listeners and the potential for psychological effects. We also have a series of long-term studies by various organisations into the morale of the home and forces populations, in which attempts were regularly made to determine the origins of particular attitudes and particular behaviours. Again, while it is unwise to take at face value many of the contemporary inferences drawn from such studies, they can provide valuable data upon which our own conclusions may be based. Moreover, it may be that the broadcasts produced effects in ways and in areas other than the mass effects hoped for by the Germans, but effects which nevertheless may well have been of value to them. It will be necessary therefore, to consider elite opinion as well as 'public' opinion. We begin with the question of the quantification of listening to German broadcasts.

Nazi wireless propaganda broadcasts attracted significant audiences in Britain during the early period of the war. They also generated a great deal of publicity in the British press and in consequence created considerable alarm in official circles. Even in the early prewar planning days of a Ministry of Information, it was recognised that the enemy would try to conduct an intensive propaganda campaign in Britain through broadcasting and other means, which it would be the duty of the new Ministry to counter. Sir Stephen Tallents, in his 1938 report as Director-General Designate at the MoI, saw one of the roles of the News Division to be providing 'replies to enemy statements'. Tallents suggested that 'provision must be made to counter quickly any announcements or propaganda statements made by the enemy. This includes arrangements for the interception of such announcements, and for speedy preparation and issue of suitable counter-statements by the News Division.'[2] Another early suggestion, which presaged many of the ill-fated attempts which would follow, was for 'a regular daily feature in the press exposing false enemy rumours. This feature could probably with great advantage be given a humourous or satirical twist.'[3]

In the first secret official response we have to German propaganda, the survey submitted to the War Cabinet by Lord Macmillan on 22 September 1939, the Minister denigrated German propaganda as lacking in subtlety and as 'sometimes downright stupid'. The Minister went on, however, to make the very good point that:

> it remains true that opinion is little impressed by argument and less by abuse, but is mightily impressed by facts – or by what it believes to be facts. When we have won great victories over the German forces, when the German people have become really hungry instead of being only underfed, when we have solved the very delicate problem of cutting off supplies to Germany and letting them through to neutrals, our propaganda will have its effect. Similarly, if facts speak for the Germans, or seem to do so, their propaganda will be listened to.[4]

From Britain's point of view, of course, the problem during the Phoney War was that no great victories had been won, and the German people were far from starving. In the final three-quarters of 1940, moreover, the position would be greatly worsened with the runaway success in the west of the German military machine. In 1939 and early 1940, however, the problem was that after the swift defeat of Poland, few military developments of any significance seemed imminent, and there was considerable official concern that the initial dogged determination on the part of the general public to see the war through might give way to a pervasive boredom and disillusion, coupled with a sagging of morale and increased willingness to consider some sort of compromise peace. Moreover, the combination of the blackout, which restricted outside leisure activities, the (albeit short-lived) closure of places of public entertainment, the much reduced, censored and consistently dull output of the BBC, as well as the only too natural thirst for information about what was really happening, ensured a sizeable potential audience for foreign, and especially German, broadcasting stations. This point was clearly made only weeks after the outbreak of war in a letter from J. S. Macgregor, on secondment from the BBC to the MoI, to Sir Kenneth Lee, Director of the Ministry's Radio Relations and Communications Division:

> In the present war, the BBC is suffering, in common with the press, from a shortage of British news, and there is no doubt but that the enemy are doing much better in quantity. For this, the character of the war is mainly to blame. If there were more stories (fully authenticated) of Allied successes, the British news bulletins would carry them, and the unfavourable balance created by the German sweep through Poland would be redressed. Surely this is the real cause of the apparent superiority of Nazi propaganda?[5]

However, this was only partly true. Certainly, the 'character of the war' dictated that Germany held the propaganda as well as the military initiative, but the BBC, the MoI and the British armed forces were responsible for the creation of the restrictions and regulations which hampered and inhibited their own efforts adequately to counter German propaganda and to discourage listening to German wireless stations by providing an attractive and informative alternative. In the first fortnight of the war, the single BBC station now available in the UK, the Home Service, broadcast some ten hours of recorded music a day, ten daily news bulletins, at least an hour daily of public service announcements and ministerial broadcasts, and a total of forty-five programmes of Sandy Macpherson at the BBC Theatre Organ. A survey conducted at the end of September 1939 revealed public unhappiness with the apparent absence of up-to-date and reliable information from official British sources, due to what was seen by 53 per cent of respondents as an overly strict censorship. The public was worried:

> They ask: 'Is there anything to hide?' They are wondering why news is so scarce, why it is out of date when it arrives, why some facts of which they themselves know, have not been released . . . Many ill-effects are ascribed to the excessive strictness of censorship. It produces rumours . . . Moreover, some feel that it will strengthen the influence of German propaganda both at home and abroad. 'We get so many reports on the radio from Germany and so few home reports, it is difficult to tell what to believe.'[6]

The BBC too came in for some vocal criticism, with its war broadcasts in particular being described as 'stupid', 'boring' and 'poor'. In addition, the BBC hobbled itself through its traditional deference to the newspapers. On 25 September the Corporation formally agreed with the Newspaper and Periodicals Emergency Council to use no information in news bulletins that had been received after 17.00 until 07.00 the next day, and to use nothing received between midnight and 05.00 before 16.00. This policy had ludicrous consequences. When Leslie Hore-Belisha resigned from his post as Defence Minister on Friday, 1 January 1940, the MoI forbade release of the news by the BBC, marking the story 'not to appear before tomorrow morning's papers'. The BBC carried the story at 12.01 on Saturday, an hour after *Deutschlandsender* and half an hour after New York stations had done so.[7] On 3 April 1940, William Joyce broke the news of the new British Cabinet to the British public, the BBC having been forbidden to broadcast the changes at 21.00, presenting, as R. T. Clark of the BBC bitterly noted, 'a marvellous scoop' to Haw-Haw:

> At 11:15 he broadcast the Cabinet changes to his English listeners who were deliberately deprived of hearing it on their own news service at nine and only by the skin of their teeth were allowed to hear it there at midnight. Is it really worth while conducting an anti-Haw-Haw campaign if he finds such efficient allies?[8]

Also in April 1940, the German wireless was first with the news of the British assault at Narvik. Bremen announced the repulse of the British landing at 19.45, while at 22.15, with no communiqué forthcoming from the Admiralty, the BBC fell back on playing gramophone records.[9] When the first British civilian was killed, in the air raid on Scapa Flow in March 1940, the BBC News Department was ordered, some twelve hours after the raid had occurred (at 19.50 on the 16th) to withhold the story until an Admiralty bulletin could be produced. The BBC first reported the raid therefore at 13.00 on the afternoon of the 17th. Germany meanwhile had broadcast her version of the raid on Zeesen in English for North America at 03.40, Zeesen in German and Spanish for the Americas at 04.15, Hamburg in English at 10.15, *Deutschlandsender* in German at 10.20, Zeesen in German for the Far East at 10.30, *Deutschlandsender* again in German at 12.30, Zeesen in French at 12.45, and Zeesen in English for North America at 12.45. The BBC's Director-General noted sourly that 'the German version of the story thus permeated the world before the BBC was allowed to mention the raid.'[10] Goebbels by contrast was delighted, noting in his diary that 'our version of events at Scapa Flow runs around the world. Churchill's tissue of lies is ripped asunder.'[11] In June 1940, the Germans again scooped the BBC with the story of Reynaud's resignation, and later still, when the Germans began systematically bombing British towns and cities, the failure of the BBC – on orders from the government – to provide adequate information on the location and extent of damage would give another fillip to listening to German broadcasts, of which more below.

Without doubt, however, the greatest inducement to Britons to tune into Bremen and Hamburg came from their own newspapers. The Germans were much assisted by the British press, which generated more publicity for their English-language broadcasts than they themselves could ever have done unaided, the invention and publicising of the 'Lord Haw-Haw' character being of special value. The traditional British press practices of simplifying complexities and personalising policies composited a ragbag of non-entities into a super-propagandist, about whom the press and the public could joke, but only in the way that they joked about Hitler – bravado disguised as humour disguising fear. Initially, the British were urged to listen in to German broadcasts since they were supposedly hilariously funny. 'I urgently ask all of you who are able to listen to broadcasts from Germany to do so,' wrote '*Cassandra*' in the *Daily Mirror*.[12] 'The more people who tune into the foreign propaganda experts, the greater the joy and the laughter,' wrote Jonah Barrington, creator of the 'Haw-Haw' nickname.[13] As late as January 1940, he was still referring to 'healthy British laughter' as the appropriate response to German propaganda.

However, even as the joke began to wear thin by the turn of the year, Haw-Haw still figured prominently in the popular and quality press, and indeed he continued to appear for the rest of the war. The newspapers regularly 'exposed' the 'latest secrets' of the German propaganda machine, and went to considerable trouble to identify (and vilify) the individual broadcasters. Geoffrey Edwards identified Eduard Dietze in the *News Chronicle* in January 1940.[14] The previous day, *Empire News* was adamant that Norman Baillie-Stewart was not one of the band of Nazi broadcasters, while the *Daily Telegraph* had been equally adamant back in October that he was.[15] In March 1940, the *Daily Mirror* identified William Joyce under the headline 'THIS IS LORD HAW-HAW', and a week later, identified his wife as a co-worker.[16] That same month, the *Daily Mail* identified James Clark and his mother, Mrs Eckersley.[17] Haw-Haw was also written into all sorts of stories, even when there was only the most tenuous connection. The *Daily Telegraph* reported in January 1940 that Mrs Sarah Ann Bellamy, aged fifty-three, of Sheffield had gassed herself after becoming depressed through listening to Lord Haw-Haw. Some newspapers took to advertising German propaganda in even more explicit ways. The *News Chronicle* – which held the publishing copyright on all surveys conducted by the British Institute of Public Opinion (BIPO) – reported on the BBC's plan to conduct a listening survey:

> BBC men are shortly to launch a nation-wide enquiry into the effect of German radio propaganda on British listeners. They will endeavour to find out: how many people listen to German propaganda broadcasts; how many listen because they believe it; and how many for amusement. A BBC official said the general impression was that people listened because they found it amusing. At the moment the chief Nazi broadcasts in English are Zeesen on 31.45 metres at 8.15 pm, and Hamburg on 331 metres at 9.10 pm.[18]

Quite quickly, however, officials in the BBC and the MoI came profoundly to regret the 'unfortunate mistake' which had been made in publicising Haw-Haw.[19] However, as the *Concordia* stations came on the air in the spring of 1940, the press again enthusiastically published details on all of the stations, again ostensibly to 'expose' them. Stories on *Concordia* appeared in the *Daily Express*, the *Evening Standard*, the *Daily Herald*, the *Evening Dispatch*, in the *Birmingham Evening Dispatch*, the *Sunday Dispatch*, the *Yorkshire Evening Post*, the *Daily Mirror*, *The Star*, the *Evening News*, the *Daily Sketch*, the *Glasgow Herald*, *The Times*, the *New Statesman & Nation*, the *Daily Telegraph* and in *The Listener*.[20] *Workers' Challenge* in particular excited considerable press interest, and the tabloids took special pleasure in being shocked at the 'Billingsgate' nature of the station's language.[21] The effect, however, was again merely to call attention to stations which could never otherwise have attracted nationwide publicity.

Since the Germans obtained most of their intelligence on the impact of their wireless propaganda from the same British newspapers, it is not surprising that they were delighted with the apparently brilliant success of their efforts. Goebbels gleefully noted the Haw-Haw phenomenon in his diary in January 1940:

> In London they're getting really worked up about our English broadcasts. They call our man 'Lord Haw-Haw'. People are talking about him, and that's half the battle. They want to put somebody up to talk against him. This would be the best thing that could happen. We'd have him for breakfast.[22]

When serious hostilities began in the west in April 1940, the press again took up the Haw-Haw story, this time reporting on an outbreak of pledges by numerous patriotic organisations and British Legion branches never again to listen to him.[23] In June, the *Daily Mirror* began its own 'Anti-Haw-Haw League'.[24] However, the damage had long since been done, as some journalists had much earlier realised. Raymond Burns had criticised the creation by the press of the Haw-Haw persona in the *World's Press News* in February 1940, asking 'was ever such a fatuous label given prominence in Fleet Street?'

> Moreover, historians of the war may well have something to say about the mistake that has been made, by reason of extravagant publicity for this dreary name in directing national attention to the only potentially dangerous system of enemy propaganda against this country's morale.[25]

Burns of course was right – the press did bear a responsibility for generating the terrific publicity which Haw-Haw enjoyed and thereby producing the very large numbers of listeners who tuned in to German broadcasts in the first year or so of the war. In fact, some attempt had been made to measure listening to German stations before war had actually begun. In April 1939, the BBC asked 4,000 General Listening Barometer 'Log-Keepers' about their habits with regard to the English news from Hamburg and Cologne. Two-thirds of the sample were able to receive the broadcasts, about half of them had known about them before asked, 29 per cent had listened at some stage, but only 7 per cent had made a point of doing so.[26] In October 1939, the BBC sponsored another survey to be undertaken by the British Institute of Public Opinion. In response to the question 'Do you ever happen to listen to foreign stations?', 53 per cent of respondents answered 'yes', and of these almost two-thirds said that the last station they had heard was German. Interestingly, when asked 'Are you satisfied with the way the BBC is doing its wartime job?', only 49 per cent of the group responded that they were satisfied.[27] Robert Silvey, of the BBC's Listener Research Department, while making no direct comparison with the April figures, conceded that it was 'certain that there has been an enormous increase in the amount of listening to Hamburg.'[28]

A wider survey was conduced using the BBC's own facilities in December 1939 at the request of the MoI, including the representative sample of 5,600 individuals who were ordinarily interviewed each week about BBC programmes. In an interim report, prepared in January 1940, Silvey claimed that during the previous month, 30 per cent of the adult population, roughly

nine million people, were listeners to Hamburg, the 21.15 broadcast being by far
the most popular. Typically, the BBC's nine o'clock news was heard by sixteen
million people, that is, over 50 per cent of the listening public. If it were
followed by a talk, this would be heard by nine million. Of the other seven
million, six million switched over to Hamburg, while the remaining million
tuned to another station or switched off. And while there was evidence that the
numbers of persons listening to Hamburg was already declining, Silvey
conceded that the broadcasts had achieved the first objective of any propagandist – to become generally known and talked about.[29]

Silvey's full report on listening to Hamburg was circulated early in March. It
was based upon information collected from 34,000 interviews, 750 question-
naires and a special BIPO enquiry of 5,000 persons representative of the adult
population. His findings were that at the end of January 1940, out of every six
British adults, one was a regular listener to German stations, three were
occasional listeners and two never listened. Throughout January and February
the habit of listening regularly had been on the decline, so that during the last
days of February only two-thirds of the number were listening who had
listened during the last week in January. All types of people listened, although
men were greater listeners than women, and people under the age of fifty
greater than those over fifty. Those whose families had been broken up by war,
or whose money incomes had declined, were no more likely to listen than those
not so affected. The one outstanding feature in determining listening was
interest in public affairs. The average listener was a more politically conscious
person than the average non-listener, and was more likely to listen to the BBC
news and take the more serious newspapers. The conclusion to be drawn was
that, rather than supplanting the BBC news service, Hamburg was an additional rather than an alternative source of information.

In terms of the impact of the broadcasts, Silvey noted that the average listener
was more likely to be aware of disunity within the British Empire, and more
prepared to credit Hitler with positive social achievements in Germany. On the
other hand, the average listener was more favourable to the operation of rationing
in the UK than the average non-listener, so that it was difficult to see that the
broadcasts had had much effect. Silvey went on to note, however, that the survey
had been conducted in the context of a relatively static period of the war, one in
which widespread hatred of the enemy did not yet exist. If there were widespread
suffering, hatred of the enemy might grow and the task of the Hamburg
propagandists would be correspondingly more difficult. If there were widespread
social discontent on the other hand, this would be Hamburg's opportunity.

In retrospect, the figures produced by Silvey's department – six million regular
and eighteen million occasional listeners – do seem extraordinarily high. In
explaining them, he cited a combination of factors which included both elements
within the broadcasts themselves and factors specific to wartime conditions:

> The black-out, the novelty of hearing the enemy, the desire to hear both
> sides, the insatiable appetite for news and the desire to be in the swim had all

played their part both in building up Hamburg's audience and in holding it together. The entertainment value of the broadcasts, their concentration on undeniable evils in this country, their news sense, their presentation, and the publicity they have received in this country, together with the momentum of the habit of listening to them, have all contributed towards their establishment as a familiar feature in the social landscape.[30]

Now, clearly large numbers of people did listen to Haw-Haw during the Phoney War period, and Silvey's findings tend to be accepted at face value by most later commentators. However, given the circumstances under which his surveys were conducted, some of his conclusions need to be treated with a little caution. It is worth bearing in mind that public opinion polling, even today an inexact science, was in its infancy in 1940, and many contemporaries were highly sceptical about the results produced by the various surveying and polling organisations.[31] Moreover, many of the results themselves suggest weaknesses in the findings. In the written questionnaire, respondents were asked to say what they thought were the chief reasons why people listened to Lord Haw-Haw. On the basis of comments already received, a list of nine possible reasons was drawn up and listeners were invited to endorse any which they felt represented their answer – space for other unlisted reasons was also provided. The result is shown in Table 4.1.

Table 4.1 'Why do people listen to Hamburg?'

	Thought to be one of the chief reasons by (%)
'Because his (Lord Haw-Haw's) version of the news is so fantastic that it is funny'	58
'Because so many other people listen to him and talk about it'	50
'Because people are amused at his voice and manner'	38
'Because they like to hear the German point of view'	29
'Because they hope to get more news'	26
'Because his anecdotes make people laugh'	26
'Because he is a good broadcaster'	15
'Because the BBC news is so dull'	9
'Because he is so clever'	6

Source: BBC WAC R9/9/4, *LR/98 Hamburg Broadcast Propaganda: The Extent and Effect of its Impact on the British Public during mid-winter 1939/40*, 8 March 1940.

As Silvey pointed out, the three reasons which head the list represent 'satisfactions' which the Hamburg broadcasts gave to those who listened to them – entertainment value and the social cachet of having heard Haw-Haw. These three had outstripped the desire to hear the other fellow's point of view and the plain hunger for news. However, a point which Silvey overlooked was that the social cachet connected with listening to Haw-Haw could and probably did lead people to exaggerate the extent of their own listening. Given that the press coverage of Haw-Haw had made Hamburg 'a familiar part of the social landscape', and given that the broadcasts were supposed to be either hilariously funny because they were so fantastic, or hilariously funny because they were so clever, to confess that you did not listen was to place yourself outside the 'knowing' social group, almost akin to confessing that you could not stand *ITMA* and firmly believed that Tommy Handley wasn't funny. In any case, as has been shown in Chapters 2 and 3, the Hamburg news and talks broadcasts were not particularly fantastic or exaggerated in their claims, and it seems unlikely that the sardonic wit of William Joyce and his colleagues would have been especially appealing or even comprehensible to the mass audience. To admit, however, to not being able to see the joke, or to being frightened rather than amused, was to admit one's own stupidity and weakness. Furthermore, during the Phoney War, when the Ministry of Information in particular and the official systems of control, regulation and censorship in general were widely held in public contempt, to 'admit' to listening to German stations, whether the admission were actually true or not, might have seemed to many a small symbol of independence of mind and even of defiance.

Of course, it is easier to make these criticisms than it is to prove them. However, the mismatch between the public perception of Haw-Haw and the content of his actual broadcasts, and the unlikely character of a great many of the Haw-Haw rumours in circulation in 1940 and again in 1942, seem to show that those who spread them and those who believed them rarely if ever actually listened to any of the Haw-Haw stations. There were therefore perfectly good and understandable reasons in the early period of the war for ordinary citizens to exaggerate the extent of their own listening to Haw-Haw, just as later on, when the war had taken a terrible and frightening turn, there were perfectly good and understandable reasons for doing exactly the reverse.

Even if one accepts, however, the premise that the very high figures for listening in the early war years are probably exaggerated, this is not to suggest the broadcasts were without an audience and had no impact. Indeed it is more likely that while fewer people listened than is normally supposed, many of these listeners took the broadcasts more seriously than is normally supposed. To be sure, the BBC produced some alarming findings on the efficacy of the material produced by the German propagandists. In another valuable BBC report, produced in February 1940, it was conceded that the Hamburg broadcasts in English had 'established a tradition of their own':

> Those who have taken to listening have been given a story which in itself was a gross distortion, but in this story there were always some elements of truth. There *is* a social problem in Great Britain, there *are* economic difficulties, and Warren Hastings or Clive *did* conquer India by force. This is the skill, therefore, of the German propaganda, that in mixing in their appeal a grain of truth the fiction becomes less apparent, and what was an allegation yesterday has become a premise to cite today.[32]

The Hamburg broadcasts did make the British listener laugh, it was argued, with their regular slips, the more general misconceptions and the traditional German misunderstanding of so many aspects of British life and character. Nevertheless, it was worth remembering that this peculiar entertainment value led people to listen repeatedly, and that the principal force of Hitler's propaganda technique lay in the effect of repetition. Many pieces of independent evidence supported the view that when people were regularly supplied with formulae for expressing grievances, at a later stage, when faced with greater hardships, they may have felt that Hamburg was right after all – the full effect could only be felt when the population was faced with real hardship or disaster. The reaction to what Haw-Haw had to say, and the attraction of it, was, however, not homogeneous:

> Although almost all listeners were to some extent critical, their attitude would depend on the degree of their own dissatisfaction and social insecurity. To an observer not personally implicated the composite Hamburg announcer might appear merely as an unorthodox form of His Majesty's Opposition, but to others who are hard hit much of what he says goes home. The range of dissatisfaction is wide; we have described how masterfully Haw-Haw distributes his appeals. In studying reactions, one is clearly faced with all the implications of the social problems in this country . . . Those who are hard hit he incites to class-warfare, those from whom no such action can be expected are at least taught to distrust themselves and their own principles. These comments, incomplete in themselves, purposely take into account only conscious or pre-conscious motivations. This does not mean that deeper layers of the mind, to which Haw-Haw – the modern 'Boney' – also appeals, are of no or even minor importance. Some listen to him with a passive fascination which reminds one of the snake's prey.[33]

Table 4.2 'Opinions about Hamburg broadcasts'

Group	% of listeners to Hamburg
1 Believe that Hamburg broadcasts contain grains of truth, that Hamburg sometimes secures news scoops	17
2 Regard Haw-Haw as first class entertainment	16
3 Believe that Hamburg broadcasts are lies, rubbish, stupid, silly, mad	15
4 Respect the skill of Hamburg propaganda	4
5 Dislike, or are angry, with Haw-Haw	4
6 Are bored with Hamburg propaganda	3
7 Fear Haw-Haw's influence	3
8 Have contempt for Haw-Haw's influence	2
9 Are suspicious of news from both sides	2
10 Desire to hear both sides	2

Source: BBC WAC R9/9/4, *LR/98 Hamburg Propaganda: The Extent and Effect of its Impact on the British Public during mid-winter 1939/40*, 8 March 1940.

Silvey's special sample had also produced some potentially worrying results on people's opinions about the broadcasts. The results are summarised in Table 4.2. The largest group thought that the broadcasts did contain grains of truth and this group certainly was larger than the one which thought they were all lies or just plain rubbish. Silvey noted that the bigger group included a large number of people who were sympathetic to all demands for social reform from whatever source they came, though they were not necessarily under any illusions about the disinterestedness of Haw-Haw's concern for the welfare of the British masses. 'I agree with much that's said but feel I have been in bad company', said a fifty-year-old Scottish employer. Others in this group regarded Haw-Haw as a salutary influence. A Manchester postman said 'Haw-Haw . . . keeps the government awake with his criticising . . . the ordinary man benefits.' Silvey noted too that the belief that Hamburg regularly scooped the British press and the BBC was fairly widespread. 'When wanting red hot news I listen to Hamburg', said a working-class housewife in South Shields. A retired Indian Army officer in Bournemouth remarked, 'I learn some things from Hamburg before our people tell us.'[34]

Silvey also remarked on the general view that the Hamburg broadcasts frequently scored some shrewd points and an attempt was made to obtain some estimate of those points which had hit home. The written questionnaire contained the question, 'Can you remember any times when the Hamburg broadcasts have made what you feel to be really good points? If so, what were they about?' The results are summarised in Table 4.3.

Table 4.3   Points scored by Hamburg broadcasts

	Regarded as good points for Hamburg by (%)
Description of British social conditions, unemployment, distressed areas, slums and working-class distress in wartime	14.5
Inadequacy of British old age pensions	5.1
Criticisms of British colonial policy and handling of India and Palestine	3.4
Allegations of profiteering, high cost of living, inflation	3.3
Inaccuracy of British news	3.2
Shortcomings of British foreign policy past and present	2.2
Problems of evacuation	1.8
Charges of corruption and inefficiency in British politics	0.8
Allegations of Jewish influence in Great Britain	0.8
Hardship of soldiers' families	0.7
A variety of other points were cited by isolated listeners	

Source: BBC WAC R9/9/4, *LR/98 Hamburg Broadcast Propaganda: The Extent and Effect of its Impact on the British Public during mid-winter 1939/40*, 8 March 1940.

Noteworthy here was that anti-Semitism, which featured so prominently in Nazi propaganda, was regarded by only insignificant numbers of listeners as one of Hamburg's 'good points', although the extent to which respondents would have shied away from aligning themselves openly with Germany on this issue may well have affected the figures. It is significant too that the points which met with any substantial measure of approval from listeners were all ones which were frequently aired in Britain herself and were, as Silvey put it, 'accepted as perfectly legitimate criticisms in no way inconsistent with a desire to prosecute the war to a successful conclusion. Genuinely defeatist propaganda appears to fall on singularly unreceptive ears.'[35]

Nevertheless there did seem to be a correlation between the holding of views which accorded with those propagated by Hamburg and the likelihood that the holder of those views was a listener. The case of Empire unity and Hitler's pre-war social achievements has already been mentioned. Members of the special sample were also asked whom they felt would gain from the war, since it was constantly repeated in the Hamburg broadcasts that whoever would gain, it would not be the ordinary British worker. The suggestions offered were: 'Soviet Russia'; 'the Nazis'; 'big business'; 'America'; 'the Jews'; 'the working classes'; 'Britain and France'; 'none of these'. The results are summarised in Table 4.4.

Table 4.4 'Who will gain from the war?'

	Persons who	
	listen to Hamburg regularly (% agreeing)	never listen to Hamburg (% agreeing)
America	57	45
Big business	39	30
The Jews	21	17
Britain and France	13	12
None of them	11	14
No opinion	9	16
The working classes	5	4
Soviet Russia	4	4
The Nazis	1	1

Source: BBC WAC R9/9/4, *LR/98 Hamburg Broadcast Propaganda: The Extent and Effect of its Impact on the British Public during mid-winter 1939/40*, 8 March 1940.

On the face of it, they might seem to show that Hamburg had had some influence, since those who listened seemed more convinced that the Americans, big business and the Jews would gain than those who did not listen. On the other hand, both groups listed gainers in the same order and the differences which are apparent may have more to do with the fact that the more politically conscious and opinionated an individual, the more likely he was to listen to Hamburg. Only 9 per cent of Hamburg listeners had no opinion as opposed to 16 per cent of non-listeners. The apparent differences between the two groups may merely reflect the more strongly held opinions of those interested in current affairs rather than demonstrating the influence of German broadcasts. The figures on the Jews too can easily be misinterpreted. Reports from Silvey's investigators revealed that many persons thought the Jews would gain because an Allied victory would signal the end of their persecution by the Nazis. That the remainder mentioned the Jews for anti-Semitic reasons merely reveals the extent to which anti-Semitism was a strong current of contemporary opinion in the UK. The differences between listeners to Hamburg and the remainder of the population are not particularly marked in this regard. What is most striking from the statistics rather is the utter certainty of both listeners and non-listeners that the Nazis were going to lose the war.

Whether or not German broadcasts were having much effect on the quite large numbers of persons in Britain who listened to them, what is perhaps just as important is the extent to which those in authority in wartime Britain thought they might be effective. Ian McLaine is probably correct when he argues that in time the ruling elite in Britain came to realise that, if trusted, the British public would demonstrate 'a very high degree of common sense'.[36] Nevertheless, for much of the early war that same elite and the middle classes from which it sprang reacted with an anxiety at times not far off panic about the likely effect of Haw-Haw upon their social inferiors. The official view on Haw-Haw was summed up by Colonel M. G. Christie in a BBC broadcast in October 1940. 'Anything coming from known German radios', he said, 'was looked upon [in Britain] as a queer form of clowning and had absolutely no effect on the sturdy British mind.'[37] Others were not so sure, however, and by the end of 1939, hundreds of letters were being received by the BBC, the MoI and the press from concerned members of the public and the political and military establishment, alarmed at what they saw as the widespread effectiveness of Nazi radio propaganda and the apparent failure of the British side to act to counter it. Only a week after war had begun, General Sir Charles Grant of Scottish Command wrote to the BBC's Director-General F. W. Ogilvie complaining of 'foul German propaganda', asking if 'the more obvious lies' were being countered in the BBC's own foreign broadcasts.[38] In mid-November, Melville Dinwiddie, the BBC's Scottish Director, was also becoming alarmed, especially at the extent of listening to Haw-Haw. He wrote to Sir Richard Maconachie, the BBC's Director of Talks:

> Recent investigation has shown that a vast and increasing number of listeners is tuning in regularly to the 'Lord Haw-Haw' broadcasts from Germany. To begin with, listeners took them as entertainment and laughed heartily at them, but indications are growing that they are being taken seriously by a good many listeners, especially women . . . The omission of references in the *Radio Times* to the timings of this nightly mixture of news and topical talks surrounds them with mystery and has helped considerably to increase their regular listeners. If such propaganda material is harmless, let no restrictions be put upon listening to it; if not, some action should be taken to counteract it in our Home Service programme.[39]

Dinwiddie went on to argue that the material was at times effective, in particular the 'subtle thrusts at the weaker points of our democratic policy' such as the burden of rationing, the ineffectiveness of British aid to Poland, help to

Jewish refugees when many British workers were 'out of work and starving', and the constant reiteration of news of British naval and military failures. Dinwiddie closed by declaring that there was a need to combat the 'subtle and oft-repeated insinuations of German propaganda'. His own suggestion was that Haw-Haw be 'flayed at the microphone, open and unabashed'. Dinwiddie's call for action against Haw-Haw presaged a long-running battle within the BBC, and between the Corporation, with some support from the MoI, and numerous other agencies and individuals, who were insistent that more overt and direct action were taken to confront Nazi propaganda head-on. The backdrop was that concern was mounting that Haw-Haw was winning. For example, on 24 November, Percy Edgar, the BBC's Midland Regional Director, expressed his anxiety at a meeting of the Corporation's Home Service Board 'at the amount of listening to these broadcasts' and said that he thought they were having some effect.[40] Basil Nicolls, Controller (Programmes) replied that Haw-Haw was being countered, by the monthly *Voice of the Nazi* talks, and by 'sporadic guying' of German news in variety programmes. The BBC received many more complaints, however, that such measures were insufficient. In early December 1939 General Sir Frederick Pile wrote from headquarters, Anti-Aircraft Command TA, that 'the [German] broadcasting is most insidious, and is nothing more or less than an attempt to foment a social revolution.' Pile's comments are interesting in that his was typical of an oft-expressed view that while the broadcasts were unlikely to have much effect upon the 'intelligent' or 'well-informed' listener, more concern should be forthcoming about their likely impact upon the working classes. General Pile had devoted a good deal of time of the preceding fortnight to listening in to Haw-Haw:

> Many of the statements one hears regarding the knowledge evinced in these broadcasts are untrue, or, at any rate, I personally have never heard anything startling. But the broadcasts are undoubtedly very clever. For the most part, the statements made are true; very often only half-true. But the man in the street, who has only a limited knowledge, believes them.

They would affect his men more than most, he argued, 'for we are pretty bored in the evenings . . . The BBC news bulletins were extremely dull, [and] when someone tunes in to Lord Haw-Haw, the whole room gets up and gathers round the wireless. After it is over, they go back to their games without comment.' Pile suggested that Haw-Haw be countered and challenged directly and immediately on the BBC every night by a working man or 'by one of the very talented men who every Sunday take up their positions at Hyde Park Corner'.[41] Similar concerns were expressed by Major H. B. Longland of the BEF about the effect of Haw-Haw's talks on British soldiers in France. In March 1940, he complained of the 'more or less consistent listening to Hamburg in the BEF', which the Directorate of Military Intelligence considered 'a grave danger to morale and [which] may be in the future a very definite penetration point for enemy propaganda.'[42] The MoI's Policy Committee was informed in June 1940 that British troops in Iceland were listening to the German wireless, 'because they did not feel confidence in news of British origin.'[43]

The Foreign Office also was keen to criticise and to make its own suggestions, often at the cost of considerable irritation within the BBC and the MoI. As early as 11 September 1939, Roger Stevens at the Foreign Office was writing to Macgregor at the MoI, with a long list of items from German broadcasts which his chief, General Charles, had decided should be taken up and refuted in the BBC's own foreign broadcasts.[44] Macgregor replied politely that BBC staff always considered the various propaganda points noted in the monitoring reports in compiling overseas news bulletins. No reasonable opportunity was lost of countering inaccurate German statements. Nevertheless he went on:

[It] must be borne in mind that the BBC are anxious not to allow the news bulletins to degenerate into verbal warfare. It is felt that the assertion of the truth is often more effective than the denial of a lie.[45]

The Foreign Office was highly critical too of what it saw as the BBC's failure to counter Nazi propaganda to the Dominions about social conditions in Britain. For example, they again complained to Macgregor in October (1939) that Britain was being successfully portrayed as a nation with soaring prices and unemployment, a collapsing currency, food shortages, generalised economic chaos, rising popular discontent and weakening support for the government. This picture was being presented in English and other languages to listeners around the world, supported by quotations from British and foreign newspapers and from statements made by political leaders. More to the point, claimed the FO, their Dominion specialists were convinced that this picture was having some effect. 'The effect varies with the type of population, e.g. the Dutch South African appears to be convinced of its truth, but even where German propaganda is discounted, a definite effect is noticed.' The only answer was that a definite 'counter-picture' be presented in BBC overseas broadcasts, with successive references to the soundness of conditions in Britain. One suggestion was that one or two housewives be interviewed, or a grocer, or wholesaler, and that they present 'a favourable view' of the situation here.[46] In January 1940, the FO suggested a committee of three, made up of representatives of the Foreign Office, the BBC and the MoI, to draw up scripts for 'debunking' German propaganda.[47]

For the BBC, the best counter-blast to Nazi propaganda was news coverage, as accurate and comprehensive as the circumstances allowed. A clearly exasperated Macgregor wrote in mid-October 1939 that:

There is far too much insistence nowadays on answering the Nazi allegations. Of course there has to be denial of certain mis-statements, but the best propaganda must be positive: we must get in first, and put the enemy on the defensive. A prompt and regular supply of significant news will be far more effective at home and overseas than the desperate effort to contradict every false story from Germany, which seems to be an obsession with so many people . . .[48]

Nevertheless, in spite of the BBC's reluctance to become involved in verbal warfare with the Nazis, specific refutations did occur, but in specially designed talks and features such as the monthly *Voice of the Nazi* programme, written and presented by the psychologist W. A. Sinclair and broadcast from December 1939 until May 1940.[49] Such talks continued to be given occasionally by Sinclair and by Lindley Fraser, the last *Voice of the Enemy* broadcast being given by Sinclair early in 1943. The Overseas Services had already had their own talks on Nazi propaganda, including one which followed all news bulletins on 1 October. Reference was made to Hitler's remarks about lies in *Mein Kampf*, and there followed a list of Nazi 'lies' which needed refuting. Another broadcast written by Michael Barkway, went out on the Overseas Service following all news bulletins on 29 October. Just as in Germany, however, the arguments continued between the various agencies in Britain who felt themselves qualified to express opinions on propaganda and counter-propaganda policy. In December, Ogilvie received yet another letter on Haw-Haw, this time from Aylmer Vallance at the War Office:

> We are getting a rather disturbing amount of reports from Public Relations Officers at Commands and from other sources which indicate that the Hamburg broadcasts in English are becoming a definite factor affecting public morale in this country. The transmissions are, I think you will agree, ingenious; and though the British public's first reaction was one of amusement, I am not sure that the constant reiteration of Lord Haw-Haw is not having a bad effect.[50]

Vallance called for some compelling diversionary programme on the BBC to draw listeners away from Haw-Haw, or a caricaturing feature on him by a humourist such as P. G. Wodehouse or '*Beachcomber*'. 'It is not for us', he concluded, 'to teach the BBC its business, but I think you ought to know that we do take a rather serious view of the Hamburg propaganda.'[51] A more heated argument broke out between representatives of the BBC and the MoI later in the month, again on the issue of counter-Haw-Haw talks. The MoI argued that since the bulk of German criticism of Britain had a leftist slant, British counter-propaganda should be directed also to the left. Sir Richard Maconachie, the BBC's Controller (Talks), was also told that the Home Secretary, Sir John Anderson, had 'represented forcibly' to Lord Macmillan, the then Minister of Information, the bad effects of Haw-Haw, and urged that 'something should be done about it'.[52] Maconachie insisted, however, that the BBC was 'completely opposed to the contradiction of particular statements, except in special circumstances, or to misdirected efforts to counter Haw-Haw's propaganda [which] might indeed do much to keep it alive and prominent'. German propaganda, he argued, would defeat itself in the long-run, as had Russian propaganda. The best solution from Britain's point of view, was straight news over the long term, aided by indirect propaganda, with no explicit references to material from Hamburg.[53]

Shortly after this row, at Christmas 1939, Director-General Ogilvie set out the BBC's position as it had by then evolved in a letter to Campbell Stuart at Electra House. The Haw-Haw question, he wrote, 'is of great importance. We have never regarded it as the joke which it is supposed to be by some . . . That Haw-Haw should be countered is, of course, agreed certainly; the only problem concerns the method.' After mentioning the idea of a regular speaker, Ogilvie added that there should be no undue publicity for Haw-Haw. 'Why had *The Times* given the times and wave-lengths of his talks and why did MPs direct so much attention to him in the House?' Haw-Haw was not a person, but 'a well informed syndicate', and what he said was clever enough 'not to admit of easy answer'. Some of his talks on working-class housing or unemployment were almost indistinguishable from articles in the *Daily Herald* or the *New Statesman*, while some of the talks about India or Pakistan or about the alleged sabotaging of the League of Nations in the last few years 'might have come straight from the *News Chronicle* or the *Manchester Guardian*'. The German news was 'reasonably accurate' and was derived from British sources. 'The Haw-Haw question', he concluded, 'merely makes it all the more important that the BBC's news service should be allowed to maintain its standards of truthfulness and speed.' The best defence was attack, and it should be attack 'on British terms not those of Haw-Haw'.[54]

Nevertheless, although the BBC view was that Haw-Haw was best ignored on the air, this did not mean that other tactics could not be employed to divert listeners away from him. One idea was the switching of some popular programmes to slots immediately after the nine o'clock news, so that *Band Wagon*, or broadcasts by George Formby or Gracie Fields might act as 'spoilers' for Haw-Haw.[55] Another was the instigation of the weekly *Onlooker* – or as they were called from March 1940 the *Postscript* – commentaries on the current news. The first speaker, in February 1940, was the lawyer Norman Birkett, although it would be his successor, J. B. Priestley, who would really capture the public imagination, making him second only to Churchill as the BBC's most popular wartime speaker.[56] That Priestley was such a terrific success in his own right, however, should not detract from the fact that the talks, broadcast immediately after the nine o'clock news on Sunday evenings, were quite deliberately designed to keep listeners from retuning to the 21.15 news on Hamburg, and to challenge and counter the ideas being propagated by Haw-Haw without actually admitting as much. It was explicitly noted at the BBC's Home Board in April 1940, that 'Haw-Haw continues to be . . . an important factor in the planning of both the Home and Forces programmes.'[57]

That there should be alarm in ruling circles about Haw-Haw is probably understandable, given the reports which were filtering up to policy-makers from organisations such as Mass-Observation (MO). Certainly, many of the 'overheard conversations' collected by MO were highly enthusiastic about Haw-Haw. A barman in Bolton was a keen listener:

> Do you ever hear that bloke from Hamburg they call Haw-Haw? I never tire of him. So where you go somebody brings him up [sic]. He has convinced thousands. I might tell you he has opened my eyes. There's no betting, he's a bloody good speaker.

A few days earlier a van driver on the East Lancashire Road in Bolton was heard to ask:

> Did you hear Hamburg last night? He said that we were only having one sausage each for breakfast in England, and lucky when we got that. Now, I've been inclined to take a bit of notice of him – but he kills his own pig when he talks like that. But there's no doubt about it – he's bloody good, he licks any one of our announcers, I hearken to him every night.

Another Boltonian, a middle-aged female habituée of the Socialist club, was overheard to recommend Lord Haw-Haw's broadcasts:

> Oh, he's good, you ought to have heard him the other night, skitting about Churchill. I always listen to him.[58]

Working-class opinion in Lambeth was divided. One woman said Haw-Haw made her blood boil: 'I feel inclined to smash the set, saying what he does about England', while a second held a different view:

> I think he is very good. He's very nice. We aren't educated enough to understand all the words he uses, but he's very interesting, and a lot he says is true.[59]

More interesting, perhaps, is the overheard snippet of a conversation between two Bolton millgirls, aged twenty-five and thirty, also from November 1939. The sentiments expressed by the older woman seem to indicate a personality of exactly the type the Nazi propagandists were aiming for, and the dialogue itself could almost have been written for the NBBS:

> 1st woman: My husband always listens to Hamburg Henry but he tells a lot of lies. Did you hear him last night? He said we were starving in England. What bunk!
> 2nd woman: *We* might not be . . . you and your husband working. What about Maggie Foster? Her husband's in the Army; they get about 30/- a week for her and five kids – she can't be so far off starving.
> 1st woman: That is true – it is a disgrace about soldiers' wives; we're allus talking about it in the top-room, but Hamburg says they are nearly all starving.
> 2nd woman: Well, if they are not now they soon will be.[60]

It would seem, however, that what might in other circumstances be disregarded merely as typical working-class cynicism came by members of the socio-economic elite to be seen in wartime as highly alarming evidence of working-class disaffection inspired by Haw-Haw. This process was already well under way during the phoney war. The BBC noted in January 1940 that broadcasts by working-class speakers were under consideration, critical of the Nazi system of propaganda. 'This suggestion is regarded as important by the MoI, since it is the "working class" which is believed to be most affected by this propaganda.'[61] Reporting on morale in February 1940, the MoI's Home Intelligence Southern Region, in the person of Sir Arthur Willart, reported that:

> Regarding news from overseas sources, two facts are worth noting: (1) the existence of a definite demand for more about the war-effort of France and the Dominions, (2) the inadvisability of taking at their face value, official reports from various parts of this Region, that enemy wireless propaganda is 'heard with contempt' or 'has no effect'. There is a steady trickle of evidence that, in spite of his obvious blunders, Haw-Haw does sometimes impress the uneducated and even the more or less educated. Thus the household of one of the leading officials in the Region was disturbed the other day by the announcement of one of the servants to an indignant kitchen, that she and her family preferred to be guided by Haw-Haw rather than the BBC.[62]

The middle-class emphasis on Haw-Haw's supposed appeal to the workers also comes through clearly in reports of the MoI's Home Morale Emergency Committee, a body which, despite the urgency and importance of its work, was staffed by individuals like Sir Kenneth Clark and Harold Nicolson who knew next to nothing about working-class life and attitudes. Nicolson himself had been concerned for a long time about the effectiveness of Haw-Haw. In January 1940 he had written to Ogilvie at the BBC, 'I remain absolutely convinced that the broadcasts are dangerous and require very urgent treatment'.[63] His Committee, moreover, assumed that disintegration of public morale would be due to five main causes: fear, confusion, suspicion, class-feeling and defeatism, although it is clear enough from their deliberations that they assumed that the latter two sentiments would be exclusive to the working masses. The Committee recommended that the anti-rumour campaign needed to be intensified and 'occasion should again be taken to discredit the Hamburg broadcasts and the New British Broadcasting Corporation [sic]. In particular an early and renewed effort should be made to dispel the legend of Lord Haw-Haw's omniscience, and of his secret sources of information.' Moreover, it was suggested that something might be done to 'diminish the present predominance of the cultured voice on wireless', again in direct response to Nazi propaganda:

> Every effort should be made to bring working-class people to the microphone, and more frequent use should be made of left-wing speakers to counteract the propaganda of our enemies regarding imperialism and capitalism. We should take an offensive rather than a defensive line under this heading.[64]

Furthermore, the Committee was clearly alarmed that Nazi propaganda based on the appeal to class differences was having some effect:

It is important to make it clear to the public that a German victory would not affect the propertied classes alone, but would bring humiliation and misery to the nation as a whole. The Nazi and Communist propagandists are instilling the idea that only the rich would suffer by defeat and that the working classes in this country would actually benefit from a German triumph. The Committee suggest that a concentrated effort should be made to establish the conviction that our defeat would not merely mean the loss of wealth, power and reputation but would also entail enslavement.

The class assumptions behind the Committee's findings should be clear enough, but such assumptions were very often expounded in starker language in correspondence both to the Ministry and the BBC. The industrialist Percy E. Goff wrote from Leeds to Vansittart at the FO in April 1940, referring to:

the most serious and pernicious effects the nightly insidious semi-truths, coupled with lying in the most ingenious and subtle manner, that the Haw-Haw broadcasts are having among the working classes in this part of the country, particularly their womenfolk . . . Even my own maids and char-women are becoming tainted, and although my wife and I tell them they are playing his and the enemy's game, and becoming undermined and disloyal, yet they quote many of his utterances that even I have difficulty to refute.[65]

In June 1940, a Mrs Ord wrote from Ribbleton, near Preston, to her MP that:

My Char-woman gives me the views of some of the working-class people around her, many of whom, I know work in the English Electric Aircraft Factory. A remark which is constantly made is 'Well, at any rate, one good thing about Hitler is – he robs the rich to help the poor'. Would it not be possible to arrange for some speakers who would appeal to the masses, such as a North End footballer or some similar 'hero' to counteract this Nazi propaganda? One cannot help feeling that there is much of this sort of thing in the whole of Lancashire.[66]

Colonel R. H. Brand wrote in March 1940 to express his alarm at the effect of Haw-Haw upon the 'locals' in rural Aberdeenshire. He was 'absolutely horrified to find what a tremendous effect these soberly-stated, quiet, German lies from Hamburg and Co. have upon them.'[67] Mrs J. E. Smith, a farmer's wife of Chelmsford, was alarmed at the impact of Haw-Haw's allegations that the Cabinet was about to flit:

It is surely time some assurance should be given the general public that there never has been the faintest idea for the Government to leave England for Canada. Lord Haw-Haw's lies to this effect are being repeated so endlessly, and although his vile propaganda is generally laughed at and despised, there is a certain section of poorly educated folk who are being alarmed. I am a Sussex farmer's wife and find that many of the farm labourers and other working folk do still listen to these German broadcasts and are being disturbed.[68]

Lady Dorothy Swan wrote to Tallents at the MoI in December 1940 that her hostess's servants 'listen in' regularly to Haw-Haw and one of them had remarked that there was probably something in what he said. A broadcaster was needed – amateur or professional – who felt strongly on the subject and could attack Haw-Haw in English and in German, 'as there are thousands of people who, like these maids, listen to him daily, and find themselves influenced by his malicious lies'. Thoughtfully, Lady Swan included a draft address of her own, lambasting Joyce as a crook and a swindler.[69]

Mr H. G. Grafton Beddells of Lander, Beddells and Crompton of London probably had different motives in writing to the BBC, but the same class assumptions are observable. Writing as late as March 1943, Mr Beddells noted:

> For some time, I have had occasion to travel regularly by a train carrying a large number of apprentices from a large war factory and have formed the opinion that many of them listen fairly regularly to the Axis broadcasts in English. Certain discussions, for example, as regards America's post-war aims, to which I have listened appeared from the arguments used to have arisen from the German broadcasts in English. Much of the present Axis propaganda is clever and well put over, and there is, I think, some danger of its having a cumulative effect on the minds of listeners unless its falsity is widely exposed.[70]

Of course, Mr Beddells had no evidence that the sentiments he had heard expressed arose from Nazi propaganda, but rather that he merely assumed that they had. If anyone in this episode had been influenced by Haw-Haw, it had been Mr Beddells himself. Moreover, second-hand information, based on unsupported generalisations, often filtered up to senior establishment figures. G. G. Thomson of the Department of Social Science at Liverpool University wrote to Ogilvie that he had been told by a lady social worker, who had met many soldiers' wives, that 'all of them' listened to Haw-Haw, 'because he discussed their hardship, and seemed to be the only person interested in them.'[71]

Now, it seems likely that fairly large numbers of politically conscious individuals of all social classes did listen to Haw-Haw and continued to do so long after the end of the Phoney War. However, for the great bulk of the non-politically conscious population, Haw-Haw in all his guises was probably just too highbrow. The following extract from a Mass-Observation report from November 1939 on the Hamburg listening habits of a Bolton family has about it the ring of authenticity, and may well have been typical:

> Woman aged 68: Now you listen to him, go on, you'll hear some home-truths you will; I always have him on at home.

> [Man 38 turns up the station and he, and the Woman 68, the woman 35 and a girl of 16 listen, silent for a minute until his economic phraseology gets a little

involved; then they continue talking about other matters, leaving the station on however.][72]

However, the extent to which members of the policy-making elite were concerned about German broadcasts is illustrated by the regular appearance of requests and demands from certain quarters that they be jammed. The issue of jamming enemy broadcasts in wartime had actually been discussed as early as December 1935, when a paper produced by the Broadcasting in War Committee was discussed by the Committee of Imperial Defence. The Committee concluded that 'We consider that counter-propaganda is the answer to enemy broadcast propaganda, and we recommend that "jamming" of foreign broadcasting stations should not be resorted to, save in exceptional circumstances.'[73] However, the issue of jamming German broadcasts reappeared almost as soon as war broke out. In mid-September 1939, the Dominions Office had asked the Ministry of Information and the BBC to consider jamming German broadcasts to South Africa. The Ministry's reply, penned by Macgregor, is instructive:

In our considered opinion, it would be a grave mistake to attempt such jamming, either from here or in the Union. The reason is twofold. In the first place, action of this kind would almost inevitably lead to reprisals, and ultimately to the destruction of broadcasting as a medium of communication, for the duration of the war. The Empire stands to lose far more that it could gain by these consequences.

The second ground is less obvious, but, we feel, equally important. The fact that jamming was being done would at once be detected, and its source would soon become known. The reaction in the mind of the listener would be to ask why. He would conclude that those responsible for the jamming were afraid of the enemy propaganda, or had something to hide. Such an attitude would be, in our view, far more dangerous than the mis-statements and perversions broadcast from Zeesen.[74]

In March 1940, the issue arose again when it became apparent to London that the French were jamming German broadcasts in French from Cologne, Stuttgart and other stations, and that the German government were in reprisal jamming French stations broadcasting in German. The British queried the wisdom of this French policy, and through the Allied Military Committee, communicated their disquiet to the French High Command, on the basis of policy agreed by the Military Co-ordination Committee on 11 March.[75] This must have caused some wry amusement to the French, and rather indicates much of the muddle and confusion in British propaganda and counter-propaganda policy in the early stages of the war, for as recently as January, British Military Representatives had been urging the French to jam the German Station *Reveil de la France*.[76] British policy now was that no attempt should be made to jam German broadcasts in English, and it was pointed out that the German Government had not attempted to jam British medium-wave broadcasts in the German language, although there had been limited and rather ineffective jamming of some British short-wave broadcasts to Germany and other countries. A jamming offensive by the Allies would, it was felt, almost certainly lead to counter-jamming by Germany, possibly on a large scale. This would have serious consequences for the Allies in that listening to Allied broadcasts by Germans and others under German control would be substantially reduced and

> since the rulers of Germany had more reason to fear broadcasts from the United Kingdom and France than have His Majesty's Government in the United Kingdom and the French Government to fear German broadcasts, it is on balance more helpful to the Allied cause to avoid an extension of jamming.[77]

It was felt too that it was in any case impractical and prohibitively expensive to stop all listening to German broadcasts, that British broadcasts to her Empire and to neutrals might be adversely affected, and that jamming might spread to commercial and military services.[78]

However, as the real and disastrous fighting began in earnest in the West, the issue of jamming broadcasts to the domestic British audience reappeared. The obsession with the supposed strength of the Fifth Column had permeated all sections of British society by the summer of 1940, and as a result even senior figures in the MoI were taken in by Nazi propaganda and had swallowed the NBBS fiction that it existed to spread information among a dedicated band of supporters in the UK. Thus in July, C. H. Wilson wrote to Sir Kenneth Clark that:

> The NBBS are continuing to put out detailed instructions for Fifth Columnists in this country . . . Mr Bernard Newman who is on the Ministry's list of speakers is anxious to know what answer to give to the queries about the NBBS that he frequently receives at his meetings. Mr Stevens agrees with me that such broadcasts have now reached a point where decisive action should be taken.[79]

The 'decisive action' which Wilson wanted was an extensive public announcement to the effect that the NBBS talk of the previous evening was an attempt to frighten the public into believing in the reality of the Fifth Column threat, whereas in fact all requisite steps were being taken to render innocuous any potentially dangerous persons. He also urged that the station be jammed forthwith and for good. The station was again discussed at the MoI's Policy Committee on 4 July, and the question of jamming it again arose at the behest of the Swinton Committee.[80] On 16 July, *Workers' Challenge* was the issue, when the Policy Committee was told that the Army found this station's propaganda particularly undesirable, and a War Office paper to this effect appeared in late July. The Directorate of Military Intelligence asked for a revision of the policy of not attempting to jam enemy broadcasts on the assumption that the combined effect of the NBBS and *Workers' Challenge* might have damaging consequences for the morale of the troops and of the civilian population, in so far as the War Office felt themselves interested from the point of view of Home Defence. The War Office were particularly worried about a recent NBBS campaign of championing General Ironside at the expense of the Prime Minister on the grounds that the former, being a soldier like Marshal Pétain, would know when to stop the war. The military took the view that 'this in itself cannot but be harmful' even though the effect might be limited by the comparatively small number of listeners whose sets were capable of receiving the NBBS. The emergence on the airwaves, however, of *Workers' Challenge*, with its campaign of 'frankly Communist propaganda in English' had given further cause for concern:

> Considered together, it appears that the two stations are working on a carefully co-ordinated programme, the object of which is to produce a situation of the kind which, to some extent, led to the collapse in France. On the one hand, the NBBS calls for support for a leading soldier who will know when to stop the war; on the other hand, the *Workers' Challenge* Station raises the Communist banner which may not only excite the Communist element in this country but is calculated also to inculcate in those who fear Communism more than anything else leanings towards coming to terms with the enemy to avoid the threat of Communism before it is too late.[81]

Ogilvie countered for the BBC that such requests from various interested parties were not uncommon, but that it was necessary 'to get a national point of view'. The NBBS used three channels, of which the BBC could jam only one, the other too being too near BBC wavelengths. As for the medium wave, on which *Workers' Challenge* broadcast, the use of one of the BBC's high-powered transmitters would interfere with the scheme of synchronisation. The BBC view was that the jamming of one or two stations locally would not be a complete answer; that to do so would further increase the BBC's inferiority of transmitters (about fifty stations were effectively under German control at this stage while the BBC controlled only twelve); that it would give the stations advertisement; and that 'it would show both to ourselves and others that we feared the effectiveness of the propaganda. The BBC thought therefore that we should concentrate on silencing this type of propaganda by strengthening public morale to resist it.' After discussion the Minister agreed that the War Office should be told that it was doubted if these broadcasts had a bad effect; even if they did, the MoI did not want to use up transmitters in jamming them, and that if an attempt were made to jam the stations, 'the public will think we are frightened'.[82]

In the absence of a commitment to jamming, however, certain officials continued to press for measures to counter Haw-Haw and the freedom stations. The question of the influence of the NBBS was raised at the MoI's Planning Committee on 8 July (1940). C. H. Wilson reported that the BBC had figures showing that 5 per cent of licence-holders in the country listened to the NBBS, and went on to say that the damage done by the NBBS was the general alarm caused rather than particular rumours propagated. In fact, no rumours could be traced to the NBBS except for those which had been taken up after they had become widespread. The possibility of doing more to publicise the fact that the NBBS was an enemy station was discussed, including the possibility of a broadcast by W. A. Sinclair. It was agreed that such a broadcast would be useful, but that something less carefully reasoned was needed, and action should also be taken in the press. After that, the broadcasts by the NBBS were not to be explicitly refuted, but the stories emanating from the station should be denied without reference to the source.[83] On the following day, members of the Committee agreed that the less publicity given to the NBBS the better, and it was even thought that a 'D' notice on the subject might be desirable. At this same meeting, the ill-fated decision was taken that the Ministry should use the term 'Silent Column' in its anti-rumour campaign.[84] On 12 July, the Committee heard that the BBC's Listener Research department advised against any talk which attacked the NBBS by name, and it was agreed not to proceed with the idea of such a broadcast.[85]

The main anxiety caused by the NBBS and its fellows was that the stations might be the source of morale-disintegrating rumour. Certainly, one of the most astonishing features of the story of German propaganda broadcasts to the UK is the wave of 'Haw-Haw rumours' which swept the country in the second half of 1940 and which reappeared at regular intervals thereafter. Very few of these rumours had their origins in any German broadcasts, but arose more or less spontaneously in the frenetic atmosphere of the imminent threat of invasion and the only too awful reality of the sustained bombing of British cities. Following the fall of France, the main topic in rumours was naturally enough the coming invasion and the supposedly imminent departure for Canada of the King, his family and his government. Home Intelligence noted on 16 September that most people expected an invasion within the next few days, although they remained confident that it would be a failure.[86] As we have seen, rumours that invasion had already been attempted and had failed were reported from many quarters. At the same time, however, there occurred a wave of rumours which would begin, 'Lord Haw-Haw said . . .' Normally the rumours took the form of a story that Haw-Haw had referred to some particular town or village and, by mentioning an item of purely local interest, revealed his detailed knowledge of British life and geography – a town hall clock five minutes slow at Eastbourne, a card school in a munitions factory disrupted by a German raid, a reference to the Golden Teapot (an advertising sign) in Londonderry. Even the War Cabinet was not immune. In a Cabinet discussion in November 1939, Churchill declared that German broadcasts clearly showed that Germany had an intimate and widespread knowledge of what was going on in Britain. Indeed, the Germans seemed, he said, to take 'a malicious pleasure in regaling the British public with details which could only have been obtained by personal observation' – for example, the reasons why Croydon would make a good bombing target; the fact that a munitions factory was being erected in a certain locality with a decoy factory nearby; the presence of the balloon barrage on the Clyde within a few hours of its arrival.[87] Whatever Churchill may have believed, however, it is a fact that the BBC's *Daily Digest of Foreign Broadcasts* for the period from September to November 1939, which was circulated to members of the War Cabinet, contains no such references.

And when the air raids began in earnest, the rumours took on a much more threatening aspect, with Haw-Haw supposedly taking the trouble to warn the dullest and remotest village that their turn was next for a visit from the *Luftwaffe*. In July it was rumoured in Devon that Haw-Haw had said that the government was building a Military Camp at Honiton, but that they would never put the roof on it. He was supposed to have said too that German planes would bomb the railway tunnel at Honiton, and to have asked why it was that Lord and Lady Sidmouth had not taken their usual Devon holiday. He knew too, apparently, that a Tiverton lace factory had been given over to munitions production and warned that German bombers would visit Tiverton soon.[88] In Bradford, Haw-Haw was supposed to have mentioned the new buildings at Bradford Grammar School, having said that 'you needn't trouble to finish it as we will finish it off for you'; 'we shall blow it up soon'; 'we shall finish it and use if for our own purposes'; 'we shall use it to manage the country after our occupation of Great Britain'; 'it will be useful for meetings of the Reichstag.'[89]

The circulation of such rumours was regarded with considerable concern, a concern reflected within the MoI by the creation of an Anti-Lies Bureau to counteract them. Charles Wilson of the Bureau was particularly concerned in June at the 'extremely widespread distribution' of the Canada rumours, and further rumours that the Royal Family was about to take flight and indeed that the princesses had already left. Even worse, and linked with these rumours, was the fact that 'people were saying that they wouldn't be much worse off under Hitler, and with their own leaders likely to run away they might as well accept the inevitable'.[90]

The reaction of the officials to these rumours does seem to suggest uncertainty and confusion as to the correct course of action to counter them, and even as to their real origins and importance. They seem, for instance, to have convinced themselves that the German wireless was the real source of many rumours, while attempting to convince the public that it was not. In June 1940, for example, the MoI had printed and circulated a leaflet drawing public attention to the prosecution of a man who had been spreading rumours in Mansfield. The Ministry believed that the wide publicity given to the case 'has had a very salutary effect in checking rumour-mongering'.[91] A clearly orchestrated press campaign was run too in May and June 1940 to discourage the circulation of Haw-Haw rumours, while the Ministry instructed MoI speakers to assert that rumours of the 'Haw-Haw has said that our town is going to be bombed' variety had been traced 'to a girl who said that she had simply made it up because she thought it would be fun'.[92] Indeed, well into 1941 and beyond officials continued to identify Haw-Haw as the ultimate source of rumours. The story about the princesses reappeared in March 1941, this time that they had been evacuated to America on the battleship *King George V*, the MoI concluding that the rumour had 'apparently originated in enemy broadcast material'.[93] The notion widely in circulation in April and May 1941, that Churchill's health was failing and that Beaverbrook was being 'nursed for Premier', was, noted Home Intelligence, 'much sounded on the German radio'.[94]

In spite of all official efforts, however, a new wave of Haw-Haw rumours accompanied the start of seriously heavy bombing in September 1940. The MoI noted that the arrival of penniless refugees from London was causing a degree of anxiety and alarm in the provinces about the fate of the capital:

> There are exaggerated stories of the damage to London circulating in the provinces. These reports are partly due to the stories told by these refugees but there is also evidence that Haw-Haw rumours have greatly increased . . . A reliable observer just returned to London from the North reports that press and radio have given an account of London damage which has an exaggerated effect. Many people appear to think that London is 'in flames'.[95]

The extent to which the German radio was ever the real source for any of these rumours is open to question, but certainly the amount of listening and the spread of rumours seemed to occur contemporaneously, whether or not the one was the cause of the other. The fact is too that listening to Haw-Haw did continue long after the end of the phoney war and at times was probably substantial. Subsequent accounts which emphasise massive listening in the phoney war followed by a collapse to next to nothing thereafter are just wrong.

Home Intelligence noted, again in September, that 'an increase is noted in the number of people listening to Haw-Haw and rumours, mostly exaggerated accounts of raid damage and casualties, have also increased considerably'.[96] No target was deemed too trivial for Haw-Haw to threaten. In October, rumours were reported in Keynsham to the effect that Haw-Haw had said between 1 and 4 October, 'By the way, we know all about Fry's', and in consequence, production at the factory was adversely affected.[97] In November, J. E. Faber, Managing Director of British Fondants Ltd of East Molesey in Surrey, telephoned the Ministry to enquire about supposed threats made by Haw-Haw to his confectionery concern. Recent German broadcasts, according to the rumour in circulation, had twice been heard to say that his works had not yet been hit, but they would be, and the time selected would be about 5.15 p.m., when the girls were leaving work.[98]

A more significant rumour appeared in mid-October 1940 to the effect that thousands of people in East London or in Liverpool had signed a petition for immediate peace overtures. MoI officials felt it was possible that the story might have been based on the deep shelter petitions organised by the Communist Party, but it was also noted that this was one of the rumours which the BBC had reported as being instigated by the German radio. It was also suggested from Bristol that listening to the German radio had increased because the BBC was so much off the air in those days. Haw-Haw rumours about places to be bombed were still common, a new version being that certain industrial concerns in Cardiff had not been bombed because of the German capital invested in them.[99] A week later, Home Intelligence reported more widespread reports of increased Haw-Haw listening for the reason noted the previous week in Bristol, while Haw-Haw rumours were common in Pimlico, Willesden, Welwyn, Stevenage and Canterbury.[100] Shortly afterwards, the 'usual crop of Haw-Haws' was reported from Ashchurch, Eastbourne, Hailsham, Lewes, Polegate and Rochester. In a good many places in North Wales, Haw-Haw was reported as saying, 'You may think you're safe in North Wales, but your turn is coming!'[101]

Noticeable too, following the very heavy raid on Coventry in mid-November 1940, was an increase in Haw-Haw rumours, especially among the middle classes.[102] Indeed, rumours on a nationwide basis seemed to have increased slightly following the Coventry raid, and stories had spread widely that the damage and casualties in the city were much more severe than official announcements made out. Rumours attributed to Haw-Haw were reported from Portsmouth, Newcastle, Leeds, Bristol, Weston-super-Mare, Exeter, Barnstaple and Northampton, taking the usual form of predictions of bombing and of promised return visits after raids.[103]

In December 1940, Haw-Haw rumours were reported to be 'extremely prevalent' and reports continued to record 'a great increase in the amount of listening to the German radio'. Haw-Haw rumours were reported in Oxford, Cambridge, Bristol, Exeter, Cheltenham, Leeds, Plymouth, East London, Nottingham, Southampton and Worcester.[104] Later in the month it was reported that the number of Haw-Haw rumours was growing, the German wireless having predicted blitzes in Peterborough, Bristol, Guildford, Nottingham, Cambridge, Reading, Aldershot, Hazlemere, Andover and Bournemouth. It was said that these rumours were causing widespread and genuine anxiety; absenteeism at one engineering works was said to have followed a Haw-Haw rumour. These rumours, moreover, were often spread by people who were normally responsible and sensible.[105] Around Christmas time 1940, rumours were still common, although slightly less so than previously. Barnstaple was to be bombed on Christmas Day; Hitler was rumoured to be saving Manchester and Hull – Hull for the invasion, Manchester for his capital. Now that the *Luftwaffe* had quashed the second of these, Haw-Haw was said to have announced the dates of Manchester's blitz in advance.[106]

As the raids eased off in January 1941, so too did the Haw-Haw rumours, so that by mid-January they had all but disappeared. By February 1941, Home Intelligence was reporting that 'Haw-Haw's stock remains low'.[107] However, following the renewed heavy blitzing of London's East End and of the provincial cities in March and April, Haw-Haw rumours began re-emerging. In Glasgow, it was rumoured that Haw-Haw had promised the city five days of peace to bury its dead. Other Haw-Haw rumours were circulating in Sheffield, Bognor, Chichester, Scarborough and Portsmouth. In May, Haw-Haw rumours were reported from Tunbridge Wells, Barrow-in-Furness and Oxford.[108]

Of course, as the MoI was forced to repeat time and again, rarely if ever did the Haw-Haw broadcasts include threats to specific towns or cities and certainly they never included references to named factories or installations, or teapots or town hall clocks. In a sense therefore the Haw-Haw rumours should not be seen as evidence of the effectiveness of Nazi propaganda, even though, as has been pointed out, the rumours and increased listening seemed to accompany one another. The Haw-Haw rumours of the Blitz period are better seen as evidence of quite natural fear and trepidation about air raids, and arose at least partly because of the government's insistence on withholding information about the locations of German raids and the extent of casualties.[109] Both the rumours and the increased listening reflect the heightened anxiety of the population and its heightened desire for news, and dissatisfaction with official sources of information. Home Intelligence noted in November 1940 for example that there were still complaints about the way in which the sinking of the *Empress of Britain* was announced. At first, it was said she had exploded as a result of bombing, while the Germans announced that she was sunk by a torpedo. The later British official announcement that the U-boat which had sunk her had been destroyed, 'once more confirms in the public mind the speed and accuracy of German news service.' Listening to German broadcasting was said to be increasing in certain parts of London, because of its recent priority with the news. A small statistical enquiry by the Lincolnshire Information Committee showed 'a surprisingly high number' of listeners to the German radio. The reasons given for listening were the good quality of the musical programmes and of the reception.[110] A week later, Home Intelligence reported on 'a slight but continuous increase in the number of people listening to Germany. The chief reason for this is said to be the poor reception of BBC programmes.'[111] Poor reception of BBC broadcasts was not, however, the sole cause of this upsurge in Haw-Haw listening. In early December, following the raids on Coventry and other provincial towns, there were reports from all parts of the country of 'indignation and exasperation' at recent BBC broadcasts and official communiqués about the raids. People failed to understand why the names of some towns were announced while others were suppressed, even when they had been mentioned on the German radio. It was claimed, too, that descriptions of damage and the behaviour of the public had often not coincided with the facts. In particular, the announcements implying that industry in Coventry was not badly affected, and that Birmingham was almost normal the day after its heavy raid had created 'serious mistrust of official news'. There were reports from many sources that this combination of official reticence with official inaccuracy and overoptimism had led to a considerable increase in listening to the German radio. Moreover, its reception in many places was still said to be better than that of the BBC. 'Only in the Eastern region is Haw-Haw listening said not to have increased.'[112]

What seems therefore to have been happening was that the public was turning to Haw-Haw from a combination of motives, but at the centre of which were anxiety, fear and exasperation, a simple fact which many officials seemed to be unable or unwilling to accept. For example, a Special Postal Censorship report for November 1940 emphasised the confidence and pride of the people as a whole, but noted a larger number of writers than usual who showed poor morale. Many complained of the strain of raids, and more of these complaints came from London and Liverpool than from the new centres of attack in the provinces. More worrying, 'a number of intelligent working-class writers adopt the attitude that "England can never win, so why not end this useless slaughter?" This attitude is coupled with the suggestion that the war is "an upper-class financial racket", run at the expense of the people'. The censors noted that such an attitude was completely absent from previous mails, and 'the uniformity of the opinions expressed lead the Censorship authorities to suggest that they are not spontaneous, but rather the result of political propaganda".[113] So just as later German historians saw in Nazi propaganda the key to explaining the support of Germans for National Socialism, wartime British officialdom saw in Nazi propaganda the explanation for declining domestic morale, a process actually easily explainable by more obvious if less palatable factors. The rumour-mongering and the increasing listening to Haw-Haw should best perhaps be seen as indicators rather than causes of lowered morale.

That this is so can be confirmed by a rapid survey of some of the major sites of heaviest bombing. Mass-Observation noted in January 1941 that, despite the heavy raids on the city in the preceding weeks, morale in Liverpool remained high, that rumour was relatively scarce and that there was no recorded mention of Haw-Haw. In Manchester, by contrast, Observers noted 'an atmosphere of barely restrained depression', accompanied by plenty of rumour, including Haw-Haw rumours, which were common. Manchester had been badly affected by two heavy raids just before Christmas, which had inflicted serious and concentrated damage to the heart of the city. Utility and transport services were much more severely disrupted than had been the case in Liverpool, while the lack of adequate local and national news coverage of the raids 'facilitated the Haw-Haw and rumour processes'. Most important of all, the local civic organisations for responding to the effects of the raids were regarded locally as wholly inadequate.[114] In Bristol too, although damage was considerably less than in Southampton or Coventry, Mass-Observation noted a greater degree of depression and quite open defeatism than in most other towns studied. Haw-Haw rumours were exceptionally abundant and investigators found more Haw-Haw listening than ever before. In Southampton, the strongest feeling was that the town was finished.[115] Morale in Belfast was badly shaken by that city's heavy raid on the night of 15/16 April 1941. Two extracts from Postal Censorship were said to be typical of the general tone: 'the idea of England's ultimate defeat is being thrown about here as a matter of time only'; 'everyone here thinks we have already been beaten.'[116]

It is worth pointing out, moreover, that the effects of bombings and conditions in the shelters were at times as bad, if not worse, than actually described in Nazi broadcasts. Even before the very heavy raids had begun, Home Intelligence reports painted a bleak picture of London life, which might not have seemed out of place in a broadcast from the NBBS:

> Lack of sleep beginning to tell on people in all districts, showing itself in paleness and lassitude of children and irritability of grown-ups. This is particularly true of poorer quarters where crowded conditions prevail and public shelters are packed and noisy at night. Unhygienic and insanitary conditions reported in large buildings used as shelters in Bethnal Green, City etc. where hundreds of people of mixed ages and sexes congregate with bedding and remain all night. Shelters not designed for mass sleeping, and responsible people fear serious consequences of impaired health and possible epidemics. School on Housing Estate in South East London has few attendances because of broken nights and head teacher states that children who come are heavy eyed and white. On some Estates, shelter marshals run public shelters and organise community singing and games of darts in public spirited manner successfully murdering sleep.[117]

And of course, once the heavy raids had begun in earnest, the situation rapidly deteriorated:

> Exodus from East End growing rapidly. Taxi drivers report taking party after party to Euston and Paddington with belongings. Hundreds of people leaving Deptford for Kent. Increased tension everywhere and when siren goes people run madly for shelter with white faces. Contact spending night in West Ham reports loyalty and confidence in ultimate issue unquenched but nerves worn down to fine point. Conditions of living now almost impossible and great feeling in dockside areas of living on island surrounded by fire and destruction . . . Extreme nervousness of people rendered homeless at being herded together in local schools with inadequate shelters. West Ham school filled to bursting point from Saturday night onwards blown up by HE bomb with many casualties. This has caused great shock in district. People angry at inadequacy of compensation for wrecked and burnt-out houses; grumbling and dissatisfaction openly voiced . . . Class feeling growing because of worse destruction in working-class areas; anti-Semitism growing in districts where large proportion of Jews reside owing to their taking places in public shelters early in the day.[118]

Clearly then, Britain at the end of 1940 and early in 1941 probably provided more potentially fertile ground for a Nazi propaganda of disintegration than is often supposed. Although morale did not crack overall, there were areas in which heavy bombing had brought many people to the brink of despair. Relationships between the various social classes were at times severely strained by bombing, and certainly there is little evidence to support the traditional view of class differences being 'levelled'. For instance, following a devastating series of raids on Plymouth in March 1941, local feelings were running high. As Home Intelligence noted, 'There are reports of sailors' children catching pneumonia through sleeping under hedges while the owners of big houses are refusing permission for sheds and garages to be used as temporary refuges by homeless and exhausted people.'[119]

Important too is the fact that the very high levels of anti-Semitism in Britain are too easily overlooked and that Nazi propaganda about Jews did not necessarily fall on deaf ears. Certainly, anti-Semitism had a long history in many parts of Britain, and seemed to be growing throughout the war, especially in those areas which took in large numbers of Jewish refugees or had large Jewish communities. Home Intelligence, for example, remarked in the first days of the London Blitz that:

> Owing to the behaviour of the Jews, particularly in the East End where they are said to show too great a keenness to save their own skins and too little consideration for other people, there are signs of anti-Semitic trouble. It is believed locally that this situation may at any moment become extremely serious.[120]

In evacuation areas too, however, anti-Semitism was regularly to be reported, even as far afield as Pembrokeshire and Cardiganshire. In the large area around London to which many Eastenders had been evacuated, anti-Semitic remarks were common. In some evacuation areas, people flatly refused to give billets to Jews.[121] Anti-Semitism was also reported in Portsmouth, Edinburgh, Inverness, Leeds and Reading. The Jews were accused of booking the best places, paying excessive prices and buying up businesses outside London.[122] In Reading, Windsor was said to be 'packed' with Jews, and the hundreds who arrived at Swindon were not very welcome. Llandudno had been referred to in Manchester as 'Jerusalem by the sea', while in Southampton the police reported the distribution of printed and written anti-Jewish slogans.[123] In Blackpool, Jews from London and Brighton were accused of buying houses, furnishing them with second-hand furniture, and selling and letting them at extortionate prices.[124] Early in the New Year (1941) an increase in anti-Semitism in middle-class and business circles was reported from the Northern Region.[125] Anti-Semitic feeling was said to be growing in Liverpool in the summer of 1941. Jews were said to be cowards, who had fled to the best billets in safe areas and who avoided fire-watching duties. One restaurant was known to have refused to serve Jewish customers.[126] At the same time, Home Intelligence noted a slight increase in anti-Semitic feeling, associated with difficulties with food supplies. Few specific instances of anti-social behaviour were brought forward against individual Jews, but general allegations suggested that 'Jews always have money to burn' and 'seem to think of no-one but themselves.'[127]

But if the atmosphere in Britain about mid-1941 was probably as potentially receptive as it would ever be for the messages produced by Nazi propaganda, the audiences in Britain were certainly smaller than during the very high levels of late 1939. One major difficulty here is once again the absence of really reliable statistics on listening. Robert Silvey at the BBC seems to have assumed that listening had all but collapsed after the fall of the Low Countries, and was reluctant to spend too much time and money on measuring it accurately afterwards. Surveys in the late winter of 1939–1940 had shown a steady decline until listening in early April 1940 was only about three-fifths of that in early December.[128] In July 1940, on the basis of replies from 200 Local Correspondents, Silvey concluded that listening to Haw-Haw was now rare, due to the growth of a feeling of revulsion towards him and a feeling that it was now unpatriotic to listen. 'From being a major topic of conversation, Haw-Haw is now rarely discussed.'[129] The existence of the NBBS was fairly widely known, but very few people listened to it. By the autumn of 1940, his view was that listening to enemy stations was of 'negligible proportions'.[130] At the end of the year, Honorary Local Correspondents were asked if they had any evidence that people had been listening more to enemy broadcasts in English. Of the 1,250 replies, four-fifths replied that they had no evidence of increased listening, while only one in six said there was. The minority who did detect an increase were more numerous among correspondents in contact with working-class listeners than among those in contact with middle-class listeners. They were also a slightly higher proportion of Midland, North and West Regional and Welsh Correspondents than of London or Scottish. About one in ten Correspondents had found some evidence of listening to broadcasts by Lord Haw-Haw, and the majority of them suggested that this was only occasional listening. The rest had some qualifying phrase, such as 'for entertainment only' and 'the effect is getting very feeble.' Correspondents mentioning *Workers' Challenge* were fewer still. A small number mentioned it only to denounce the vulgarity of its broadcasts. There was no evidence that its political ideas found very much approval. Nevertheless the minority view was that *Workers' Challenge* had 'a heavy following . . . The novelty was in the language, but the feeling grows that a lot of his remarks are true.'[131] In April 1941, in response to further promptings from Whitehall on the extent and effects of listening, Silvey reiterated his view that the Haw-Haw craze was long dead. Listening to Hamburg had ceased to be socially the thing to do and become instead something not done. He went on that there were no doubt

> 'some listeners [to Haw-Haw, who were] either openly or in secret fascists or pro-fascist . . . Apart from these, we think that by far the greatest cause of any listening to German broadcasts which exists arises from the insatiable appetite for news. In so far as our own News Bulletins are regarded as, or come to be regarded as, untrue, inadequate, or tardy, people turn or will turn, to other news in English to some extent.

The problem of course would lie in measuring this, since 'there has become a flavour of sin about listening to enemy broadcasts, [and because] people are reluctant to admit that they do this, enquiries are liable to prove abortive.'[132]

Silvey's words were wise ones, and it seems therefore less wise to take at face value some of his earlier findings that Haw-Haw listening was negligible when it is frankly admitted that there were intense societal pressures upon individuals to lie about their private listening habits. Indeed, it is as likely that the figures for listening from the spring of 1940 onwards are deflated by these pressures as it is that the figures for listening earlier in the war were inflated by different but equally real pressures. Indeed, the point about Haw-Haw's audience being directly related to faith in British sources and to the general state of public morale, was well illustrated by events over the next few months. German advances in Africa in April and the British withdrawal from Greece in May and dissatisfaction with the news which was filtering back to the population at home again seemed to give a boost to listening to the German radio broadcasts. Home Intelligence reported that it was widely complained at home that 'our failures are still being minimised, and that trivial successes against "a single Messerschmitt" are given undue importance.' In this connection, BBC news bulletins were regarded as the worst offenders. 'The delay in official news, and the publication of communiqués from Axis sources, which subsequently turn out to be true, are said to be causing more and more people to listen to Haw-Haw's broadcasts in order to learn what is really happening.'[133] While there was little trust in German Air and Naval communiqués, it was generally believed that their military communiqués were true. The silence maintained by the British broadcasting authorities during the Greek evacuation in particular had serious consequences, said Home Intelligence; to begin with, it gave rise to rumours that the worst was being kept from the public, but secondly, led directly to an increase in the number of listeners to Haw-Haw.

> This has been reported from many sources. The German broadcasts are not regarded as more reliable than ours, but as being almost as reliable, and so much fuller that this outweighs their untruthfulness. It is thought not to be enough to discredit them on the grounds of lying while they continue to give more up-to-date news that we do.

Moreover, among those who listened regularly – notably those with relations in the Navy and Merchant Marine – Haw-Haw's prestige had increased through the intensification of the Battle of the Atlantic: 'On several occasions lately he is said to have given the first news that a ship, mentioned by name, has been torpedoed, and this has later proven correct.'[134] It was, however, impossible to discover the actual volume of Haw-Haw listening, and many reported cases may have been merely garbled versions of what other people said he had said.[135] By mid-May, however, not only was there increased listening, but an increased tendency to believe what was heard. Of twenty-two Police Duty Room Reports from Chief Constables, six mentioned continued listening and Regional Information Officers made similar observations. 'Nothing but a prompter, more comprehensive explanation of what has happened, will reduce the amount of listening to German broadcasts, which has undoubtedly increased during the last month.'[136] Home Intelligence reported at the end of the month (May 1941) that there was 'substantial agreement between the Chief Constables' in one region that it was the 'unimaginative tardiness' of the news services that was turning listeners towards Haw-Haw and the NBBS. 'Chief Constables report that the recent change in the transmission times of the NBBS has brought enquiries as to what the new times were.'[137]

Since this insatiable appetite for news and a certain degree of political consciousness and sophistication seemed to go hand in hand in wartime Britain, it is sometimes suggested that Haw-Haw's audience was protected against his propaganda by dint of its very sophistication.[138] There may well be something in this, but it is worth remembering that for much of the early war – and indeed well into 1942 – the politically sophisticated outlook was as likely to be that Britain's position was more or less hopeless and that the rational thing to do would be to come to some sort of terms with Hitler. Moreover, there were many politically sophisticated individuals in Britain who read the serious papers, listened to the BBC news and were in the upper income bracket, and who at the same time held extreme right-wing political views, who were anti-Semitic, and who cared nothing about European affairs except to the extent that they had a fear and hatred of communism. The irony is that amid all the middle- and upper-class anxiety about the effects of Haw-Haw on the workers, it is more likely that his broadcasts found their most attentive and receptive listeners among the ranks of the bourgeoisie.

These issues are taken up again in the conclusion. In the meantime, we turn back to the broadcasts themselves, and consider in the next two chapters propaganda and its reception in Britain as the war expanded into a global conflict.

Notes

1 PRO INF 1/849, *Covering Note for Paper on Extension of the BBC's Overseas Services*, 30 January 1941.
2 PRO CAB 102/375, *CID. Standing Sub-Committee to Prepare Plans for the Establishment of a Ministry of Information*. Report by Tallents, October 1938.
3 PRO CAB 102/374, *International Propaganda and Broadcasting Enquiry, Memo No. H.P. (v) 24*, undated, May 1939.
4 PRO CAB 68/1 WP (R) 39 17.
5 PRO INF 1/161, *BBC Overseas Service: Countering Nazi Propaganda, Macgregor to Lee*, 5 October 1939.
6 PRO INF 1/261, *BIPO: Public Opinion during the Week Ending 30th September, 1939*.
7 BBC WAC R28/121/1, *SNE to C(P)*, 8 January 1940.
8 BBC WAC R28/121/1, *SNE to C(P)*, 4 April 1940.
9 BBC WAC R28/121/1, *SNE to C(P)*, 14 April 1940.
10 BBC WAC R34/639/3 File 2a, *Oglivie to Lee*, 25 March 1940.
11 Goebbels, *Tagebücher*, entry for 20 March 1940.
12 *Daily Mirror*, 25 September 1939.
13 *Daily Express*, 2 October 1939.
14 *News Chronicle*, 8 January 1940.
15 *Daily Telegraph*, 4 October 1939.
16 *Daily Mirror*, 2 March 1940 and 9 March 1940.
17 *Daily Mail*, 12 March 1940.
18 *News Chronicle*, 2 November 1939.
19 The remark was made by the BBC's Director-General, F. W. Ogilvie, at a meeting

in July 1940 of the MoI's Policy Committee. See PRO INF 1/849, *Minutes*, July 1940.

20 *Daily Express*, 26 February 1940; *Evening Standard*, 26 Febuary 1940; *Daily Herald*, 27 February 1940; *Evening Dispatch*, 13 March 1940; *Birmingham Evening Dispatch*, 13 March 1940; *Sunday Dispatch*, 31 March 1940; *Yorkshire Evening Post*, 5 April 1940; *Daily Mirror*, 24 April 1940; *The Star*, 29 April 1940; *Daily Herald*, 9 May 1940; *Daily Sketch*, 10 May 1940; *Glasgow Herald*, 27 June 1940; *New Statesman and Nation*, 13 July 1940; *Daily Telegraph*, 19 July 1940; *Sunday Dispatch*, 25 August 1940; *The Listener*, 17 October 1940.

21 See, for instance, *Sunday Dispatch*, 25 August 1940, which ran a *Workers' Challenge* story under the headline, 'BILL BLASTER (the Crimson Cockney) TAKES THE AIR. And he swears!'

22 Goebbels, *Tagebücher*, entry for 5 January 1940.

23 *Daily Sketch*, 11 April 1940; *Daily Mirror*, 19 April 1940.

24 *Daily Mirror*, 6 June 1940.

25 *World's Press News*, 1 February 1940.

26 BBC WAC R9/14, *LR/74 The British Audience for German Bulletins in English*, 16 May 1939.

27 PRO INF 1/261, BIPO Set 63 – October 1939.

28 BBC WAC R36/369/1 File 1A, *BIPO Report, Silvey's Comments*, 17 November 1939.

29 BBC WAC R9/9/4, *LR98 The Effect of Hamburg Propaganda in Great Britain, Interim Report by the BBC*, (January 1940).

30 BBC WAC R9/9/4, *LR/98 Hamburg Broadcast Propaganda: The Extent and Effect of its Impact on the British Public during mid-winter 1939/40*, 8 March 1940.

31 When Silvey's full report was forwarded to the MoI, it was reportedly well-received, although the Minister himself 'professed disbelief in the technique'. BBC WAC R34/639/3, File 2a, *DHI to C(PR)*, 15 March 1940.

32 PRO FO 371/24393, *The Voice of Hamburg*, 14 Feburary 1940.

33 PRO FO 371/24393, *The Voice of Hamburg*, 14 Feburary 1940

34 PRO INF 1/161, *Hamburg Broadcast Propaganda*, 8 March 1940.

35 PRO INF 1/161, *Hamburg Broadcast Propaganda*, 8 March 1940.

36 The remark was made by Stephen Taylor of the MoI's Home Intelligence Division in October 1941, cited in McLaine, *Ministry of Morale*, p. 251.

37 *The Listener*, No. 614 (Vol. XXIV), 17 October 1940, p. 551.

38 BBC WAC R34/639/1 *Policy: Counter-Propaganda File* 1A, *Grant to Ogilvie*, 10 September 1939.

39 BBC WAC R34/639/1, *Dinwiddie to Maconachie*, 16 November 1939.

40 BBC WAC R34/639/1, C(P) to DT, *Minute 95 of Home Service Board*, 24 November 1939.

41 BBC WAC R36/369/1, *Pile to Sir Robert Gordon-Finlayson*, 5 December 1939.

42 BBC WAC R34/693/3, File 2a, *Longland to DMI*, undated, March 1940.

43 PRO INF 1/849, *Minutes: Policy Committee*, 4 June 1940.

44 PRO INF 1/161, *BBC Overseas Service: Countering Nazi Propaganda, Stevens to Macgregor*, 11 September 1939.

45 PRO INF 1/161, *BBC Overseas Service: Countering Nazi Propaganda, Macgregor to Stevens*, 12 September 1939.

46 PRO INF 1/161, *BBC Overseas Service: Countering Nazi Propaganda, Spry to Macgregor*, 7 October 1939.

47 BBC WAC R34/639/2, File 1b, *Pealie to Maconachie*, 4 January 1940.

48 PRO INF 1/161, *BBC Overseas Service: Countering Nazi Propaganda*, *Macgregor to Lee*, 19 October 1939.

49 Transcripts appeared in *The Listener*, 21 December 1939, 4 January 1940 and 1 February 1940.

50 BBC WAC R34/369/1, File 1A, *Vallance to Ogilvie*, 11 December 1939.

51 In fact, Wodehouse was at this stage living in France, and would later broadcast on the Nazi wireless system to Britain and the United States. See p. 15 above.

52 BBC WAC R34/369/1, File 1A, *DT to C(P)*, 19 December 1939.

53 BBC WAC R34/369/1, File 1A, *Minutes*, MoI Home Publicity Division, 19 December 1939.

54 BBC WAC, R34/639/1, File 1a, *Ogilvie to Campbell Stuart*, 26 December 1939.

55 Nicholas, *Echo of War*, p. 54.

56 See Briggs, *The History of Broadcasting in the United Kingdom.*, pp. 149–154, and pp. 210–212.

57 BBC WAC R34/693/4 File 2b, *DPP to ADPP*, 9 April 1940. In March it was recommended that simultaneous broadcasts on the Home and Forces broadcasts at 9.15 p.m. were to be avoided, since a choice of listening had a better chance of distracting listeners from Haw-Haw. *DDG to C(P)*, 12 March 1940.

58 [M]ass-[O]bservaton [A]rchive, Radio 1939–1945: Box 1: Radio During the War: File 1/B: *The Voice of Lord Haw-Haw.*

59 'Public and Private Opinion on Lord Haw-Haw', in *Us* (Mass-Observation's Weekly Intelligence Service), No. 9, 29 March 1940.

60 MOA, *The Voice of Lord Haw-Haw.*

61 BBC WAC R34/639/2, File 1b, *DT to C(P)*, 1 January 1940.

62 HO 199/436, *Public Sentiment Report*, February 1940.

63 BBC WAC, R34/639/1, File 1a, *Nicolson to Ogilvie*, 10 January 1940. He copied this message to Sir Samuel Hoare, Sir Edward Bridges, Aylmer Vallance at the War Office, Sir Kenneth Lee at the MoI, Vansittart at the Foreign Office and Sir John Anderson.

64 PRO FO 898/5, Home Morale Emergency Committee. *Report to Policy Committee*, 4 June 1940.

65 BBC WAC R34/639/3, File 2a, *Goff to Vansittart*, 2 April 1940.

66 PRO INF 1/252.

67 BBC WAC R34/639/3, *Brand to C(P)*, 28 March 1940.

68 PRO INF 1/265, *Smith to Ministry*, 13 August 1940.

69 BBC WAC R34/639/5, *Swan to Tallents*, 29 December 1940.

70 BBC WAC R34/639/7, *H. G. Grafton Beddells to BBC*, 22 March 1943.

71 BBC WAC R34/639/4, File 2b, *Thomson to Ogilvie*, 26 May 1940.

72 MOA, *The Voice of Lord Haw-Haw.*

73 PRO CAB 21/838, *Webb to Howard*, 27 May 1937.

74 PRO INF 1/161, *BBC Overseas Service: Countering Nazi Propaganda*, *Macgregor to Carr*, 22 September 1939.

75 PRO CAB 21/838, *Makins to Harvey*, 25 March 1940.

76 PRO CAB 21/838, *Extract from the Record of the Twenty-second Meeting of the Military Representatives*, 20 January 1940.

77 PRO CAB 21/838, *Makins to Campbell*, 25 March 1940.

78 The only dissenting voice to the agreed view that the French should be urged to desist was Churchill's.

79 PRO INF 1/267, *Wilson to Clark*, 1 July 1940.

80 PRO INF 1/849, *Minutes*.

81 PRO FO 895/5, *Jamming German Broadcasts*, 22 July 1940.

82 PRO FO 898/5, *Minutes*, MoI Policy Committee, 22 July 1940.
83 PRO INF 1/249, Planning Committee, *Minute 129*, 8 July 1940.
84 PRO INF 1/249, *Minute*, 9 July 1940.
85 PRO INF 1/249, Planning Committee, *Minute 141*, 12 July 1940.
86 PRO INF 1/264, *Daily Observations*, 16 September 1940.
87 PRO CAB 65/4 WM 68 (39) 7 *Confidential Annex*.
88 PRO INF 1/268, *H. F. Kallaway to MoI*, 22 July 1940.
89 Letter from R. B. Graham, *Manchester Guardian*, 6 June 1940.
90 PRO INF 1/267, *Wilson to Stevens*, 17 June 1940.
91 PRO HO 199/462, *Rumours: Miscellaneous Correspondence and Reports*, *Wilson to Parker*, 14 June 1940.
92 PRO INF 1/251, *Ten-Minute Talk No. 3. Rumour*.
93 PRO INF 1/292, *Home Intelligence Weekly*, 20 March 1941.
94 PRO INF 1/292, *Home Intelligence Weekly*, 8 May 1941.
95 PRO HO 199/436, *Daily Report on Morale*, 12 September 1940.
96 PRO HO 199/436, *Daily Report on Morale*, 11 September 1940.
97 BBC WAC R34/639/5 File 2C, *Mitchell to Abrams*, 14 October 1940 and *Abrams to D.EUR.S.*, 16 October 1940.
98 PRO INF 1/266, *Miss B.L. Hornby to Faber*, 27 November 1940.
99 PRO INF 1/292, *Home Intelligence Weekly*, 15 October 1940.
100 PRO INF 1/292, *Home Intelligence Weekly*, 22 October 1940.
101 PRO INF 1/292, *Home Intelligence Weekly*, 29 October 1940.
102 PRO INF 1/292, *Home Intelligence Weekly*, 19 November 1940.
103 PRO INF 1/292, *Home Intelligence Weekly*, 5 December 1940.
104 PRO INF 1/292, *Home Intelligence Weekly*, 12 December 1940.
105 PRO INF 1/292, *Home Intelligence Weekly*, 19 December 1940.
106 PRO INF 1/292, *Home Intelligence Weekly*, 2 January 1941.
107 PRO INF 1/292, *Home Intelligence Weekly*, 13 February 1941.
108 PRO INF 1/292, *Home Intelligence Weekly*, 15 May 1941.
109 In July 1940, the War Cabinet had decided that casualties following air raids were only to be described as 'slight', 'considerable' or 'heavy'. PRO CAB 65/8, *Conclusions*, 3 July 1940.
110 PRO INF 1/292, *Home Intelligence Weekly*, 12 November 1940.
111 PRO INF 1/292, *Home Intelligence Weekly*, 19 November 1940.
112 PRO INF 1/292, *Home Intelligence Weekly*, 5 December 1940.
113 PRO INF 1/292, *Home Intelligence Weekly*, 5 December 4 1940.
114 PRO HO 199/442, *Report on Liverpool and Manchester*, 10 January 1941.
115 PRO HO 199/442, *Report on Bristol, Southampton and Cheltenham*, 22 December 1940.
116 PRO INF 1/292, *Home Intelligence Weekly*, 15 May 1941.
117 PRO HO 199/436, *Daily Report on Morale*, 31 August 1940.
118 PRO HO 199/436, *Daily Report on Morale*, 10 September 1940.
119 PRO INF 1/292, *Home Intelligence Weekly*, 8 May 1941.
120 PRO HO 199/436, *Daily Report on Morale*, 9 September 1940.
121 PRO INF 1/292, *Home Intelligence Weekly*, 15 October 1940.
122 PRO INF 1/292, *Home Intelligence Weekly*, 22 October 1940.
123 PRO INF 1/292, *Home Intelligence Weekly*, 29 October 1940.
124 PRO INF 1/292, *Home Intelligence Weekly*, 5 December 1940.
125 PRO INF 1/292, *Home Intelligence Weekly*, 16 January 1941.
126 PRO INF 1/292, *Home Intelligence Special Report on Conditions in Merseyside* (undated, probably June 1941).

127 PRO INF 1/292, *Home Intelligence Weekly*, 24 July 1941.

128 BBC WAC R9/14, *Listening to Hamburg*, April 1940.

129 BBC WAC R9/14, *The Public and German Radio Propaganda*, 19 July 1940.

130 BBC WAC R9/14, *LRD to C(H)*, 23 November 1940.

131 BBC WAC R9/9/5, *LR/210 Listening to Enemy Broadcasts*, 20 January 1941.

132 BBC WAC R/19, *LRD to DPP*, 29 April 1941.

133 PRO INF 1/292, *Home Intelligence Weekly*, 24 April 1941.

134 PRO INF 1/292, *Home Intelligence Weekly*, 8 May 1941.

135 PRO INF 1/292, *Home Intelligence Weekly*, 15 May 1941.

136 PRO INF 1/292, *Home Intelligence Weekly*, 22 May 1941.

137 PRO INF 1/292, *Home Intelligence Weekly*, 22 May 1941.

138 Nicholas, *Echo of War*, p. 61.

5

Propaganda in the Global Struggle

More than any other political belief-system in the twentieth century, German National Socialism was a negative ideology, defined as much by what it stood against as what it stood for. And while it stood for love of race and love of country, it stood against Judaism and against Marxism as the supposed twin pillars of racial degradation and destructive internationalism. For the first year and a half of the war, however, Nazi propaganda was hamstrung by the Hitler-Stalin Pact which robbed the propagandists of half their armoury. The massive brooding presence of the Soviet Union was dealt with in 1939 and 1940 in propaganda both for the Germans themselves and for the rest of the world largely by ignoring it, notwithstanding the occasional and exceptional linkage of Germany, Russia and Italy as 'the young nations of Europe'.[1] When Germany invaded the Soviet Union in June 1941, however, the propaganda shifted its focus to reflect the dramatic shift in the nature of the conflict. Until this point, the war had been portrayed as a struggle between the old decadent plutocracy represented by Great Britain and the young dynamic Germany of National Socialism. After this point, Germany proclaimed herself the defender of centuries-old European civilisation against the onslaught of barbaric Asiatic Bolshevism. The bridge between these divergent representations was anti-Semitism.

The events of June 1941 and after had major consequences for Nazi propaganda to the UK. Overnight Britain's position was transformed. From being the chief orchestrator of the world's ills, she was relegated to a secondary role, a process accelerated when after December 1941 the conflict escalated onto a truly global plane. Nevertheless, a substantial and sophisticated wireless propaganda organisation for the UK continued beaming news and talks into British homes from Germany in the relentless pursuit of the same goal – the creation of national disunity within Britain, and international disunity between the Allies.

In the days and weeks leading up to the invasion of the Soviet Union, Russia disappeared from the official stations broadcasting to Britain. On 21 June for instance, the 'white' stations focused on such issues as *Luftwaffe* raids on British ports and Rommel's seizure of Sollum in Egypt. The freedom stations – in particular *Workers' Challenge* and the NBBS – did comment on Russia, but only to suggest that rumours of a coming Russo-German war were no more than a ruse to cover the imminent attack on Great Britain. Of course, the suggestion that an invasion of Britain was planned in 1941 was itself no more than a gigantic ruse organised by Goebbels in the hope of diverting world attention away from the real target of German aggression, and the Minister even lied to his closest colleagues, announcing at his ministerial conference on 5 June that England was indeed about to be invaded.[2] When the invasion of Russia did actually begin, the task of propaganda was not only to explain and justify the attack – launched without a prior declaration of war – but also retrospectively to explain away the 1939 Pact which Germany had unilaterally shattered.

These tasks were attempted in a number of ways. On the one hand, the Pact was portrayed as a genuine attempt on Germany's part to come to reasonable terms with Russia. For instance, the home audience was told on the morning of the invasion that, 'if ever in history there has been an attempt to live at peace with your wicked neighbour, this was the case with the Germano-Soviet Pact of 23 August 1939.' In the same broadcast, there was even the suggestion that Bolshevism might have been reformable. At the time of the Pact, said Zeesen, there were 'many signs that Bolshevism, after 20 years of sanguinary reign and efforts at political corruption of the world . . . would gradually develop into a tolerable part of human society.'[3] Hitler had made the same point in his long personal statement to the German nation on the morning of the 22nd – a rambling rehearsal of the same self-pitying platitudes which Hitler had been touting since the early 1920s – which was read on the wireless by Goebbels, and delivered on the English service at 7.10 a.m. Hitler earnestly insisted that he had genuinely attempted to set the Russians at rest with regard to his territorial ambitions. The Pact had been concluded 'from a sense of responsibility towards the German people . . . above all in the hope of achieving a permanent relief of tension, and of being able to reduce the sacrifices which might otherwise be demanded of us.' Hitler was in any case a man of peace, a responsible statesman, and 'no responsible statesman would fail to attempt gaining his ends in a peaceful way. Only when all peaceful means have failed, does he take up the sword.'[4]

On the other hand though, and often in the same broadcasts, the Pact was openly admitted to have been an act of temporary expediency. Germany had been under threat from a new encirclement, just as in 1914. She once again was the victim of a plot between Jews and Democrats, Bolsheviks and Reactionaries with the sole aim of 'inhibiting the establishment of a new German national state, and of plunging the Reich once more into powerlessness and misery.'[5] William Joyce on Bremen for the UK on 23 June claimed that the pact with Russia was actually Britain's fault:

> When in August, 1939, Hitler made a pact of friendship with Stalin, some of you may have wondered if Hitler had betrayed western civilisation. Yesterday in his proclamation, the Führer was able to speak openly for the first time. He said that it was with a heavy heart that he sent his Foreign Minister to Moscow. England left him no other choice. She had worked hard throughout the summer of 1939 to build up a coalition against Germany. Hitler was compelled in self-defence to conclude a pact of friendship with Russia in

which the signatories agreed not to attack each other and defined spheres of interest.[6]

The decision to launch the attack too was justified in a whole series of different ways, again often within the same broadcasts. In the first place, it was claimed, the Russians had cynically betrayed Germany by systematically breaking the Pact and under cover of war operations in the west, had made an uninterrupted series of attempts at blackmail. Of course, the Bolsheviks would never have had the courage to do so alone, but were being encouraged by Britain. Britain in fact was still determined to form a pact with Moscow to encircle Germany, the plutocrats of London and Washington being not at all fussy about their choice of allies (a breathtaking example of Nazi doublethink, given that the subject under discussion was Hitler's own pact with Bolshevism). So, scarcely had the war with Poland ended, before Russia suddenly demanded all of Lithuania. Estonia, Latvia and Lithuania were all openly annexed and Bolshevised in violation of the Pact. Stalin had treacherously taken advantage of Germany's preoccupation with the war in the west to turn the screws on Finland and Romania. Russia now constituted a direct threat to the Reich. In fact, so serious was this threat that by August 1940 Germany had been forced to withdraw large reserves of army, air and naval forces from the western front. Bolshevik duplicity had in fact made it impossible for Germany to proceed with the projected attack on England.[7] Worse, they were now preparing an attack on Germany herself. The Führer had wisely acted to forestall a Bolshevik stab in Germany's back. Stalin, it was alleged, had well-advanced plans for an attack on Germany, concocted in a plutocratic-Bolshevik conspiracy with Britain. It was revealed on 25 June that enormous Soviet troop concentrations of four armies, forty-nine infantry divisions, three armoured divisions, twelve armoured brigades and seven artillery divisions were to attack Germany from north of Warsaw on 7 July.[8] So not only was Hitler justified in attacking Russia, he had had no choice.

So, having explained and justified the invasion of the Soviet Union, the next task of Nazi propaganda was to garner support at home and among neutrals and allies for the latest war effort, the ploy being to portray the war not as a German war of aggression, but as a war in defence of European culture. For the British, the task was naturally different – to foment disunity and disaffection by pillorying the government's linkage of its own struggle with a state which represented the enemy of European civilisation and culture. Hitler had set the tone here in his announcement on 22 June, styling himself not only the leader of the German Reich, but 'a conscious representative of European civilisation and culture'.[9] The Bolsheviks, it was claimed, were preparing a war not against Germany, but against Europe, a continent of which they had never been a part:

This is no mere war between two States. It has developed into the greatest Crusade in history against the evil, soul destroying force of Bolshevism which must be hurled back into the orient if Europe is to live. It is not a war against the Russian people as such; it is a mighty movement for which the civilised world has been longing, against the enemies of God and man . . . it is a revolt of Europe against the persecutors of Christianity and the destroyers of morality.[10]

William Joyce told his listeners in Britain and the US on 11 July that the Soviet plan to Bolshevise Europe had backfired. Stalin had 'welded the people of Europe into a League of Nations with the common aim of crushing communism.' At the head of this League stood the German Führer, the guarantor of European culture.[11] But the British people needed to ask themselves why and how their government had allied itself with the Bolshevik criminals:

There must be in Britain very many people to-day – I know some – who realise that Hitler is doing a work which they have long known to be necessary. Britain was never more isolated than she is to-day; Germany never had so many friends. Whatever the dreary blunderers of Downing Street and the designing Hebrews of Wall Street many think or say, Europe as a whole will save herself from the Red Menace . . . To-day the Red Front is being broken. Let Stalin look with his mind's eye on the blood-spattered faces of the priests and nuns whom his assassins tortured and murdered. These martyrs are being avenged, and the ideals for which they died shall live. When the Red Front is finally broken, the lackeys of reaction who shelter behind it shall not escape. Stalin and Churchill represent the old union of Red Front and reaction. As he has broken it before, the Führer shall, by the grace of God, break it again. Victory is the only possibility. It is decreed![12]

The world, according to Nazi propaganda, had now divided into two camps – the one representing all that was good and healthy in the world, the other all that was evil and corrupt. Hilversum in English had told the British on the morning of 22 June that:

this morning we woke to find a new war, involving the world's greatest armies, representing two conflicting ideologies. The Red Army, standing for destruction and annihilation of civilisation and the betrayal of treaties, is fighting the White Army, the army of liberty, the protector of personal property, of patriotic transition and the defender of native soil.[13]

In fact, as Luxembourg told British listeners on 25 June, Germany was even fighting for Britain:

Even in Britain, many people are praying that the Bolshevists will be beaten, for they realise that a Red victory would mean a Communist dictatorship in the British Isles. In spite of the bitter war between Germany and Britain, the Führer is fighting the battle, not only of Europe, but also of the ordinary decent British people to whom Communism would be worse than death.[14]

Here again was the demonstration of another standard propaganda technique: the vast oversimplification of complex issues into simple stereotypes of good versus evil, black versus white. The stereotypical Jewish-Bolshevik had been the central hate figure for Nazi propaganda since its inception, and the Russian war now allowed this stereotype to be rehashed and dusted off to good effect. The Soviet Union could now be revealed as the festering centre of an international Jewish-Plutocratic-Bolshevik-Anglo-Saxon conspiracy, a union of the combined forces of disintegration and reaction against National Socialist Germany, the guardian of European culture. The Jews, of course, were at the heart of the conspiracy, and for the Jews who ruled the capitalist West with a rod of gold, international communism was merely a weapon with which to create anarchy and confusion from which the parasitical Jewish financiers could only benefit. The New York Jews, said William Joyce, had financed the Russian Revolution. Their purpose was to create a vast storehouse of inter-national unrest, capable of bringing any nation to its knees if it opposed the sacred decrees of high finance. Whenever a government showed signs of a desire to model its policy on national interests, the sub-men of Moscow crawled forth, armed with the most powerful propaganda weapon in the world, the natural and all too well-founded envy of the poor against the rich. The Soviet Union, said Joyce was 'a dunghill of Kremlin vipers':

> Bolshevism is a psychological poison which degrades and debases the human mind to such an extent that its addicts have less feeling for decency than brute creatures which are satisfied with killing their prey. Only in the light of this terrible fact can we understand the awful and obscene atrocities, the shameful mutilations which have been perpetrated by the Soviet sub-men on German prisoners and wounded who have fallen into their hands.[15]

The Germans and their allies of course, in Nazi propaganda, did not commit atrocities. These were the exclusive preserve of the Bolshevik sub-men, and atrocity propaganda was another staple of the material for home and foreign consumption. At his ministerial conference on 5 July, Goebbels had ordered that his staff make made maximum use of stories and pictures of the massacre of 3,000 Ukrainian nationalist prisoners in Lvov by the fleeing secret police.[16] Sure enough, all the propaganda outlets, including the English language stations, covered the massacre in semi-pornographic gory detail:

> Before the Bolshevists fled from Lemberg they ran amok in a blood orgy. They murdered their victims wherever they could find them. Persons in prison were shot or beaten up. The Bolshevists applied the most horrible forms of torture. Hundreds of bodies were found by the Germans after they had taken Lemberg. Women and children were nailed to prison doors. Corpses were stuck through with bayonets. When the murderers saw they could not finish their work before the Germans came, they threw gasoline over their victims and set them alight. Innocent people were slaughtered. The methods used could be seen in the third degree cells, where a thick layer of blood covered the floor, the walls, and even the ceiling . . . The bodies of many of these defenceless victims were hacked to pieces with axes. Two

young Ukrainian girls had their stomachs slit open, and it was evident that they had been raped. Boiling water was poured over the bodies of men, and their skin was torn from them . . . This blood bath shows the methods by which the Bolshevists hoped to destroy European civilisation and culture.[17]

The point of this type of material was to contrast the image of Hitler as guardian of Europe, with Churchill, the 'Cockney guttersnipe', the 'paid hireling of the Jews', the 'Gentile steward to Jewish capital', the 'betrayer of Europe', the 'betrayer of Christianity'. While Germany and Hitler defended Christian European civilisation, Churchill allied himself with atheistic Jewish Bolshevism. '*Mary Fraser*', on the NBBS, expressed the indignation of the ordinary British public at the very idea of fighting alongside Russia:

Since I last spoke to you events have taken a frightening turn. We are now an ally of Russia. Why should we lay ourselves open to the evils which may arise from a too close association with such a state as Russia? The Government would do far better to put our own house in order than go acquiring military (interest) everywhere. There were a lot of things which needed attention before the war started. Conditions are worse now. Why talk of supporting Soviet Russia when people of England have a job to get food enough to eat? If the Ministry of Food were less slack and badly organised we should have a sufficient quantity of food. Then too the question of decent air raid shelters has not been solved. Why not do something here, instead of promising aid to Russia? We shall soon be faced with Communist ideas. Do you remember the anti-God campaign? Our new ally not only permits, but encourages atheism, co-education of the worst type, the breaking-up of family life. Why should we fight for them?[18]

But if Germany was fighting to preserve Christian civilisation against the demonic Bolshevik monster, was not the implication that Germany was fighting in defence of the old world against the new? This apparent problem was again dealt with simply by ignoring it, and the Nazis attempted to represent themselves as at once the champions of centuries-old European Christian civilisation, and at the same time as crusaders for the efficient New Order against the corrupt and inefficient past represented by Britain. Naturally in these circumstances it was inevitable that the German New Order would begin to exert its influence outside the Reich, and would meet thereupon with the ferocious hostility of the Old Order in its death-throws. William Joyce produced on 27 July an ingenious theory, elegantly linking the downfall of capitalism and Marxism with the emergence of the New Order:

In the whole of the war, there has perhaps been nothing more appropriate than that Churchill, who has pretended to oppose Communism for so many years, should find himself marching arm-in-arm with Stalin. For the very philosophy of Marxism reeks of the last century. It was a natural answer to that Liberal Capitalism which is now breathing its last and can never rise again. The ancient Capitalism which Churchill represents was of a nature to

draw forth the hatred of the workers, and the survival of these old values only
means the perpetual strife of class against class. The natural development of
the twentieth century was a synthesis of all the best in Nationalism and all the
best in Socialism. Such a synthesis had to come, unless the human race were
to perish through disintegration. It was the work of Hitler and Mussolini to
build a new Socialism on a Nationalist basis, to reconcile the people with the
State, the individual with the community. Because this work was succeeding,
those who are not satisfied to have less than the whole world under their sway
made a last bid to retain the obsolete. By the grace of God, they will vanish
with it.[19]

That Britain had allied herself with the 'Moscow sub-men' was, of course, a
national disgrace and a 'terrible mortification' for decent English people.[20] And
it was Joyce as usual who was most vituperative in his denunciations of
Churchill and his disgusting alliance with Bolshevism. In a broadcast in July
– described by Electra House as 'revolting' – Joyce contrasted the attributes of
National Socialism with the iniquities of communism, as represented by the
sub-men with whom he had had to deal in England:

National Socialism condemns wealth without responsibility, privilege without merit and it works to unite all classes in the common task . . . Communism (for the benefit of the few) preaches the law of the jungle.
Communism is based on the lowest tendencies of rapacity . . . In England
I have seen crowds of sub-anthropoid creatures using razor blades and pieces
of lead piping . . . against disabled ex-Servicemen who happened to belong to
patriotic movements . . . or to the Conservative Party. In almost every case,
they were led from behind by Jews. It is with creatures of the same kind that
Churchill has made his pact. Small wonder that the truth is not to be
expected from him. Small wonder that the darkness deepens over England as
Europe sees the dawn of a New Order.[21]

Churchill had betrayed Europe in making an alliance with the Bolshevik sub-
humans, but had only succeeded, however, in uniting the continent still more
solidly against Britain and the Churchill-Stalin-Roosevelt combine of Jewish-
international finance and communism: 'the Pact . . . is significant only in so far
as it demonstrates the anti-European union between British plutocracy and
Bolshevism. Churchill thus proves his readiness to betray Europe to Bolshevism.'[22] Instead, the solidarity of the European peoples was demonstrated now
by what Hamburg called 'their enthusiastic adoption of the Viktoria "V", the
sign of the Victory of the New Order in Europe, and of the just rising of all the
nations on the European continent against the common foe'.[23]

The invasion of the Soviet Union might have been expected to have caused
particular embarrassment for *Workers' Challenge*, given that the fake station, by
now a year old, presented itself as the voice of true British socialism. Since its
inception, *Workers' Challenge* had presented the war as one for the preservation
of capitalism and exploitation, and one therefore which no true worker could

support. Now that socialist Soviet Russia had been directly attacked by Germany and was engaged as a belligerent ally of Britain, how could this line be maintained? The answer lay in the simple construction that Stalin had been tricked into joining the war on Britain's behalf by Churchill, in a vain attempt to pull the capitalist chestnuts out of the fire. The consequences would be dire, and the great Russian socialist experiment would be liquidated. There was therefore no reason why British socialists should now surrender to capitalism by supporting capitalism's war in the futile hope that they could thereby assist the Soviet Union which was already doomed. As usual, the answer lay in the establishment of real British socialism at home:

> Will you wait till you are in the hopeless position of our Russian comrades, or will you avoid the tragedy by acting now and ending the war before Hitler has the chance to turn all his forces against us?[24]

Of course, the problem for Nazi propaganda of this sort aimed at the UK, was that the outbreak of Russo-German hostilities and Britain's subsequent alliance with Moscow was greeted in Britain not with indignation but with relief and delight. The reception of the stunning news was reported as 'jubilant', albeit a jubilation tinged with a strong current of caution. There was little confidence in Britain in Russia's military capacity, which was judged by her poor performance in Finland in 1939, and a large section of the public felt that the best they could hope for was that she would hold out long enough to give Britain some real advantage. There was also some confidence that Hitler's real aim was not the Ukraine and its riches but the desire 'to make 100% sure that he would not be stabbed in the back while attacking England'. There was eagerness that Britain herself should in some way 'strike now, while the Nazis are tied up, before it is too late for us to strike at all.' Churchill's pledge on the part of the country to give aid to Russia was generally accepted as practical and logical, and it was felt that he 'discharged a difficult task well when he spoke of our support for Russia, after he had for many years voiced his contempt and at times his abhorrence, for the Bolshevik regime.' His speech – which had been soundly rubbished by the Nazi wireless service – was 'greatly admired, and has more than offset the recent fear that his touch was not quite as sure as it had been.'[25] Indeed, the very fact of Russian resistance provided a terrific fillip to public morale. While people were aware that a Soviet collapse would have the gravest consequences for Britain, the expectation was quite widespread that Russia would be able to offer resistance throughout the autumn, so that the German High Command would be faced with the grim prospect of continuing to wage war in the midst of a Russian winter.

At the same time, however, there remained considerable cause for concern about certain trends in public morale. Home Intelligence noted 'a growing apathy towards the whole war effort, particularly on the part of less intelligent and wishful-thinking people.' This view manifested itself in two different ways. The view became more widely expressed that 'even if Hitler managed to conquer this country, it wouldn't matter very much.' Commoner still was the belief that the war was nearly over, and would indeed be over by Christmas. Moreover, there appeared to be developing among fairly large numbers of people a new fascination with the occult. Rumours were widespread of the prophetic utterances of gypsies and astrologers foreseeing the rapid end of the war, while natural history was sometimes blended with the occult to bolster the view that the war was nearly over. Thus, the last time broad beans grew upside down was said to have been in 1918, at a time when the Allied cause looked black, yet the war ended that year. In 1941, the beans were apparently observed to be doing the same thing. As Home Intelligence dryly remarked, 'this pattern has even more variants than the projected invasion story.'[26]

Haw-Haw rumours too continued to flare up mysteriously from time to time. In early September, for example, one (unidentified) MoI Region reported, 'a sporadic outburst of Haw-Haw rumours, the first for a considerable time.'[27] There was evidence too, however, that 'scarcity of real news in the Russian bulletins, and our own, is causing more people to turn to enemy broadcasters to know what is happening on the Eastern Front'. It was also feared that more reliance was being placed on enemy bulletins. It was thought too to be most damaging to BBC news services when 'a German claim is followed by BBC protests that it is unconfirmed, suggesting that the German news agency has falsified a statement; and then follows the Russian admission of its truth.'[28]

However, by early winter, the initial sense of jubilation and relief at Russia's entry into the war had given way to a growing admiration for continued Russian resistance, and an accompanying sense of frustration, guilt and even shame that Britain was not doing more to help her Soviet ally. This sentiment was strengthened following the failure of the Germans to capture Moscow at the end of October, when the city's collapse had been widely predicted for some weeks. The public was said to be 'united in deploring the effect which they fear upon both Russian and American opinion if we continue to appear unable or unwilling to act vigorously'. In many quarters, the desire for more aid for Russia was deflected into 'severe criticism of the Government'. According to one Regional Information Officer, 'the feeling seems to be gaining ground that our capitalists will hold up help to Russia in the hope that both Germany and Russia will exhaust themselves'.[29]

This discontent with government policy, however, was not necessarily to Germany's advantage, any more than similar grumblings about the inadequacy of Britain's war effort had been back in the spring of 1940. Goebbels had indeed argued in those days that Germany's interest lay in overthrowing whatever government was in power in enemy countries, regardless of whether this government or that might be more acceptable on points of detail. What mattered was the unsettling and weakening effect.[30] Of course, this policy had inherent dangers which the Minister ignored. In May 1940, a weak British administration might indeed have been undermined by Goebbels' propaganda, only to be replaced by another much more determined to wage aggressive warfare against Germany. And while this government was frequently unpopular, German propaganda may paradoxically have bolstered it. By repeatedly pointing out the government's many shortcomings, rather than provoking its collapse, the Nazis may merely have stimulated it into a more vigorous conduct of the war.

Certainly, there is evidence that this was so at least as far as news policy was concerned. In November 1941 there again seemed to be an increase in the tendency to give greater regard to Allied or even enemy communiqués than to official British announcements. The sequence of events was said to conform 'with amazing regularity' to a given formula: the position was described as 'confused'; the Germans claimed to have taken a certain position; this was neither confirmed nor denied; the place for the first time was mentioned without comment by the Russians; it was reported that the Russians had evacuated it. The result of this was said to be that 'our war news is considered to be less reliable than that of the Germans.' Apparently, some individuals took to asking that the times and wavelengths of Russian broadcasts in English should be published, and also those of American news bulletins, 'which would give a better balanced view of the war than the BBC bulletins.'[31] The higher regard in which the BBC was held by the public at the end of the war than at the beginning of it probably stemmed in no small measure from the salutary effects of a dose of competition from German and other sources.

Of course, it is difficult to know the extent to which the Nazi wireless broadcasts were implicated in the growing cynicism around this time about the extent of Britain's war effort, and the greater willingness of members of the public to attack senior figures, including the Prime Minister himself. What we can say for sure is that senior officials and politicians maintained an interest in and anxiety about the activities of the Nazi broadcasters. In November 1941, for example, Churchill received from Desmond Morton the following extract from an NBBS broadcast:

Extract from New British Broadcasting Station, broadcast 28th October, 1941.

The Aid Russia mass meetings and demonstrations are changing their tone. Gradually they're taking on a different aspect, and are adopting a definite political objective, apart from the demanding of all-out assistance for our Red ally. Their aim, it's now clear, is to cause the overthrow of the present Government. The speakers are cleverly turning the indignation mania of their audiences against the War Cabinet, and particularly against the Prime Minister. Eyewitness reports which have reached us from all parts of the country, indicate that attacks on Mr Churchill are now frequent, and are not prevented, but are even welcomed by a large section of the people. Among the demonstrations which took place yesterday and today, were big meetings at Coventry, Swansea, Hull, Leeds and Liverpool. Though there's ample evidence that the originator of this wave of demonstrations was the Communist Party, its lead has been taken up by discontented people of all shades of opinion, and the vast majority of the participators are far from being Communists.

Morton had accompanied the extract with a covering note stating: 'You may care to see the line now being taken by the German Broadcasting Station, pretending to be British (known as the NBBS or *New British Broadcasting Station*). I have no evidence that this nonsense is having any effect here.'[32] Nevertheless Churchill was sufficiently interested to ask Bracken personally for a report on the station. The Minister replied that he had

> no evidence to suggest that it is widely listened to; still less that its account of public feelings in this country bears any relation to the facts. Our Home Intelligence Reports during the past few months record no deterioration in public confidence nor in the public's esteem for their Prime Minister.[33]

Bracken may not have been wholly candid here, since as has been shown, there was increasingly a mood of cynicism and disquiet among sections of the general public, although of course the NBBS wildly exaggerated its extent.

Some further indicators of the public mood can be gleaned from Postal Censorship reports. These reports for December 1941, for example, reveal that the great majority of the population still remained cheerful and confident of ultimate victory.[34] On the other hand, a quarter of letters intercepted revealed a lack of confidence, despondency and even in a small number of cases outright defeatism – a quarter of the 25 per cent of letters which revealed depression and a lack of confidence could be described as actually defeatist. Given that censorship of the mails was no secret, the reports may underestimate the true feelings of the public, but they do at least reveal that there were still individuals and groups to whom Nazi propaganda might still make a potent appeal. For example, one correspondent, doubtless unsuspectingly, echoed the sentiments so often expressed on the *Christian Peace Movement*:

> Oh, how stupid it all is and how futile, I think the world's womanhood should rise and compel our mad manhood to stop before they have annihilated themselves, things in the end will have to be settled by negotiation so why not *now*.[35]

Another – again untypical it must be said – reflected views commonly expressed on the NBBS or *Workers' Challenge*:

> Life in a luxury hotel lets one see the funny side of life as it is lived today. The government howling for a tax on the worker's wage, shouting to the house-wife, typist and shopgirl not to spend. Every penny saved builds a Spitfire. But not a word to stop excessive extravagance by the idle rich, who although heavily taxed, still have sufficient to squander.[36]

Even the entry of the United States into the war in December 1941 did not appreciably brighten the public mood. Home Intelligence noted in the early spring of 1942, for instance, that although 'a large proportion of the civilian population are still whole-heartedly and actively forwarding the war effort', other sections continued either to 'profit from the War', or to 'play no part in the war effort'. Since mid-January 1942, moreover:

A number of people have been encountered whose mood suggests a slackening of effort and a feeling of lack of purpose. This mood does not appear to be confined to any definite social classes or occupational groups, and has been encountered in members of the professional, small business, industrial and agricultural classes.[37]

That this should be so is scarcely surprising, given the terrific series of blows to British prestige in the early months of 1942 with the fall of Singapore and the dash through the Channel of the German battle cruisers *Scharnhorst* and *Gneisenau* and the heavy cruiser *Prinz Eugen*. The Nazi wireless made fullest use of these humiliations, and as usual William Joyce was blisteringly sarcastic:

Japanese troops have entered the city of Singapore. And now we ask the British whether their Government is capable of learning through experience. Of course, in England a man cannot be regarded as a serious politician until the first stages of arterial sclerosis have set in, by which time he may be described as a coming man. When senility has caused severe damage to the brain, he is a rising man, and when local mortification has begun, he is recognised as a success, fitted to receive the votes of confidence irrespective of circumstances. Under these conditions, it is not surprising that the British concept of war should be somewhat antiquated . . .

But what must the British think when they learn that the city of Singapore has been entered by Japanese troops? . . . In Norway, in the West, in the Balkans, Crete, North Africa, and in Russia the German Command has given proof of its mastery of a war as a science. The Japanese too have demonstrated their modern efficiency by the tremendous scope and rapidity of their successes. Remember: They've entered Singapore. [38]

The NBBS was certain where the guilt lay for the fall of Singapore, and used the disaster to suggest that Britain herself would be the next target unless the public took action:

Singapore reports that the Union Jack still waves over the town, although most of the island is in the hands of the Japanese. Evacuation continues under enormous difficulties, the enemy Air Force has vastly superior numbers, and transport ships are being subjected to a savage bombardment. Many have been sunk, and casualties are heavy. The Japanese claim to have penetrated the centre of Singapore this morning, and say our forces are resisting near the reservoirs . . . [B]ehind it all was Churchill. If the Government genuinely believed in the strength of Singapore, it was guilty of a fearful blunder and criminal irresponsibility. Fools are no better fitted than knaves to rule a great nation. This great catastrophe has come as a climax to a series of disasters, all of which bear the mark of the man Churchill. The Norwegian campaign, our failures in Belgium, France, Crete, Greece and Libya represent the logical development of his ill-considered policy. We are a long-suffering people, and we have been complacent. But perhaps we were not to blame, for we were victims of the greatest fraud ever practised by a Government. That fraud has at last been discovered. The complacency is finished. The question which now remains is how long it will be before the nation takes revenge on its betrayers. The people are bewildered and while they hesitate Singapore proves that not even this England of ours can be regarded as a stronghold. We cannot tell where the next blow will fall, but we can be saved even now if we throw out Churchill and his clique, and replace them by men who will make peace. We are still unconquered, and a just and manly peace can still be made. But we must call on the people to join at once in vigorous and fearless action. Time is very short indeed.[39]

It should be borne in mind, however, that while the British were suffering defeat and humiliation in rapid succession in this period, the Germans too suffered their own defeats, and the extent of Russian resistance and the impact of the Russian winter on the stalled campaign on the Eastern Front came as a shock. Goebbels more than any other German leader realised that the war was far from over, and certainly his pronouncements on propaganda take on from these months a more realistic hue. At a ministerial conference in January 1942, for instance, he stated his belief that the war could not be ended by the moral collapse of a people, but only by a military decision or a compromise.[40] Nevertheless, he went on, 'in our propaganda for abroad . . . these aspects of [moral] breakdown in Britain may be used quite legitimately.'

And certainly there is evidence of discontent and disillusion in Britain at this stage about the country's military performance and her chances of ultimate victory. The fall of Singapore was received in Britain with 'a silence too deep for words'. The general feeling was summed up by one of the MoI's Regional Information Officers, who wrote that 'not since the Norwegian fiasco has there been such grave and wide-spread doubt regarding the adequacy of the high direction of the war in general and of our staff work in particular. The dominant sentiment appears to be one of frustration that after two and a half years of war, and nearly two of the Prime Minister's leadership, we should, except for the Battle of the Atlantic, be still apparently incapable of conclusive victory over anybody except Italians'. There was a feeling that 'we have got to the stage when it is time to stop accepting excuses, and try a change of Government.'[41] Depression was reported from several MoI Regions, and in a few areas there were said to be 'some signs of defeatism'. The passage of the German ships through the Channel appeared to have shocked the public far more than the fall of Singapore, during what was described as 'the blackest week since Dunkirk', causing not only 'shock, bewilderment and anger, but also a feeling of humiliation and disgrace'.[42] The desire to criticise was very widespread and, although the service chiefs were greatly blamed, the main weight of public criticism seemed to be directed at the government, and no longer excluded the Prime Minister. Many people were said to be once again taking seriously the possibility of German invasion as a direct result of the escape of the German battleships.[43] Later in the month Home Intelligence noted a widespread sense of despondency, pessimism and anxiety, and indeed there was said now to be some realisation that Britain might actually lose the war, and that 'victory does not come automatically just because we are British.' There were also said to be 'disquieting signs of an increasingly 'questioning' mood, with doubts as to the worth-whileness of the struggle'.[44]

Moreover, just as the Blitz had done in 1940 and 1941, the defeats of early 1942 gave a renewed boost to Haw-Haw and produced renewed criticism of the BBC. In the weeks before the collapse of Singapore there was 'growing dissatisfaction' with BBC news bulletins. Early in February, their 'completeness and veracity' was questioned. 'Lack of real news' was said to arouse suspicion that bad news was being withheld while inducing listeners 'to give greater credence to the exaggerated claims' made on the German wireless. Objection was made to official statements still being 'too often tinged with that sort of hearty, almost perfunctory, optimism, which, in the past, events have often failed to justify.' Criticism was again made of the practice of boosting the importance of territorial gains, and if they were afterwards lost, of making them out to be of trifling value.[45] And when Singapore did fall, there was some evidence of 'renewed interest' in enemy broadcasts, caused by the feeling that 'the announcements of our misfortunes are delivered with greater promptitude and clarity than at home'.[46]

The Postal Censorship reports for the period from the middle of February to the middle of March 1942 revealed a similar picture. From a total of 84,691 letters examined, only 46 per cent showed confidence, 34 per cent criticism and 19 per cent pessimism. The highest number of criticisms concerned 'muddle, weakness and refusal to get down to reality', but 'slackness, complacency, apathy, selfishness, greed, inefficiency, pleasure seeking' were all mentioned and strongly condemned. Noticeable too, as the censors put it, was 'a wave of despondency' in comments mentioning the progress of the war, one correspondent noting that, 'we seem to be pretty good at losing one way and another and now they say our shipping losses are running up again. Makes me feel sick when I think about it and I guess I'm not alone. Do you suppose we can ever do right and shall we ever be fully prepared?' Other comments were outright defeatist, and again sentiments of *Workers' Challenge*-style class feeling were sometimes evident:

> Everything is in such a state of upheaval that I don't know what to say about it only that it will be a good thing for all the working classes when it is all over. The working people all over the world had nothing before the war and only a lot of lip from the bosses and now the war is on they (the workers) are the ones who are getting it in the neck. After it is all over they will be the ones who will have to clean up after all the dirty work is finished. What a mess the world is in right now. However – it's up to the people themselves – if they want to stop

the Silly Slaughter they could do it – just don't do anything – sit down strike as it were.[47]

And interestingly enough, the censorship reports reveal that some people were indeed still avid listeners to the fake workers' station and believed it to be British in origin:

> We turn to secret British Communist Station which comes on at 10 past nine each night. Do we have fun – what names he calls the Cabinet. When Cripps was made the leader of the Commons he was charmed, and then after a few days when it became known he was going to India, all his hopes of an English Russia vanished and then music, or I should say language, 'tis very amusing after the proper BBC accent.[48]

The point does need to be made here that comments of this nature were the exception rather than the rule, and there were just as many anti-communist and pro-government comments in Postal Censorship reports. It is rare enough too to find, as in this case, direct evidence that the Nazi freedom stations had much of an audience after 1940. Nevertheless, it is easy to be misguided by the traditional picture of a wartime Britain in which equality of suffering and sacrifice was universal and seen to be universal. The MoI reported in mid-March 1942, for example, that there was 'growing evidence of a feeling among certain sections of the public that "everything is not fair and equal and that therefore our sacrifices are not worth while".' In particular, there was some belief that the rich were less hit by rationing than ordinary people, having access to more and better foodstuffs, and were receiving preferential treatment at retailers. Moreover, the same report drew attention to the continuation of feelings of inequality of sacrifice – 'frequently mentioned in these reports' – between the services and civilians. Ill-feeling between the two was said to be growing as tales of slacking in factories, high wages, and black markets increased the belief among servicemen that civilians were not pulling their weight.[49] Moreover, as the Army's Morale Committee noted in the spring of 1942, when confronted by bad war news or by apparent instances of inefficiency or unfairness, an increasingly large number of soldiers were not inclined to blame their national or military leaders but the whole of 'the existing system', and expressed a resolve that the system must be different after the war. Unfortunately from the point of view of the Nazi propagandists, the reaction of these soldiers was not to seek to come to terms with Germany, but 'to point a contrast with Russia, which is apparently believed to be a paradise of complete freedom and perfect efficiency.'[50] Nevertheless, admiration for Russia notwithstanding, there were grounds for anxiety within the Army about the average soldier's feelings towards the war and towards Germany, and about his likely susceptibility to German propaganda:

> Full realisation of what would be involved in defeat would show that the enemy is indeed the common enemy of all, and thus go far to create the feeling [of] solidarity which is so much to be desired. No such realisation

seems to exist amongst soldiers, and though there are no positive signs in the Army at home of war weariness, apathy, or the tendency to ask 'What difference does it all make?', such as the MoI reports show to exist among civilians, the troops, in their present state of mind and feeling, might well fall victims to propaganda which aimed at producing such an attitude. It is reported that it is not uncommon for soldiers to ask lecturers whether Hitler has not done a great deal for the trade unions in Germany, and similar questions which reveal that they have no idea of the kind of enemy they have to face, and two Commanders' reports state that 90% of the new intakes at P.T.Cs. lack enthusiasm and interest in the war and betray ignorance of the issues involved in it.

Even more alarming for the Army was the fact that British troops in certain sectors seemed to be taking decidedly the wrong attitude to the enemy. For instance, troops in the Middle East were said to be 'remarkably well disposed' to their enemies in the *Afrika Korps* and the fear was expressed that enemy propaganda was to blame:

There are frequent expressions in the troops' letters to the effect that 'Jerry' is a good chap and it is difficult to see why we are fighting him, and that after all the interests of the common man in all countries are really the same. Whether this is the result of a planned policy on the part of the Germans is not clear; but it is clear that no planned policy could have succeeded more swiftly or more advantageously from their point of view.[51]

This mood of goodwill towards the men of the *Afrika Korps* did evaporate at the end of the year, following the long-running dispute between Britain and Germany over each side's retaliatory shackling of prisoners of war. By this stage, however, the War Office was directly attributing the former goodwill to 'German propaganda'.[52]

So while it remains difficult to prove a connection between Nazi propaganda and this discernible lack of enthusiasm for the war on the home and fighting fronts, to an extent at least there remained a potentially receptive environment for it. As Home Intelligence reported in March 1942, the prospect on the industrial and home fronts was 'still viewed with depression. It is stated that the possibility of defeat is openly discussed in some quarters, coupled with the question: "Do we deserve to win?" '[53]

And as the war ground remorselessly on into 1942, there was little enough news which might be expected to lighten the public mood. The raids on St Nazaire in March and Dieppe in August merely served to illustrate the enormous difficulty to be expected come a fully-fledged invasion of Europe. It has to be said too that there was considerable cynicism in Britain about the country's brash new ally from across the Atlantic. The prevailing British sentiment in December 1941 was, not surprisingly, one of 'great satisfaction and relief', but one tinged too with a certain 'malicious delight' that the Americans would be now forced by military necessity to do what they would not do before in co-operation in the fight for democracy.[54] Antipathy towards the Americans was reported to be 'strongest among working people, who most admire the Russian resistance.'[55] There was a widespread feeling that America was 'too damned wealthy', that Americans were too mercenary-minded, and that the hardship and suffering of war would 'do them a lot of good'. That said, however, America was 'not really regarded as a foreign country, to be wooed with praise, but as a close relative to be chided freely for her shortcomings'.[56] Home Intelligence conducted a large-scale survey on British attitudes to the Americans in early 1942 concluding that 'there is no very burning interest in America. The picture which people have in their minds is mainly of a pre-1929 America, in which Trades Unionists are ignored or attacked, corruption is common, social legislation primitive and commercialism rampant – a cock-sure country, with a high standard of living and a great capacity for mass-production.'[57]

And again, while acknowledging that much German propaganda for Britain on the United States was flawed by its grounding in Hitler's Jewish-conspiracy theory, a good deal of it was well-chosen to play to British prejudices about Americans. William Joyce was adamant that the war in the Pacific had begun because of Roosevelt's Jew-inspired provocations of the Japanese. There was no menace from Japan to British interests, but Churchill and the US President foolishly believed they could intimidate the Japanese, 'a proud people who have long since repudiated the theory that the Far East should be ruled by a Committee of American and British Hebrew financiers':

> There may be some sections of the British public who rejoice at the thought that America is now belligerent in the sense that she and Britain are fighting against Japan. Such rejoicing, I think, is very ill-founded. The U.S.A. have cost Britain much as a non-belligerent associate; they may cost her far more as a belligerent Ally. We must wait events and scrutinise them carefully. But this much may be said at once: every extension of hostilities which the Jewish warmongers have planned has only led in the end to a worsening of their own positions. They have challenged Japan at a time when Europe is rapidly making good its claims to complete independence. They have not yet found out the difference between declaring a war and waging it successfully. Their object has been to spread the flames of war as widely as possible. But it is by these very flames that they and their order will be consumed.[58]

That the alliance with the United States would bring only disaster upon the British was explained by Joyce in a long talk in April 1942. In the Great War, forced upon Germany by international finance, when England's sons were sacrificed on the battlefields of Europe, the USA had done profitable business at England's expense. The markets of South America and China, even those of India and Africa, were flooded with American goods. Whenever English companies were compelled to sell their assets, New York was delighted to buy them. Wherever an English firm went bankrupt, one of the Jewish firms of Wall Street opened there. England soon ceased to be the world's banker and became the world's debtor instead. With the proceeds of the war supplies which England was forced to pay for in gold, the Americans not only built up a vast new industry in their own country but also acquired enormous new investments abroad. Whereas before 1914 there had only been a few ridiculous out-of-date tramp steamers sailing under the Stars and Stripes, an American merchant navy was now created which soon rivalled that of Great Britain:

> Involuntarily we ask ourselves whether things will be different in this war. It is true the war is not yet finished, and if Roosevelt gets his way it may not be for many years to come; but once again we observe the same phenomenon – England is in a bad way, because being too deeply engaged in the war she cannot devote herself to business. Again she must transfer her foreign assets to the Americans – she must even cede her naval bases to the Americans – she must fight on the seven seas, and the Americans do not even take the trouble to help Australia. While the British people must pay 50 per cent and more of their income in war taxes, taxation rates in the USA are still far below the level of Britain's peace time taxation. While in England one great firm after another has to close down, the businessmen of Wall Street cannot even find enough clerks to take the place of the Englishmen who have left. Indeed, Wall Street knows only too well what business means, and where there is something to snatch from the English they take it, and this time for good.
>
> We are not prophets like Churchill, we believe we know what things are really like. One thing is certain; anybody who can read facts can predict this will be the end of it all. America has been profiting in the years 1939 to 1942 just as she did in 1914 to 1918, at the expense of England, who must bear the burden of the war. And just as in the last war, England will lose wherever the USA gains, till finally she ends by becoming a colony of Mr Roosevelt.[59]

This talk provides a good example of a number of the propagandistic techniques at which Joyce was adept. In the first instance there is the simple assertion of unsupported generalisations, including the (highly tendentious) contention that Germany was forced into war in 1914 by the Allies, a war which she would have won had it not been for the outbreak of a Jewish-Bolshevik revolution in Berlin in 1918. Secondly, Joyce pitches an emotional appeal to his British listeners, by recalling the sacrifices of British lives in 1918, while projecting feelings of animosity away from the German enemy of 1918 onto the American ally. Next comes the careful selection of material from the long and complex history of interwar financial and economic relationships once again to prove that Jewish Wall Street interests had wrecked the British economy, ignoring among other things the fact that the impact of the Depression was far more severe upon the United States than it had been upon Great Britain. Finally comes the simplification of this whole mass of complexities to the easily graspable notion that Britain will end the war as a colony of the United States, which itself is personalised into the character of President Roosevelt. Moreover, this extract is informative, since contrary to the perceived view of Nazi propaganda as merely a tissues of lies, much of it is substantially true, albeit a truth refracted through the distorting lens of Nazi ideology. Britain had suffered severe economic loss as a result of the Great War, she had been converted from the world's leading creditor into the world's leading debtor nation, she had gone through a period of serious economic hardship in the interwar period, and it seemed clear that now in 1942 she looked ahead to a grim economic future. It was also true that the economy of the United States had been substantially boosted by the Great War, and there were very many Britons in 1942 who were convinced – rightly – that the United States would be boosted a second time by this bigger war. The fact that his listeners might fail to follow Joyce's logic all the way to his desired destination, or might fail to see the Jews at the root of all evil, does not necessarily mean that his material would be wholly ineffectual.

Moreover, while it is easy enough now to see as rather silly some of the talks on the freedom stations like *Workers' Challenge* or the *Christian Peace Movement*, it is worth bearing in mind that following the disastrous first few weeks of 1942, Home Intelligence noted the increasing trend for two new factors to come to the fore in public opinion. More and more people of all classes were said to be taking to a kind of 'home-made Socialism', which did not owe allegiance to any particular political party, but which expressed 'a resentment of the system which had given so much power to so few people'. This feeling was said by no means to be confined to factory workers and the industrial middle class, though it found its strongest expression in that section of the community. The second factor was 'the religious or spiritual aspect of our lives'. It was observed that 'compared with eighteen months ago, an increasing number of people are said to be talking of Christian principles, and "regretting that this country has so far departed from them as to make this war possible".'[60] Such sentiments would probably not have sounded out of place in one of Donald Grant's little sermons on the *Christian Peace Movement*.

Again, although the Nazi obsession with a Jewish world-conspiracy probably undermined much of the propaganda material for non-German audiences, it is also worth recalling that anti-Semitism was by no means an exclusively German phenomenon. Goebbels noted in his diaries that 'the anti-Semitic bacilli naturally exist everywhere in all Europe; we must merely make them virulent'.[61] Certainly the Germans tried hard to whip up hatred of Jews in their propaganda for the UK, and regular outbursts of anti-Jewish feeling had been reported throughout the UK in 1940 and 1941, and continued to be reported for the remainder of the war. In the early part of the period, the emphasis seemed to be on increased general indignation at black-marketeering, with which Jews were often associated in the public mind, both as instigators and customers 'willing to pay anything to get what they want'. In October 1941 Home Intelligence noted that there was 'unquestionably a feeling about that Jews in big business are behind the black markets' and recent disclosures were said to have intensified 'acute and bitter anti-Jewish feeling' which existed in some quarters.[62] Gradually the connection between Jews and the black market became more pronounced, and by mid-1942 extreme and generalised anti-

Semitic sentiments seemed much more common. In January (1942) in a special report into anti-Semitism, Home Intelligence reported that the phenomenon was 'latent . . . in most districts'. While there was no indication of any feeling that as a nation Britain was 'Jew-led' on the lines suggested by German propaganda, some people were said to have a 'sneaking feeling that by getting rid of the Jews, Hitler and those of like thought through the ages were right.' Anti-Semitism was said to be increasing in areas where Jews had evacuated themselves from danger spots and in towns with a large percentage of Jews in their normal population. Specifically mentioned were: Oxford, Reading, Luton, Brighton (where anti-Jewish sentiment was said to 'run very high'), Camberley, Farnborough, Colwyn Bay, Llandudno, Glamorgan and the south-west of Scotland. The situation in Glasgow had been described as 'a banked fire which could easily flare up if fanned'. At Sheffield and Leeds 'the close contact between Jews and the population has led to a continuous simmering of anti-Jewish feeling'.[63]

A month later, Home Intelligence noted that 'it is felt that there is a lack of severity in the punishments which are being meted out [to black marketeers], and that the fines are wholly inadequate. Some satisfaction is reported where these activities and prosecutions can be traced to Jews'.[64] In April 1942, continued anti-Semitism was attributed chiefly to 'the number of Jews appearing before the courts over black market dealings', and to 'the presence of Jews in hotels and restaurants where expensive meals are to be bought.'[65] In May, the growth of anti-Semitism was reported from widely separated areas, according to the North Midland Region report. Infringements of the rationing orders, dealings in black markets and 'deliberate cunning evasions of measures instituted by the Government to meet war-time conditions' were said to have aroused strong public feeling. Allegations were made of 'enormous numbers of young Jews' boasting of evading the call-up; the expression of 'open indignation' was feared unless measures were adopted 'to bring home to this race that they are inviting a similar revulsion to that which they have experienced in other countries.' This view was confirmed in another MoI region, from which the comment was reported that 'one thing Hitler has done is to put those damned Jews in their place'.[66] In June, a 'flare-up of the always underlying feeling against the Jews' was again reported from four MoI regions. In black market operations Jews were considered the worst offenders and it was said that 'they rob us while we fight for them'.[67] In December 1942 anti-Semitism, aggravated by reports of 'regulation dodging' and prosecutions for black-market offences, was again mentioned from three regions, at the same time as reports on the wholesale murder of Jews in Poland were said to have caused 'extreme horror'. Much of the feeling on the atrocities, however, seemed to be along the lines of 'I don't care for the Jews, but this is terrible'.[68] Just before Christmas anti-Jewish feeling was referred to in five MoI regions, one of which suggested that it might have been on the increase, and that the atrocity stories emanating from Poland had given rise to talk of Jews and black-markets after a period when it seemed to have decreased.[69] Later in the month, Home

Intelligence reported anger and disgust at the behaviour of the Germans, but 'no evidence that the popularity of Jews in this country has increased.' As one regional report put it: 'Abroad – greatest sympathy; in England – general feeling that they badly want controlling'.[70]

That this view was quite widespread was confirmed in the New Year when it was reported that 'as a result of the publicity [about the atrocities], people are more conscious of the Jews they do not like here'.[71] Towards the end of January 1943 it was reported that there were 'increasing signs' of anti-Semitism. Talk was 'cropping up again' of Jews being thought 'to contribute nothing to the war effort: they dodge the call up, wangle out of the Army, and you never see any in factories or working as labourers.' It was suggested also that 'they are at the bottom of the conspiracy in almost every black market prosecution' and are 'always at the head of queues'.[72] It was also suggested in the North Midland Region that 'rumours are going around of the number of Jewish turns – especially in variety shows – being broadcast by the BBC; and any preponderance of Jews in any particular industry or department does get an Englishman's goat.'[73]

The obvious question here though is whether or not the incessant emphasis in Nazi wireless broadcasts on the influence of the Jews had much effect on encouraging sentiments of these kinds. As always there is the difficulty of making a causal link, but we can say for sure that at times and in some parts of the country at least listening to Haw-Haw was still quite widespread, although BBC data and material produced by Home Intelligence often tell a different story. A BBC report on attitudes in the Services to wireless news in June 1941 found little evidence of listening to Haw-Haw, although it was conceded again that 'tardiness in the announcement of news acts as an encouragement to listening to enemy broadcasts'.[74] There seemed more generally to be evidence of increased listening immediately after the preliminary announcement of some item of exciting war news. In April 1942, for example, Home Intelligence noted that 'there was not a bar parlour for miles' in one area of Scotland 'where the German version of the St. Nazaire raid wasn't being discussed.'[75] In the following month an organiser of 'informal discussion groups' on Clydeside reported to the MoI that Haw-Haw broadcasts were being 'fairly widely listened to and discussed' by Clydeside workers. Haw-Haw was considered by many of them to be 'a very good speaker' who very often 'hits the nail on the head', and was only condemned for his exaggeration.[76]

People were also, however, reported to be listening to enemy broadcasts 'for the pleasure of hearing the excuses being made for Axis reverses in Russia and Libya'. It was also remarked that these reverses had 'curbed Lord Haw-Haw's arrogant self-confident tone'.[77] Likewise, at the end of May 1942 following the RAF's first massive raid on Cologne, many people tuned in to Haw-Haw on the Sunday evening, 'gleefully hoping that for once he would be at a loss'. Joyce's statement, however, that the raid on Cologne was a reprisal for the big Russian defeat at Kharkov puzzled some listeners and, though not widely believed, disturbed many. It was, said the MoI, considered 'a clever twist'.[78] Moreover,

British glee at the raid on Cologne soon evaporated when only a few weeks later it was announced that Rommel had taken Tobruk, with 35,000 Allied prisoners, shocking the public out of the optimism of previous weeks. Disappointment, exasperation, shame and rage were only a few of the very widespread reactions which were reported. While the people seemed to have been fairly well prepared for unfavourable developments, the sudden capitulation of Tobruk appeared to have constituted what in four MoI regions was described as 'the greatest single blow to public confidence since Singapore'.[79] Particularly worrying for the authorities was the fact that the government as a whole and Churchill in particular were being criticised for the recent unhappy turn of events. Moreover, the government was again strongly criticised for its handling of news. 'People are stated to be absolutely fed up with misleading news, saying: "we were led to expect differently".' The public were also said to be irritated by the habit of breaking bad news gently and by the fact that Axis news seemed frequently to forestall Britain's own. In direct consequence, listening to enemy broadcasts was said to be increasing.[80] The public's willingness to listen again to Haw-Haw was said to be due to a growing readiness to consider the German news more reliable than the BBC: 'We were told everything was all right at Tobruk, while the enemy were announcing its fall.' Also cited was the desire for the facts about British shipping losses and to hear which towns in Britain were raided by the Germans.[81]

Complaints about the paucity of information from official British sources were also used to justify listening to German stations by the relatives of men serving in the forces, and provide some evidence of the success of a technique widely used by the Nazi radio authorities which was to broadcast lists of names of prisoners and also short messages from them to their families.[82] In August 1942, the postal censorship authorities drew attention to the following remark, intercepted in the mail: 'What do you think of Richard's name coming over the wireless from a German station last Monday? So he's a prisoner! Haw-Haw gives six names every night, quite a few heard it.'[83] In early 1943 Home Intelligence noted again that the families of servicemen reported missing were listening to Haw-Haw in the hope of hearing that their loved ones had been taken prisoner. One woman was said to have listened for months, until she heard her son's name, and thereafter advised others to do the same. It was suggested that there might be less listening to Germany if 'those whose relatives are missing could be assured that official quarters are following the German announcements and will inform the next-of-kin if anything is heard of them'.[84]

By mid-July 1942 the tendency to listen-in to Haw-Haw was still being reported from MoI regions (from five out of thirteen in fact), and 'opinion is said to be growing that German claims are far more truthful than the Press or the BBC admit; it is remarked that we are forced to confirm them, sometimes within a few days, sometimes after a considerable interval.'[85] By mid-August, 'the desire to hear both sides' had re-emerged as an explanation for the 'sporadic listening by many' to the German news.[86]

Although public confidence in ultimate victory was still said to be strong at this point, the morale analysts at the MoI thought that it had been considerably shaken as far as immediate prospects were concerned, an effect augmented by fears of the 'ominous threat' to Allied shipping and doubt at Britain's ability to maintain a heavy bombing offensive. A slight increase in war-weariness, not unmixed with defeatism, was reported, and there was a recurrence of the belief that Britain was 'in for a long war'.[87] Moreover, as the year dragged on, there seemed little cause for optimism about the future. Indeed, Bracken reported to the Cabinet in October that postwar conditions seemed to be more a cause of anxiety as to what they might bring to the individual in the shape of unemployment and distress than of hope for the blessings that they might bring to the nation at large. The public was regarding the coming winter (1942/43) 'as a period dominated not by hunger but by cold, darkness and irksome transport difficulties. The prospect of air raids grows more formidable.'[88]

That the public should be war-weary by mid-1942 is hardly surprising, and the new series of raids on historic towns and cities in April and May placed proportionately much greater stress upon the inhabitants of towns like York, Bath, Exeter and Norwich than had been endured by Londoners some two years earlier. However, the contrast between the nature of the propaganda on the new raids produced by the German wireless and the British public's perception of it is instructive. A broadcast by William Joyce on Breslau on 28 April was typical, the bulk of the analysis being devoted not to threats but to allocating blame for the raids upon Churchill, who had ordered terrorising raids on German cultural shrines in order to prove himself a worthy ally of the barbarians in the Kremlin. The one passage which could be construed as a direct threat reads as follows:

> Concerning these raids [on Germany], *The Times* remarks, in effect, it would be idle to assert that the damage was restricted to industrial objectives, for the photographs of Luebeck show how street after street was laid in ashes and ruins. Very well, then on a matter of such importance it is certain that *The Times* would not have made such an admission without the assent and indeed the approval of Churchill himself. Now, in Germany we are not whining or repining, but the people are very naturally and justly demanding reprisals and it is only necessary to make it crystal clear where the responsibility for such retaliation lies. It lies with Churchill. Exeter, Bath, and Norwich have already received proof that the capacity to retaliate exists and their fate must be taken in earnest that Germany's commitments elsewhere will not prevent her from repaying blow for blow in this terrible kind of warfare, which the Führer, with all his victories to his credit, would have preferred to spare the civil population of Britain.[89]

Just as in 1940, the new raids, however, led to a massive wave of rumours, with again Haw-Haw figuring prominently as the supposed source of most of them. In May, the MoI noted that rumours were widespread, including one about a death-toll of 30,000 at Bath. Haw-Haw was again supposed to have named numerous other towns to be bombed, as well as having provided the dates on which the attack was to take place and, as before, showing that he had at his fingertips local circumstantial details.[90] And just as in 1940, the Enemy News and Counter-Propaganda section at the MoI was forced to produce a standard letter which, *mutatis mutandis*, was sent to its numerous correspondents on Haw-Haw rumours:

> On checking our records of enemy broadcasts, there has been no threat to bomb Kings Lynn. Since the renewal of the German bombing of this country, we have had very many rumours of exactly this nature reported to us, and in no case has there been any foundation for the rumour. It is quite foreign to the character of German broadcasts to threaten specific places or objects in those places. They have on occasions mentioned large cities such as London or Liverpool, but for obvious reasons no actual threat has ever been given. The Germans are naturally unlikely to give us any information of this sort which would be advantageous to the planning of our defences.[91]

And as before, the rumours were found in the unlikeliest places. Newton Poppleford in Devon was reported by one correspondent to be 'a hotbed of "Haw-Haw" rumours', while July seemed to be a particularly fervent month for rumour-mongering.[92] Mrs Jellicoe of the Enemy News department wrote to ask if it were true that Haw-Haw had mentioned that Lord Hankey had attended a luncheon party in London. Captain Kamm of South Midland District Headquarters reported a rumour that Haw-Haw stated that the number of US troops in Cheltenham was known and that the *Luftwaffe* would be visiting them shortly. Mr R. H. Baker rang to ask if on the morning after the last raid on Weston-super-Mare at 07.00, Haw-Haw had said that they 'haven't finished with Weston yet'. A correspondent in Cambridge asked for confirmation that Haw-Haw had said that Norwich was due for a visitation at the full moon. Major de Bere rang on behalf of Canadian Military Headquarters, saying that they were anxious to check a rumour that Haw-Haw 'knew perfectly well that Dunsford Aerodrome would never be completed'. Captain Barret, of the American Army HQ, telephoned from the US embassy to check for an alleged Haw-Haw broadcast claiming to know the exact location of General Clark's HQ and promising that a visit would be paid to him in the near future. The Chief Constable of Cardigan enquired about a rumour to the effect that Haw-Haw had stated that the date of the National Eisteddfod, which was to be held in Cardigan, had been noted, and that Hitler would visit the district. And the flood of rumours and enquiries continued throughout the remainder of the year and into 1943. Haw-Haw supposedly promised bombings for Wolverhampton, Hereford, Norwich, Torquay, Leicester, Leeds, Bargoed, Wellingborough, Northampton, Biddington, Penzance, Aldenham, Cheltenham, Truro, Liverpool, Aldburgh, London, Beckenham, Bexhill, Sunderland, Grimsby, Cleethorpes, Great Ashfield, Weybridge and Somerton.[93] C. H. Symon wrote from Torquay in August that the town was alive with rumours that Haw-Haw had promised them a bombing when the town would be full of munitions workers for the Bank Holiday. When the raid actually did take place, the 'I told you so' brigade was legion.[94] In Cambridge, Haw-Haw was said to be in possession of excellent recent photographs of Shorts, the Pye Radio Works, Chivers' Jam Factory and the Cambridge Fire Station.

It is of course most unlikely that Haw-Haw or anybody else ever mentioned Chivers' Jam factory on the wireless, but for our purposes this is not really the point. The sometimes near universal spread of Haw-Haw rumours in Britain meant that actually it did not matter what Joyce or his colleagues really said, just as it did not really matter how many people actually listened to them. Haw-Haw was a bogeyman known to everybody to whom any far-fetched rumour or scare-story could be attributed. No doubt there were many people in Britain who sought and gained a perverse enjoyment from frightening themselves and others by circulating Haw-Haw stories, but there were many others too who were simply frightened and alarmed by them. The creation in 1939 and 1940 of the Haw-Haw personality had done the trick, and for Haw-Haw to continue to frighten and alarm it was merely necessary that he continued to broadcast.

Of course, it would have been much easier for William Joyce to frighten and depress the British at the end of 1940 than it was at the end of 1942. The Anglo-American landings in Tunisia and Morocco in November followed rapidly upon the heels of Montgomery's victory over Rommel at El Alamein, and at last the British had something to cheer about after years of defeat and disaster in depressing succession. There seemed, noted Home Intelligence, to be a fairly general conviction that 'the tide has turned in our favour'.[95] There were reports of some increase in listening to the German radio although 'not for the news it gives, but rather to see what excuses they offer for their difficulties.'[96]

Those tuning in, however, in the hope of hearing a downbeat or depressed William Joyce would have been disappointed, for he steadfastly refused to be downhearted, and dealt with defeats largely by ignoring them:

In the speech which the Führer delivered yesterday on the eve of 9th November – a historic date in the annals of the German National Socialist Party – there was one characteristic which dominated: the note of calm and complete confidence in victory, based not only on feeling and faith, but upon reason; upon the knowledge that Germany has in her hands the means of winning this war; that the raw materials at her disposal are sufficient for the purpose; that her food supplies are assured; and that, as the Führer said, wherever the battle front might be, Germany would always parry every thrust and go over to the offensive. No doubt the press and radio, secure in the knowledge that the vast majority of their public understand no German, have given quite a different impression of the speech, in accordance with their established custom. But every German who listened to the Führer yesterday must have realised more clearly than ever what immense reserves of strength his country possesses, and what singleness of purpose actuates its leaders. As Adolf Hitler said: 'We shall not fail, and in consequence it is our enemies who will go down.' The words are simple enough, but they express the fundamental and historic truth in which we live . . .

From the Egyptian Front I have not much detailed information to give you. It is evident that the Axis Forces are opposing a fierce resistance to the enemy. In the vicinity of Mersa Matruh, German aircraft destroyed a number of British tanks, as well as enemy columns of motor vehicles. It is announced by the German Supreme Command that a German formation, commanded by Major/Gen. Ramcke, which had been temporarily cut off, inflicted heavy losses on the enemy, during an engagement of three days' duration, and succeeded in capturing a large number of British motor vehicles by means of which it was enabled to rejoin the main body of the Axis Forces. This is merely one instance of the resolution and resourcefulness with which the Axis troops are fighting in the Egyptian theatre of war. It is moreover an indication of the spirit in which they will continue the struggle. As the Führer said yesterday, the British have often advanced before in North Africa, only to retire again. It is not the fluctuating tide of the movement in the desert that counts; it is the power to deliver the decisive blow, and the final issue will show that this power belongs to the Axis.[97]

Joyce might well have been forgiven his optimism, given that most people in Germany regarded North Africa as something of a side-show and the real war was being fought in the East. And Hitler had boasted in his November speech that Stalingrad had all but fallen and that the terrific battle for the city was practically over. The astonishing and audacious counter-attack launched by the Russians at Stalingrad, however, appeared to take the propagandists as well as the military men by surprise. Goebbels, let alone Joyce, seems to have been as much in the dark about the real position there as anyone else outside the highest military circles, and even there confusion and recrimination seems to have been widespread.[98] Stalingrad was more or less written out of domestic propaganda until well into January and the stations for the UK followed suit. *Workers' Challenge* did produce a rather weak line on the Russian offensive, its supposedly pro-Soviet but anti-Churchill line forcing it to see every Russian victory as a defeat:

To put it bluntly, Stalin was compelled to make this move simply because Churchill and Roosevelt let him down. The Nazi forces and positions in this part of Russia are very strong. It is possible for a Soviet force to break through, but when it has broken through it may be cut off and wiped out, because it looks as if the Nazis have enormous reserves, behind their first line of defence. Now all this was known perfectly well to the Soviet High Command. They didn't go into this thing with their eyes shut. It was, to put it plainly, neck or nothing. In other words, Stalin was informed on the best authority that unless he took some action very rapidly the Nazis would complete their hold on the Caucasus – would completely collar Stalingrad – and would quite possibly then be in a position to bring about the collapse of the Soviet Union next year. Make no mistake about it workers, this offensive means a terrific sacrifice by the Soviet Army. This could have been (?spared).

This could have been evaded if only we had set up the Second Front in Europe as we promised.[99]

The white stations, however, maintained a more or less complete silence on the subject of the surrounded and embattled Sixth Army. Joyce's New Year broadcast at 22.30 on 31 December 1942 mentioned the ferocious battle only in the most oblique terms:

> We are approaching the end of a year signalised by the magnificent triumphs of Germany and her allies which have laid the sure basis of their victory, a year in which the Führer and the forces under this command have made a great advance towards final victory . . . as the year draws to a close we are witnessing the dramatic spectacle of the Soviet Union dissipating its forces, squandering its reserves and smashing its war potential to pieces on the adamant rock of German resistance. Next year, when the German offensive is resumed, we shall see the real significance of the desperate and prodigious sacrifices which Stalin is now making. Even before that time comes, the world may well be able to perceive the tremors which will precede the earthquake of economic collapse in the Soviet Union, and before the German and allied forces move forward in their next great attack, there will probably be much strife and discord between the Soviets and the Allies, for even if shipping space were available in plenty to Britain and the USA, as it certainly is not, the war production of the two countries combined would not yield a sufficient quantity of arms and munitions to replace the losses the Bolsheviks have suffered during the last month . . .[100]

On New Year's Day 1943, German listeners received practically no news about the military position on the Russian front, and of the several hours broadcasting in English, there was only one short mention of Stalingrad, in which Germany's Sixth Army was now surrounded and on the brink of destruction:

Stalingrad Area: Luftwaffe Activity

German bombers and dive bombers were active in the Stalingrad area. Over 114 motor vehicles and 60 horse-drawn vehicles were destroyed, and a further six tanks and a large number of lorries were heavily damaged.[101]

And aside from the reading of the vague and non-committal High Command communiqué the only other comment on Russia in a day's broadcasting dominated by the war at sea came from William Joyce:

> There for the present the task of German arms is to maintain the defensive. It will not always be so. The reserves, the resources, the manpower, the armaments that Stalin has been sacrificing so prodigally in recent weeks must be subtracted from the means of resistance that will remain at the disposal of the Soviet Union when the Führer once more gives the order to

advance. Not a day goes by that does not weaken still further the basic power of the Bolsheviks to hold back the German forces in 1943.

He then proceeded to rehash the figures for Allied shipping losses as reported in recent special announcements to the effect that seventy-eight vessels had been sunk in December alone, concluding rather weakly;

> I can well understand the view of those who believe that no military results on land, however striking, can have a more profound influence on the result of the war than this colossal drain on the enemy's tonnage which makes talk of replacement sound almost pathetic.[102]

The admission that von Paulus and his Army was surrounded did not in fact come from German propaganda until 16 January, when it was reported that a fresh Russian attack had been repulsed 'by our troops which have been engaged for weeks in an heroic defensive struggle against an enemy attacking from all sides.' However, Joyce's talk that day dealt again only obliquely with events in Stalingrad, preferring to see in events there only enormous losses for the Soviet side:

> [I]f we look back upon the last two months, we find that the first Soviet attack in the South failed; then the attack in the Central Sector came to grief; a renewed attack in the Southern Sector was once more repulsed; south-east of Lake Ilmen, one onslaught after another was hurled back by the German forces; in the Caucasus, ambitious Bolshevik undertakings were frustrated; the hopeless Soviet attempt to recover ground in the Don area broke down, and finally, the attacks in the region of Stalingrad have foundered on the rock of implacable and tenacious German resistance. For the layman, it may be hard to guess what exactly was the Soviet Command's intention in the first place. No doubt, it was hoped that out of a number of major drives, at least one would succeed, but that hope was doomed to failure. And so the Soviets were expending and dissipating their vital forces, no longer in the hope of gaining a useful decision, but solely to maintain the outward appearance of a campaign which has already lost its strategical purpose . . .
>
> The extent of the enemy's sacrifices has been colossal and cannot be maintained. In the Stalingrad Sector, above all, the Soviets have been employing heavy forces and their losses have been proportionately high. Day after day, more Soviet tank losses have been reported and at the same time, the ratio between the German and Soviet air losses is incomparably in favour of the *Luftwaffe*. For example, it was reported yesterday that sixty-seven Soviet aircraft had been shot down as against four German losses; on Tuesday, the ratio was fifty-two to one in our favour. As might be expected, the *Luftwaffe*'s superiority has dealt a hard blow at the enemy and it is now reported that the Soviets are being compelled to use untrained personnel in their larger bombers . . .
>
> Whether in the North, by Lake Ladoga, or in the South and in the Stalingrad area, the picture is the same – enormous masses of Bolsheviks

launched, irrespective of training and with no clear view as to the results, against the solid and impregnable defences prepared by the German forces for this very contingency.[103]

Even as accomplished a propagandist as William Joyce, however, could not talk away the terrible disaster which was befalling von Paulus in Stalingrad. Of course, Joyce's problem was that he, like von Paulus, had been placed in an impossible position by Hitler. The Führer had determined that surrender at Stalingrad was unthinkable and Joyce and the other propagandists could therefore only describe and enthuse about the 'solid and impregnable defences' cunningly prepared by Germany. After months of predicting the imminent collapse of the Russians at Stalingrad, Hitler had ensured that the whole affair would end as 'an astounding propaganda fiasco'.[104]

Joyce's talk on 3 February, after the Sixth Army had finally surrendered, represented the triumph of wishful-thinking over unthinkable reality, delivered with all the passionate advocacy of the true believer:

[I]t would be a profound, a cardinal error to suppose that the German nation does not know how to take one defeat after so many victories. Nor, if the truth must be told, am I convinced that Stalingrad was, in the worst sense of the word, in the most essential, in the psychological sense, a defeat. Let us look at the facts. I think it was Napoleon who said, 'In warfare the moral is to the physical as three to one'. So far as divisions, brigades and battalions are concerned, Stalingrad was a German defeat. But when a Great Power like the National Socialist Reich is waging a total war, divisions and battalions can be replaced. If we review the position in sober and cold calculations, all sentiment apart, we must realise that the fall of Stalingrad cannot impair the German defensive system as a whole. Whatever individuals have lost, whatever they may have sacrificed, there is nothing in the position as a whole to controvert the view that the main objectives of the enemy offensives have been frustrated. Stalingrad was a part of the price which had to be paid for the salvation of Europe from the Bolshevik hordes.[105]

Now, to see the saga of Stalingrad as in any sense a German victory was stretching credibility beyond breaking point, and the very best that could be said of his remarks here is that Joyce was trying to put a brave face upon a terrible catastrophe. It has been suggested here though that news and talks on the official German stations, while at times vigourously exaggerating and selecting, stuck probably as much to objective truth about the bare facts of war as the BBC did. The defeat and surrender at Stalingrad was a watershed. The whole German propaganda machine systematically lied about the surrender of the Sixth Army, and Joyce was no exception:

The Special Communiqué from the Führer's H.Q. describes how the defenders honoured their standards with their last breath. Two Rumanian divisions and a Croat regiment shared the fate of their German comrades . . .
[T]he German officers and men did not consider that the time had come to

surrender when the ammunition gave out. When there were neither shells nor cartridges there were bayonets, and if the bayonets snapped there were rifle-butts, and if the rifle was torn away from the German soldier by many hands even then he resisted with all that was in him, until movement became impossible, and he covered with his body the place where he stood.

And rather than say nothing at all, and for the want of anything better, Joyce ended his peroration with the kind of wordy but empty rhetorical flourish, which would have been familiar to listeners of Hitler's own performances:

> The lesson that Germany's enemies have to learn and shall learn is that if Germany was strong before she will be doubly strong in the future, and as the shades of the heroes of Stalingrad march side by side with their living comrades, they will march to a glorious victory which will redeem their sacrifice and stamp upon the tablets of history the proud legend: Thanks to these men and their like Europe lives in freedom and in peace.[106]

A BBC LRD enquiry into the extent of listening to German broadcasts, undertaken in December 1942, found that there had been very little change from the fairly low levels discovered at the end of 1940. However, at the same time, Home Intelligence noted a report from the MoI's South Western Region, which suggested that there was 'a fairly numerous regular audience for German broadcasts . . . especially in Cornwall', where reception of them was said to be better than that of the BBC. It was further noted that the principle motive of those who now listened seemed to be a desire to hear the Axis version of the news, though there was little anticipation of this being very truthful. The general view in Home Intelligence seemed to be that, from the standpoint of morale, such listening as there was gave 'no ground for concern'.[107] The years of triumph now behind them, the Nazi propagandists faced a different and more difficult task in the years of disaster and defeat. Chapter 6, the penultimate chapter, considers Nazi wireless propaganda and its effects in the closing stages of the war.

Notes

1 DEUT IGFG 13.50 5.9.39.
2 Semmler, *Man Next to Hitler*, p. 39 and Boelcke, *Secret Conferences*, p. 174.
3 ZEE IGFG 09.00 22.6.41.
4 ZEE IEFENA 07.10 22.06.41.
5 ZEE IEFENA 07.10 22.06.41.
6 BREM IEFE 18.10 23.6.41.
7 BREM IEFE 18.10 23.6.41.
8 DEUT IGFG 20.00 25.6.41.
9 ZEE IEFENA 07.10 22.06.41.
10 HAM IEFE 21.30 28.6.41.
11 ZEE IEFENA 21.30 11.7.41.
12 HAM IEFE 19.30 26.6.41.

13 HILV IEFE 22.07 22.6.41.

14 LUX IEFE 21.30 25.6.41.

15 BREM IEFE 13.30 27.6.41.

16 Boelcke, *Secret Conferences*, p. 178. In Russian *Lvov*; in Polish *Lwow*; in German *Lemberg*.

17 ZEE IEFNA 04.20 12.7.41.

18 NBBS IEFE 20.30 26.6.41.

19 BREM IEFE 13.30 27.6.41.

20 BREM IEFE 21.30 28.6.41.

21 From a broadcast by Joyce given at 10.30, 13 July 1941, cited in PRO INF 1/251.

22 HAM IEFE 00.30 14.7.41.

23 By this point, July 1941, Hamburg broadcasts in English and other languages were preceded by the morse 'V', coupled with the station signal in a rather obvious attempt to undermine the British 'V' campaign which was running at the same time.

24 WC IEFE 21.10 9.7.41.

25 PRO INF 1/292, *Home Intelligence Weekly*, 26 June 1941.

26 PRO INF 1/292, *Home Intelligence Weekly*, 14 August 1941.

27 PRO INF 1/292, *Home Intelligence Weekly*, 4 September 1941.

28 PRO INF 1/292, *Home Intelligence Weekly*, 1 October 1941.

29 PRO INF 1/292, *Home Intelligence Weekly*, 22 October 1941.

30 Boelcke, *Secret Conferences*, p. 38.

31 PRO INF 1/292, *Home Intelligence Weekly*, 5 November 1941.

32 PRO PREM 4 101/4A, *Morton to Churchill*, 5 November 1941.

33 PRO PREM 4 101/4A, *Bracken to Churchill*, 10 November 1941.

34 PRO PREM 4/100/1, *Postal Censorship*, 1 December 1941. Postal Censorship reports were compiled on the basis of examination of outgoing letters, mainly to the USA, to Canada, to Eire and to Northern Ireland, and on letters to and from certain prohibited areas.

35 PRO PREM 4/100/1, *Postal Censorship*, 1 December 1941.

36 PRO PREM 4/100/1, *Postal Censorship*, 1 December 1941.

37 PRO INF 1/292, *Home Intelligence Weekly*, 11 March 1942.

38 BRES IEFENA 22.30 11.2.42.

39 NBBS IEFE 20.30 13.2.42.

40 Boelcke, *Secret Conferences*, p. 202.

41 PRO INF 1/292, *Home Intelligence Weekly*, 18 February 1942.

42 PRO INF 1/292, *Home Intelligence Weekly*, 18 February 1942.

43 PRO INF 1/292, *Home Intelligence Weekly*, 25 February 1942.

44 PRO INF 1/292, *Home Intelligence Weekly*, 4 March 1942.

45 PRO INF 1/292, *Home Intelligence Weekly*, 11 February 1942.

46 PRO INF 1/292, *Home Intelligence Weekly*, 25 February 1942.

47 PRO PREM 4/100/1, *Postal Censorship*, 4 April 1942.

48 PRO PREM 4/100/1, *Postal Censorship*, 4 April 1942.

49 PRO INF 1/282, *Home Intelligence Weekly*, 25 March 1942.

50 WO 32/15772, *Morale Report February – May 1942*.

51 WO 32/15772, *Draft Morale Report May to July 1942*.

52 PRO WO 193/453, *Morale Report – August to October 1942*.

53 PRO INF 1/282, *Home Intelligence Weekly*, 25 March 1942.

54 PRO INF 1/292, *Home Intelligence Weekly*, 10 December 1941.

55 PRO INF 1/292, *Home Intelligence Weekly*, 17 December 1941.

56 PRO INF 1/292, Home Intelligence Division, *Public Attitude towards the USA*, 24 December 1941.

57 PRO INF 1/293, *British Public Opinion and the United States*, 23 February 1942.
58 BRES IEFENA 22.30 8.12.41.
59 BRES IEFNA 22.30 1.4.42.
60 PRO INF 1/292, *Home Intelligence Weekly*, 18 February 1942.
61 *Goebbels' Diaries*, Taylor (ed.), entry for 10 May 1943.
62 PRO INF 1/292, *Home Intelligence Weekly*, 1 October 1941.
63 PRO INF 1/293, *Anti-Semitism*, 15 January 1942.
64 PRO INF 1/292, *Home Intelligence Weekly*, 25 February 1942.
65 PRO INF 1/282, *Home Intelligence Weekly*, 1 April 1942.
66 PRO INF 1/292, *Home Intelligence Weekly*, 28 May 1942.
67 PRO INF 1/292, *Home Intelligence Weekly*, 4 June 1942.
68 PRO INF 1/292, *Home Intelligence Weekly*, 17 December 1942.
69 PRO INF 1/292, *Home Intelligence Weekly*, 24 December 1942.
70 PRO INF 1/292, *Home Intelligence Weekly*, 31 December 1942.
71 PRO INF 1/292, *Home Intelligence Weekly* 7 January 1943.
72 PRO INF 1/292, *Home Intelligence Weekly*, 21 January 1943.
73 PRO INF 1/292, *Home Intelligence Weekly*, 28 January 1943.
74 BBC WAC LR/290, *Summary of Opinion of Listeners in the Forces on the News*, 24 June 1941.
75 PRO INF 1/292, *Home Intelllligence Weekly*, 15 April 1942.
76 PRO INF 1/292, *Home Intelligence Weekly*, 28 May 1942.
77 PRO INF 1/292, *Home Intelligence Weekly*, 31 December 1941.
78 PRO INF 1/292, *Home Intelligence Weekly*, 4 June 1942.
79 PRO INF 1/292, *Home Intelligence Weekly*, 25 June 1942.
80 PRO INF 1/292, *Home Intelligence Weekly*, 25 June 1942.
81 PRO INF 1/292, *Home Intelligence Weekly*, 2 July 1942.
82 A recording of such a broadcast on the German European Service from September 1944 may be heard on the CD at Track 18.
83 PRO INF 1/292, *Home Intelligence Weekly*, 27 August 1942.
84 PRO INF 1/292, *Home Intelligence Weekly*, 14 January 1943.
85 PRO INF 1/292, *Home Intelligence Weekly*, 16 July 1942.
86 PRO INF 1/292, *Home Intelligence Weekly*, 13 August 1942.
87 PRO INF 1/292, *Home Intelligence Weekly*, 25 June 1942.
88 PRO INF 1/284, WP (42) 454, *Report on Home Opinion*, 9 October 1942.
89 BRES IEFENA 22.30 28.4.42.
90 PRO INF 1/292, *Home Intelligence Weekly*, 6 and 13 May 1942.
91 PRO INF 1/265, *A. F. Hutcheson to Mrs R. Goodrick*, 3 July 1942.
92 PRO INF 1/265, *Helen Pearman to Churchill*, undated.
93 PRO INF 1/265, *passim*. Somerton was actually bombed at the end of September 1942, and a rumour rapidly circulated to the effect that Haw-Haw had issued a warning to the Somerton people that he would return again the same night and finish the job he had started in the morning.
94 PRO INF 1/265, *Symon to MoI*, 2 August 1942.
95 PRO INF 1/292, *Home Intelligence Weekly*, 26 November 1942.
96 PRO INF 1/292, *Home Intelligence Weekly*, 5 November 1942.
97 BRES IEFUK 22.30 9.11.42.
98 Balfour, *Propaganda in War*, p. 306.
99 WC IEFE 21.10 25.11.42. Evidence that any of the *Concordia* stations had much of an audience by this stage is hard to come by, and certainly the unit's staff had few illusions about the number of their British listeners. The standing joke in the *Concordia* offices, amongst everyone except Dr Hetzler, was that NBBS had by

now only one listener in Britain, and he was the gentleman at the BBC whose job it was to take down the broadcasts. See PRO WO 71/1112, Spillman's evidence.
100 CAL IEFUK 22.30 31.12.42.
101 CAL IEFUK 23.30 1.1.43.
102 CAL IEFUK 22.30 1.1.43.
103 BRES IEFUK 22.30 16.1.43.
104 Kershaw in Welch (ed.), *Nazi Propaganda*, p. 198.
105 BRES IEFUK 22.30 3.2.43.
106 BRES IEFUK 22.30 3.2.43.
107 PRO INF 1/292, *Home Intelligence Weekly*, 21 January 1943.

6

Nazi Wireless Propaganda
in Collapse and Defeat

That Germany was seeking from 1943 to avoid defeat rather than to obtain outright victory naturally had consequences for propaganda for foreign audiences. As has been shown, in 1940 or 1941 Goebbels believed that his propaganda for the UK – by flailing and exposing British politicians and the plutocratic system they represented – could assist Germany's war effort by undermining the morale of the British public, although as the war dragged on and on he became less and less confident of its potency. By 1943, Goebbels was far more interested in bolstering German domestic morale and in seeking the widest powers for his own obsession with mobilising Germans for total war, and propaganda for the UK figures less and less frequently in his diaries and ministerial briefings. Nevertheless, the wireless services for the UK continued throughout this period; some of the freedom stations were dropped, other stations were added, and a number of new personalities appeared who, for a while, grabbed a few headlines in the UK. William Joyce remained the dominant figure in German wireless propaganda in English, however, and it would seem that he continued to hold onto an audience. However, the tide had turned against Germany, and public opinion in the UK at last had war news of a cheering sort. Joyce had few enough triumphs to trumpet now, and ever more disasters to explain away. We consider here the content of wireless propaganda in the last years of the war in Europe, once again in the context of the British public opinion within which it had to operate.

The war in the East continued to dominate propaganda and public opinion in the first half of 1943. German propaganda strategy was simple enough – to cause a rift between the eastern and western Allies by terrorising the populations of Europe with visions of their coming enslavement to Bolshevik tyranny. So great was Goebbels' determination to stoke up world-wide fear and hatred of the Bolshevik menace that he concocted what he called a 'tactic of calculated pessimism', allowing German successes to be underplayed or even unreported both at home and abroad, while Soviet victories were to be built up. 'What a turnaround compared with last winter!', the Minister noted in his diary. 'Then we went out of our way to rubbish the enemy's exaggerated claims of victory; now we're doing all we can to supply them with the necessary force.'[1] Rudolf Semler, who worked as one of Goebbels' press officers in the Propaganda Ministry, also kept a daily diary and noted in mid-March that his Minister was delighted with the success he believed his propaganda was having:

Of this success Goebbels is as proud as a general is of his successful operations. He is already talking of open distrust between the Russians and their Allies. Every shrewd observer, he says, can see the evidence of this growing tension, and it is a short step from open distrust to an open breach. Goebbels believes it is the secret hope of the Western Allies that Germany and Russia will completely exhaust one another in this struggle. Yesterday he said that German propaganda of the last three months would be worth analysing for a doctor's thesis. It would be found to offer a classic example of the art of political propaganda because cause, opening stages and effects could be observed so close together in time.[2]

And at his ministerial conference on 14 March, Goebbels spoke of the palpable fear of Western statesmen, when three hundred miles of Germany's eastern front had been torn open by the Red Army and the whole line seemed in danger of collapsing. 'I shall now try by every means to stimulate this fear, until at last there comes a breach between East and West. That is the great long-term object of my work, which I hope to attain by this summer.'[3]

Apparently perfectly calculated to promote the breach between East and West was the story carried on 13 April on all German stations of the discovery in the Katyn forest near Smolensk of the decomposed bodies of some 10,000 Polish officers, murdered by Soviet forces in 1940.[4] The long and gory accounts given of the find in the forest were clearly determined to convince listeners throughout Europe of the horrific fate which awaited them at the hands of the Bolshevik sub-men, should their leaders get their way and fail to assist Germany in her struggle against the Judeo-Bolshevik conspiracy. Certainly, American monitors believed that the Katyn material was well handled by the Germans: 'every conceivable propaganda theme was cleverly tied into this story of "Russian bestiality"', including the opportunity once again to blame the Jews. Eyewitness accounts were said to prove that the assassins 'were all Jews. The orders of execution of the OGPU were made by Jewish officials'.[5] The British and Americans too, of course, were implicated in this Jewish butchery. The world, said Berlin on the 15th, 'has waited in vain for a word of protest from London. The English Jews, and naturally the American Jews too, make every effort to hush up the crime of their racial brothers in the USSR . . . The civilised western nations must conclude that England feels herself identified with the criminal elements of Bolshevism and its Jew allies.'[6]

William Joyce devoted his talk on Breslau on 16 April to 'the gigantic and hideous massacre' of Poles by Bolshevik butchers:

> I am used, of course, to the fact that Bolshevism is criminal, remorseless and unscrupulous. There is no account of any Jewish-Bolshevik atrocity which would be brought before me that could surprise me, and yet there does seem to be a particularly macabre element in this discovery. The work of exhumation has been carried out by Poles. These men must be wondering as they go about their gruesome task how much British guarantees are worth. For after all, the pledges given to Poland by the British Government did not

specify that Polish sovereignty was to be protected against Germany but surrendered to the Bolsheviks. So far as the Poles knew, the guarantee was perfectly general. It is not merely that Britain is the ally of the Soviet Union, the associate of these Jewish-Communist murderers whose character, if it has changed at all in the last quarter of a century, has altered for the worst . . .

Blind confidence has often been inculcated by the wily Jew in the unsuspecting Gentile. [N]ever has there been a more flagrant abuse of human credulity than the Jewish attempt to convince the British people that Bolshevism is harmless. How harmless it is the thousands of corpses dug up in that pine forest near Smolensk will testify, with a silence more expressive than words could be.[7]

Cleverly handled as the Katyn massacre may have been by the Germans – and the issue certainly led to a rift between the Soviet Union and the Polish government in London – the problem facing the propagandists in 1943 was that as far as the bulk of the British public was concerned, the Soviet Union could do no wrong. In the Army, ignorance about the Soviet Union amongst the ordinary soldiers was such that 'that country is evidently looked upon as a paradise of freedom and justice, with a benevolent Government which provides unlimited scope for the individual, and "Joe" Stalin is a figure among political leaders second only in affectionate regard to the Prime Minister himself.'[8] Among civilians, a most common sentiment was an almost unbridled admiration for the Soviet Union in general, and for the Red Army in particular, since for so much of the war it was the Red Army which had borne the brunt of the fighting and seemed at last to have Germany on the run. British 'Russomania' was particularly noticeable during the defence of Moscow and Leningrad in 1941, throughout the latter half of 1942 during the long and desperate resistance at Stalingrad, and again in the autumn of 1943 when the Russians were making terrific strides against the German forces, when by contrast the Anglo-American invasion of Italy seemed to be petering out. A BIPO survey conducted in May 1943 found that no less than 50 per cent of Britons nominated Russia as the country of the United Nations which had so far made the greatest single contribution towards winning the war, as against 42 per cent who favoured Britain. As many as 57 per cent of those aged twenty-one to twenty-nine named Russia as the leading nation.[9] Home Intelligence reports continued to reveal, as they had done in 1941, that the sentiments of the majority of Britons about Russia were not fear of the Bolshevisation of Europe, but rather guilt, humiliation and even shame that Britain's leaders seemed unwilling or incapable of doing more to assist their heroic ally. In November 1941, for instance, Home Intelligence noted that the 'great admiration felt by the public for Russia's courage and endurance continues to grow with every week of her resistance.'[10] Nearly a year later, it was concluded that 'feelings about Russia combine profound gratitude and admiration with a considerable sense of frustration that more overt help cannot be given.'[11] In November 1943, admiration for the Red Army was now being described as 'boundless'. The

Moscow Conference of the same month was received with 'general satisfaction' and great relief at the dispelling of doubts about Allied unity. Particular pleasure was expressed at what was seen as 'the blow to German propaganda' which the Conference represented.[12] The 'German propaganda story' of the 'Polish graveyard' at Katyn was 'said to be disbelieved, though in Scotland it is reported to have caused "bitter discussion" and "much ill-feeling".'[13] According to Home Intelligence, the difficulties between the Russians and the Poles were widely discussed among all classes, and although a large section of the public declined to take sides, 'sympathy appears to be mostly on the side of the Russians. Only in Northern Ireland is opinion reported to be strongly in favour of Poland.' Elsewhere, even among those who sympathised with the Poles and thought that 'there may be some truth in the German allegations', the general attitude was said to be that 'she should subordinate her interests to those of her Allies.'[14]

Nevertheless, that there was a constituency in Britain for anti-Soviet propaganda – however small – seems clear. Home Intelligence noted in January 1943, just before the revelation of the extent of the Soviet victory at Stalingrad, a minority who were 'anxious that Russia should not be allowed to feel she is the only victor' and 'dominate the peace'. According to one regional report, a few said: 'We shall have to fight Russia yet', and it had even been rumoured that 'we are soon to pack up the war with Germany in order to join with her in an attack on Russia.'[15] There was also a more generalised anxiety at a predicted coldness in relations between the Allies. The Intelligence Branch of the Ministry of Home Security noted, for example, in April 1943, that 'people were anxious because they believe that grave differences exist between the US and Great Britain on the one hand and Russia on the other.'[16] In preparing its own weekly reports into civilian morale in October of the same year, the MoI came to similar conclusions. It reported that there was said to be increasing awareness of the possibility of postwar difficulties in the international sphere, and a growing fear that 'the end of the war will not mean the end of strife'. Fears chiefly concerned Russia and the USA. On the one hand, it was felt that we 'may not be as eager to be friendly with Russia as we might'; on the other, that 'we shall be dominated by the USA'.[17]

And if there was an anti-Soviet constituency in the later years of the war, it is also clear that dislike of Jews remained commonplace, even as Germany was forced onto the defensive. Again, no causal connection between Nazi propaganda and British anti-Semitism can be proved, yet it is important to realise that a constituency existed, despite the growing revelations of the horrors being committed in Europe against Jews by Germans. For example, in February 1943, Home Intelligence noted that sympathy for the plight of European Jews was said to be about equally balanced by unfavourable references to Jews living the UK.[18] When 178 persons died in the Bethnal Green Tube disaster in March, the panic was attributed in three MoI regions to East End Jews. Two of these three regions, London and North Western, had been most consistent in reporting anti-Semitism. The suggestion that 'the trouble was occasioned by the Jews is reported from all parts of London, with the exception of Bethnal Green where there is full knowledge that any such statement is untrue.'[19] At the end of the month Home Intelligence noted that nine of its thirteen regions referred to 'the prevalence of anti-Semitic feeling'. There was reported to be resentment at the influence which Jews had in financial and trade circles and at the number of young Jews not in the Army. 'They are getting everything into their hands – building, land, tobacco, food, catering trades, etc.' The number of prosecutions against Jews for various offences was also said to have given rise to comment. The same report noted that five regions reported sympathy for the Jews in Europe, and it was generally thought that something should be done to help them, although it was often added, 'we don't want any more in this country'.[20] When Herbert Morrison refused to publish the findings of the enquiry into the Bethnal Green disaster, there was talk that 'the decision not to publish the findings is proof that the Jews did, in fact, panic.'[21] In May, anti-Semitism was said to be on the increase, again in London and the North Western Regions, but also in the North Midland Region, an increase which in some areas was said to be 'deliberately organised and fostered'. It was suggested, for instance in Hornsey, that 'anti-Semitism due to ignorance and prejudice is exploited by Fascist elements'.[22] In August, although a general reduction in reports of anti-Semitism was noted, in the Northern, North Midland, London and South-Eastern Regions, anti-Jewish feeling was still said to be on the increase. The usual accusations of black-market activities and 'funking' of military service were laid, and attacks were made upon the Jews as 'rank exhibitionists', driving around in fancy cars 'as if there were no petrol restrictions'. Jews were also accused of putting 'the small shopkeeper' out of business, and Jewish financiers were 'responsible for the prolongation of the war'. The belief that anti-Semitism was being stimulated intentionally was again reported from two regions.[23]

Interestingly enough, the Germans increased their anti-Semitic output in 1943, when a new and ferociously anti-Jewish freedom station, Peter Adami's *Radio National*, began broadcasting in July. The following extract from a talk by Francis Maton as '*Manxman*' is a typical example of the station's output:

It is the duty of every sane-thinking Britisher to denounce the race of parasites and aliens who have brought the might of our empire into this terrible war. This race as we know are the Jews, who by their financial manipulations in London, New York and Moscow have plunged the European nations into untold misery, sacrificing Christian lives so that they can emerge the victors and become the rulers of the world . . .

If the Japs and Chinese and the South Americans want to kill each other off and to live a life of continual war and horror, let them. It is not our direct affair. It is only the business of the Yids in England who wish to supply them with the means of killing each other. But for Joe Smith and Bill Higgins it is no matter or consequence. We can take our place as Britishers amongst the intelligent and Christian peoples of the world and live peacefully and fairly well just as we did before the Jews decided to change our mode of living for us. To wage this war, when we have everything to live for and so much to lose, just for the sake of Judah, is hypocritical and beyond comprehension . . .

Once more I say, people of Great Britain, just think for a moment and you will realise how much we are losing, individually and as a nation as a whole. The sooner we stop this senseless slaughter and come to our right senses and furthermore kick the Jews out of our country, the sooner we shall be able to secure peace for ourselves and for the rest of the world, and above all, shall we secure a return to the high British standards of living that are so dear to us all. Let them remain, and we shall find ourselves sold to everlasting Jewish bondage and our children will only be able to turn round and say that we were the generation who delivered the empire to the Jews.[24]

Maton of course was a nonentity, and there is little evidence that anyone in Britain listened to *Radio National*. John Amery on the other hand was famous, his father being a prominent member of the British government. Amery had little in common with William Joyce, other than their shared obsession with Jews and Bolsheviks, and his tiresome, poorly delivered rants on the German wireless reflected his pathological hatreds:

Here is the New Year. Despite all that has happened we must look forward with hope. We can only do that if we add to hope, determination. In Washington the champagne flows. The Jews raise their glasses – 'cheerio – the British Empire is sold!' Hong Kong, Singapore, Burma – so many places, so many riches sacrificed to our American Allies, so many British lives lost – for what? The British gold reserve in Washington, Honduras, the West Indies sacrificed to our American ally, so much British capital lost – for what? Millions of tons of our ships at the bottom of the ocean. The 365 days of the year have run out. Everywhere on every front, we lost, that world Jewry may survive. At home we suffer restrictions, humiliations from the American troops who occupy our England, and from the Communist agitators we must tolerate demonstrations and Red flags. The gaols are full of patriots who dared to tell the truth, whose only crime was to desire England for the English. The Lord Mayor is Jewish, the press, the cinema, the BBC . . . At whatever cost, be it even civil war and bloodshed, this war must be stopped. We cannot remain any longer on the wrong side. Our place is with civilisation, hand-in-hand with our German cousins, against Bolshevik barbarity and American Jewish domination. That must be our New Year resolution, and if we all resolve together, then there won't be even any bloodshed at all . . . But the parasitical Jewish intermediaries who enrich themselves on the brains of the leaders and the work of the masses must once and for all disappear from our social structure. Don't you see how marvellous it would be to see all the lights in Piccadilly Circus again? How much better life will be when one can have a drink amongst Englishmen in an English pub without the American soldier, the insolent Jew, or the professional Communist agitator? . . . It can never be treason in wartime, or at any other time, to love one's country ardently, to take up arms because all the things that are sacred to us are being systematically violated. The public, the free Englishmen did not declare this war, but a disheartened old gentleman, pressed on all sides by the men who wanted this, the Jews.[25]

It might be thought that, given his notoriety, Amery should have been able to attract an audience in Britain far in excess of anything which the merits of his talks might have warranted. His first broadcasts from Berlin were heard and discussed, at least in Scotland, and aroused widespread comment there and in Northern Ireland.[26] However, his talks seem to have passed more or less unnoticed in other parts of the country. The chief reported reactions were 'sympathy with his father', and condemnation of his anti-Jewish sentiments.[27]

Nevertheless, Home Intelligence again noted the prevalence of anti-Semitism in a report in February 1944, remarking that intermittent criticism of Jews had been recorded during the previous eighteen weeks. In two MoI regions, anti-Semitism was said to be particularly apparent among workers. Many believed for instance that Jews were largely responsible for black-market offences, a belief said to be encouraged by Jewish names seen in the press in this connection. There was a feeling too that Jews were trying to monopolise industry and business and 'have a finger in every pie' (five regions), and some belief that Jews would make money at other people's expense in the postwar period (three regions). Jews were also accused of wasting petrol, of escaping service in the Forces, the Home Guard and Civil Defence (two regions each) and of buying up property at exorbitant prices (one region).[28] Criticisms of Jews were again referred to in a report in June 1944. In the North-Eastern Region there were complaints that Jews were fomenting industrial unrest and that Jewish Communist agitators were concerned in a recent coal strike.[29] A month later, it was noted that anti-Semitic comment continued at a low level, although in some areas, apparently as a result of discussion of German atrocities against Jews and of evacuation difficulties, there had been some increase. Criticisms had been chiefly on the grounds of Jews being 'first out' when the flying bomb raids started (seven regions), of Jewish 'wealth and ostentation' (three regions), of their 'evading National Service' (two regions), and of Jewish 'black market activities' (two regions). In November 1944 an increase was noted in anti-Semitism, following the assassination of Lord Moyne by Jewish terrorists.[30]

Of course, even if it were possible to show that German broadcasts had the effect of encouraging anti-Semitic feelings in Britain, it is a long step from this to showing that anti-Jewish propaganda had the effect of diminishing the public's determination to see the war through to its conclusion. After all, there is a gulf between the type of obsessional anti-Semitism of fanatics like Amery and Joyce who saw in the Jews a malignant force bent on global domination, and the nasty but everyday bigotry, jealousy and petty spitefulness of very large numbers of people against out-groups, which might well be brought to the surface by the stressful circumstances of wartime. Moreover, while many

Britons may have disliked Jews, by 1943 they hated Germans. In September 1939, only 6 per cent of Britons had seen the German people as their chief enemy, while 91 per cent saw the Nazi government in this role. By April 1943, 43 per cent saw the German people as the chief enemy, while 51 per cent named the government.[31] The British people were therefore no more likely to run 'hand-in-hand with our German cousins, against Bolshevik barbarity and American Jewish domination' than they were to fly to the moon.

This may be demonstrated by reactions in the UK to Germany's intense propaganda campaign at the end of May 1943 on the indiscriminate Allied bombing of German cities, which claimed that British incendiary attacks on Germany were almost exclusively directed against civilian dwellings, women and children, hospitals and schools, churches and cultural monuments. In June, Home Intelligence reported that the attitude of the majority of the British public appeared to be 'unqualified approval of relentless bombing of Germany, with little or no thought of enemy civilian casualties'. A number said freely that 'it is a good thing to kill the Germans, not so much from vindictiveness as from policy.' What appeared to be a large minority regarded the bombing as 'horrible but necessary'. They took no pleasure from the news since they realised the suffering produced by the raids, but the majority 'warmly approve the policy as a right means towards winning and ending the war' and 'have no wish to see the raids reduced in number and intensity.'[32] In the light of such attitudes, German attempts to evoke feelings either of sympathy or guilt from the British, were futile.

Moreover, events by now were rapidly moving against Germany. Mussolini was overthrown in July 1943 and Italy threw in the towel in September. The loss of Italy was obviously a major blow for Germany, and one which would naturally present serious difficulties to the propagandists, the more so since it is now clear that Mussolini's overthrow came as a surprise to the Nazi leadership. No mention of his downfall was heard on the German wireless until five hours after the announcement from Rome. Such stories as did appear were generally anodyne reportage, repeating the news as transmitted from Italy, adding lamely the suggestion that the Duce was perhaps ill. Here now was evidence for the simple fact that even the Nazis could not make bricks without straw. Having no control over events in Italy and unable lightly to dismiss the downfall of Il Duce, the German propaganda experts were floundering. Joyce had little to say about Mussolini's downfall until 29 July, when he paid a sentimental homage to the fallen Duce:

> And now, today, I could not discuss any aspect of European politics without paying a tribute to Benito Mussolini, whose birthday it is. Perhaps this is a subject upon which I can speak from a personal as well as a national point of view. The German people honour this man, who, in the fateful days after the last war raised the standard of Fascism against the Communist menace and brought the spirit of regeneration to his country, which, though technically among the victors, was treated very much as a defeated Power. In the period

before Mussolini marched on Rome there were many Italian cities in which an officer or a soldier who had fought at the front could not wear his uniform or his decorations without being mobbed, spat upon, and treated like a public enemy. Mussolini's path to power was not strewn with roses. All the bestiality of Moscow's agents, all the atrocious venom of the Communist sub-men, all the hatred of which the enemies of nationalism were capable, were directed against this heroic figure and his gallant followers. Many were the martyrs that gave up their lives in order that an Italy redeemed should take her place with pride amongst the nations.

Joyce then went on to close with a remarkably personal and apparently sincere passage in which he remembered Mussolini's impact upon his own early conversion to fascism. Note though how no opportunity is wasted to press home the attack on the Bolshevik enemy of humanity:

> And, for the personal point of view, if that be allowed to me, I can only say that when I joined the first Fascist movement in Britain on 6th December 1923 I saw that night in Battersea the mob violence, the Red Flags, the broken heads and the broken bodies, the typical evidence of the disruption which Communism can bring into a nation; and while I heard the dismal wail of the 'Red Flag' intoned by the sub-men out for blood, I thought of Mussolini and of what he had been able to do for Italy. I was not pro-Italian, I was merely pro-human; there were many millions of people throughout the world at about that time who had the same thoughts; and when I look back upon these 20 years I can only say that Mussolini has, in that period, become one of the greatest figures in history. The shades of the great Romans up to the time of Augustus, and unborn generations of Italian people, can pay homage to this great leader whose stature time can only increase.[33]

Joyce may well have sincerely held these views about Mussolini and felt his downfall acutely. His sentiments, however, were shared by few in Britain, where Mussolini was universally regarded with contempt. To picture him as a modern Caesar must have made Joyce sound rather ridiculous in Britain in 1943.

More likely to be effective was the consistent use of the one strong card which Germany could still play in 1943, which was the situation at sea and the continuing onslaught upon Allied shipping by the U-boat fleets. The official German claim reached its peak in the whole war in March 1943, when it was triumphantly reported that 926,000 tons of Allied merchant shipping had been lost. As Michael Balfour has shown, German claims for Allied shipping losses were not for the most part wildly exaggerated and at times even underestimated the real total of shipping lost.[34] Even in this area though, the optimistic claims of Nazi propaganda began to be tempered by the real decline in the strike rate of the U-boats, as Allied counter-measures began to take effect as spring turned to summer. For April, the claimed figure was only half that for March.

On the Eastern Front too there was little good news to report. The extraordinary turnaround in the Russo–German war was reflected in a constant series of retreats and twists in the German propaganda line throughout 1943. Immediately after Stalingrad a manpower shortage in the East was admitted and the total mobilisation of Germany's military and productive forces was declared. At the same time, a new German offensive was promised for the summer. By March, the Germans were declaring that their lines had been stabilised, the Russian offensive was declared a failure, and Germany's new 'defensive front' supposedly held possibilities for future offensive action. But when this German action came and failed in the summer, it was claimed that the precipitated Russian offensive at Byelgorod-Orel had been completely thwarted. Instead, a battle of materiel had developed, which would lead to attrition of the Russian forces. There was still no hint of any large-scale German withdrawal, although following the fall of Mussolini, a coming two-front war was announced. Towards the end of August the term 'elastic defence' became prominent, and on 8 September, a few hours before the announcement of the Italian surrender, the High Command stated that strategy was based on the needs of fronts other than the Russian, and it was not of decisive importance to retain Russian territory. Rather, the object was to prevent a breakthrough and save manpower to retain sufficient reserve. Next, it was stated both at home and abroad that the new reserves gained as the result of total mobilisation had been withheld from the eastern front to meet an Allied invasion of western Europe. This had dictated the decision to withdraw from Russia. During this period, no indication of the extent of the withdrawal was given and when the retreating German armies reached the Dnieper, propaganda both at home and abroad claimed that the retreat had now come to an end. When it had become plain by October 1943 that the Russians could and would advance far beyond the Dnieper, home propaganda began to diverge sharply from propaganda abroad. At home, propaganda still refrained from speaking of a planned strategic withdrawal and explained the retreat on the need to avoid encircle-ment and the German success in wearing down the Russian forces. Abroad, propaganda began to suggest that the planned withdrawal was still continuing, accompanied with hints at the armies which were being held in reserve to defeat invasion in the West.[35]

The whole tone for Nazi propaganda for the new year, 1944, was set by Hitler himself and this leading colleagues in their various New Year proclama-tions. The contrast with similar proclamations a year earlier was striking. In 1943, Hitler had spoken of German invincibility, German determination to reach a decisive victory and the prospects of an Allied collapse. In his 1944 speech, however, he said it would be a question of survivors and annihilated, and not of victors and vanquished. He made this point, however, not in reference to the annihilation of the Allies, but to stress the fact that Germany would be annihilated in the event of an Allied victory. Goebbels' speech, too, reflected a new tone. Like his Führer, he said that 1944 was the year in which a final decision would be reached, though again he made no specific pledges of German victory. The reason for his certainty that the war was in its endgame was entirely a negative one: namely that the Allies' attempt to deal a knock-out blow in 1943 had failed.[36]

For the broadcasting propagandists, the New Year too began in a wholly negative tone. The day 5 January saw the appearance of another of the frequent directives to the propaganda editors, this time from the *AA*, headed 'New Themes for Propaganda to England'. The themes to be pressed were that Britain could not win the war, and that any action she undertook against Germany benefited only Bolshevism. In any case, even if Germany could be defeated, it would involve a military campaign lasting years which would entail the destruction of Europe.[37] This negativity in German propaganda was reflected in a rehashed 'New Order' campaign, which began around this period. Back in 1942, when such material had been at its height, prominence had been given to German power and the process by which she would bring the 'New Order' into being. By 1944, however, circumstances had changed, and as PWE pointed out, Europe as a whole figured more prominently, while stress was laid on Germany's difficulty in accomplishing her mission. However, if Germany were to be defeated, then the future for Europe would be bleak, and the entire continent, as well as Eastern Asia, would be divided between the rapacious giants of US imperialism and Soviet Bolshevism.[38]

Germany's defeat came a giant step closer when the Allies finally invaded western Europe in June 1944. The 'second front' had figured in German propaganda at various times since 1942 – the St Nazaire and Dieppe raids of that year for instance had been used to illustrate to the world the ferocious reception which any invader could expect. In March 1943, Goebbels had launched another 'second front' campaign designed in part at least to discourage the British from trying their luck, and by early 1944 the official German line was that in the unlikely event of a bridgehead being established in western Europe, the invaders would be driven back into the sea. Both for domestic and foreign audiences, the certainty of severe Allied casualties, and the resultant fear which this certainty excited in Allied minds, continued to receive prominence.[39]

Certainly in Britain, there was little enough optimism that the German defenders of the European continent would prove a pushover, and even in the spring of 1944 the end of the war seemed still a very long way off. For a time, in December 1942, after the victories over Rommel and the Anglo-American landings in North Africa, some very optimistic souls predicted victory by Christmas 1942, while most were more cautious, seeing victory, however, by Christmas 1943 at the latest.[40] At the time of the collapse of Italy in September 1943, the news again raised people's spirits to a very high pitch, and while only a minority now believed that it would all be over by Christmas 1943, the more cautious majority still felt the war would not be over until 1944.[41] Quite naturally, however, these disappointed expectations had a serious long-term effect on morale, particularly as the Italian victory quickly became a hollow one and was not followed by the opening of any meaningful second front. The MoI reported in April 1944 that 'spirits remain at a low level'. Although invasion of

Europe was expected, it was the cause of widespread tension and expectancy. People wanted to get it started, to bring the end of the war nearer. 'There is much war-weariness and tiredness and people are beginning to fear there may be another black-out winter in store.'[42]

When invasion did come, the German wireless once again scooped the Allied propagandists by announcing the landings ahead of the BBC. As has been shown, persistent criticism of BBC news bulletins had been accompanied since the beginning of the war by reports of listeners tuning in to German stations in the hunt for information. Although the BBC had been praised back in 1942 for its overall handling of events in North Africa, there was still criticism of tardiness, padding and over-optimism in BBC broadcasts. Complaints had been received from five MoI regions of delay in the release of news by the BBC: 'We are always behind the German bulletin'.[43] And in 1943, German stories on Allied shipping losses seemed to be gaining credence in some areas in the almost total absence of official British accounts.[44] Similar criticisms were voiced in December 1943 following the Tehran conference, when the BBC was accused of 'getting the news last'. Home Intelligence reported that delays which allowed the German radio to make announcements before the BBC tended to make the public listen to and believe other items in enemy broadcasts.[45] And as the build-up to D-Day intensified throughout the spring and early summer of 1944, and the tension in Britain became almost unbearable, once again much irritation was recorded in Home Intelligence reports that information and news was being withheld, again with predictable consequences. Home Intelligence noted in May 1944, that 'this week there are more complaints of too much repetition and padding (seven Regions), and of the withholding of news (four Regions)'. A commonly expressed view was: 'If you want to know anything, go to the U.S. or German wavelength.'[46]

Even so, the BBC and the press were almost unanimously praised for the way in which they presented the news of the invasion of Europe when it did come. Eye-witness accounts were particularly appreciated, but there was special praise for the BBC's 'hot' recordings. The Corporation's *War Reports* after the 21.00 news were said to be the high spot of the day's news, and were particularly praised for the vivid impressions they gave of battle conditions. Even so, as Home Intelligence wryly noted, 'the fact that the Germans announced the invasion before we did is a matter for some regret'.[47]

Certainly, William Joyce on the evening of 7 June appeared to take considerable pleasure in what he claimed to be the authoritative position of the German wireless system as regards news about events in western Europe. While he seemed to have little concrete information about military developments there, nevertheless he was more that cautiously optimistic that the outcome would be favourable for Germany:

[O]n the first day of the invasion, on D-Day in fact, the world, including Britain, had to accept the reports issued by the German authorities as the sole criterion of events. Not only in neutral capitals, but even in London, the dominant question was, 'What is the latest information given by the German radio?' Naturally it must be allowed that the German Supreme Command is in a superior position with regard to the appreciation of the military situation on the Normandy coast. The defences have been systematically prepared for more than three years. The German commanders have perfected their knowledge of the country and have organised their communications with the thoroughness which the enemy sometimes like to describe as 'Prussian' . . .

[I]n dealing with the German Supreme Command, Mr Churchill is not dealing with a class of junior field officers at Camberley, or with American generals whose experience is compounded of memories from the last war and reminiscences of the exploits of Buffalo Bill . . . On the whole, I can now assure you that Germany's military position is now better than it has been for some time. The enemy in the West has been so obliging as to select the very ground upon which the German Command desired the decisive battle to be fought. Not all at once, not in every skirmish, will the accumulated strength of the German reserves manifest itself. When in due course the campaign can be assessed on the basis of established fact, the optimism which Churchill nurtured amongst his people will sink into ashes and dust. Before us lies a period in which many riddles will be solved and in which much that has been obscure will become clear.[48]

Joyce's colleagues also had plenty to say on the butcher's bill to be paid by the Allies for the landings in Normandy. Edward Bowlby's remarks were intended for British troops in France, but his broadcasts were receivable in Britain too:

The terrific casualties suffered by the Allied Forces in the first ten days of the invasion, which show that the British Government has not the slightest regard for the life of its soldiers, have been compared by the highest German military experts with the useless mass slaughter of the British troops at Paschendaele, in the last war. British troops have been forced into tank traps when storming bridges, in such numbers that literally mountains of dead bodies have to be climbed over by those who are following behind. There is no need for me to give details of this terrible and useless massacre because those of you who are now taking part in the fighting are fully aware of what is going on.[49]

Bowlby and Joyce of course were obsessive anti-Semites who saw in the invasion of Europe the Jews' latest onslaught in their war of hatred against Germany. Eduard Dietze probably regarded himself as more sophisticated, and certainly in his *Views on the News* on 22 June Dietze never once mentioned the Jews, preferring instead to concentrate on Churchill's betrayal of European civilisation to Bolshevism. Nevertheless, Dietze ended his talk by reading with approval a piece of anti-Semitic doggerel composed by William Joyce:

'The Great Day'

Oh, D-Day was a great day in the history of the world,
When the Allied flags of freedom were so bloodily unfurled.
The boys who did the fighting were engulfed in Hell on earth,
Whilst the Jews at home delighting watched their stocks increase in worth.

Oh, D-Day was a grand day on the good old Stock Exchange,
For the paratroops of pockets, well outside the German range.
Like the vultures, they descended on the battlefield of gain;
By the time the day had ended, they'd made sure 'twas not in vain.

Oh, D-Day was a great day, when they gathered up the loot,
These money-grubbing Hebrews who'd never launched a 'chute;
While England's lads were dying amidst the hellish roar
And their heroes' blood was drying on the fatal Norman shore.[50]

In his talk, however, Dietze had also drawn attention to what he called 'the first and mild prelude to German retaliation for the terror raids on German cities . . . roaring across the Channel, spreading death and destruction in southern England and in the metropolis.' The unleashing of the so-called *Vergeltungswaffen*, or 'vengeance weapons', against Britain had been threatened in German propaganda for over a year. In Hitler's November 1943 speech, the Führer had promised that he would retaliate for the British terror bombing of the Reich. 'Even if for the present we cannot reach America', he said, 'thank God that at least one country is near enough for us to tackle, and on that country we are going to concentrate. The hundreds of thousands of our bombed-out people will become the advance guard of revenge.' In consequence, the general public and the authorities in Britain were widely aware and apprehensive about the threat from a German secret weapon. Aerial reconnaissance had revealed experimental works at Peenemunde and later the launch sites in northern France, and plans had been under consideration since May 1943 to deal with the censorship and publicity aspects of the new threat as and when it arrived. Numerous press reports speculating on the new weapon were in circulation in Britain as early as September 1943, and editors were briefed by Herbert Morrison and Brendan Bracken at a secret meeting on 12 October.[51] Such was the delay in the first-use of the weapons, however, that there were suspicions in senior Allied circles that the threats and indeed the sites were part of a gigantic hoax operation designed to divert bombing raids from more significant targets inside Germany.[52]

The MoI sought to play down the effect that this German propaganda might be having, referring, for example, to 'mild speculation and slight uneasiness' in Britain about likely attack by German secret weapons.[53] Others, however, were less sure. Air Marshall Sir Richard Peck reported to the MoI the comments of a friend, senior in the Women's Voluntary Service. 'She meets a large number of people in all walks of life during the course of her work. She finds that this German propaganda about retaliation with a secret weapon is undoubtedly having considerable effect on public morale and, indeed, that alarm is somewhat widespread.'[54] Home Intelligence reported that in the run-up to Christmas 1943, 'in London, it appears that a majority are now giving some thought to the possibility of a retaliatory secret weapon. Indeed many are anxious about it, though there are still a large number who laugh at the idea.' It was rumoured, in fact, that rockets had already fallen, in Park Lane, the Borough High Street and somewhere in the West End. It was reported too that theatre and cinema attendances were thought to have declined.[55]

The arrival of the first of the pilotless aircraft in June 1944 rapidly displaced the Allied invasion of Europe as the main topic of conversation throughout the country. Although most people were fairly confident that a technical answer to the V-1s would be found in time and that their military effectiveness in the long-run would be limited, a considerable minority was less sure. In London itself most people confessed to feeling considerably shaken, despite their calm behaviour. Only at the scenes of some incidents had there been anything approaching panic. The main feeling was one of 'incredible tiredness' from lack of sleep, coupled with nervous anxiety, arising in part from the 'weird and uncanny' nature of the device and in part from the strain of listening for and to their approach. Aerial reprisals had been expected from the Germans, but nothing quite like this.[56]

The weirdness and appalling destructive power of the new weapons were themes consistently reiterated on all of the German stations for the UK. The NBBS prominently featured the latest developments in its *Uncensored News Review* for 17 June:

> The new weapon attacks against this country have continued practically without pause during last night and again today. Our aircraft have been hammering away at the Boulogne area in a determined effort to damage the bases from which the formidable flying destroyers are dispatched . . .
>
> According to some reports, the Flying Frankensteins have no great penetrating power, although they cause great devastation by the unusual amount of blast and heat development. Various types of these winged monsters must have been employed by the enemy, however, as one report from a South Coast town tells us that one of the things flew low over the roof tops then crashed through the wall of a whole row of houses before it exploded. Our experts say that these Flying Frankensteins, from the point of view of effectiveness can best be described as super-mines. One interesting thing which has come to light is that the monsters, after the little light goes out, fly all over the place so that nobody can tell where they will land.[57]

Radio National joined in as well, claiming in its news bulletin on 27 June that Vernon Bartlett MP had been injured in his home in a flying bomb attack on the village of Elstead in Surrey. This small place, said *Radio National*, had received no less than fourteen direct hits in the previous eight days.[58] In July, this particularly scurrilous station had some fun at the expense of the head of Britain's Anti-Aircraft Command:

> And this General Sir Frederick Pile, who's in charge of our defensive action against the flying bombs, must be suffering from piles, for it's about time he jumped up from warming his office seat, and did something about destroying the bloody things. He admits that he's known about this weapon for many months, but as yet has found no effective measure of combating it.[59]

A week after the onslaught had begun, William Joyce was warning of more terrible weapons to come:

> London and southern England have now been under bombardment for more than a week. For nine days, with very little interruption, the V-1 projectiles have been descending on the British capital. May I remind you, the name V-1 has been given to them officially. 'V' is the capital letter of the German word 'Vergeltung', which means 'retaliation', and its use to denote the concept of victory must be familiar to nearly all of my listeners. The very term V-1 implies, of course, that Germany has other new weapons which have not as yet been employed against the enemy. That is a fact, and is a fact which even the British Government is beginning to realise . . .
>
> The emergence of V-1 has provided a surprise for Germany's enemies and I believe they will have several other surprises 'before the autumn leaves fall', if I may borrow a phrase which Mr Churchill used on a certain occasion. Germany's military policy in this war is based not on slogging and on squandering but upon a scientific economy and application of energy, but this is the kind of policy the details of which must never be disclosed before the right time. It can reasonably be assumed that the battle in the East against the Bolshevik foes of civilisation will be hard and fierce and there is every reason to believe that the battle in the West against the capitalist agents of Jewish international finance will attain a climax of violence possibly without precedence. But in the closing rounds of this war it will be seen that Germany has conserved her strength to a degree that will confound her enemies.[60]

An NBBS broadcast, in mid-August, attempted further to alarm the British by talking up the technological miracle which the V-1 represented, and the seemingly limitless capacity of the Germans to dream up new horrors for their unfortunate victims:

> Two new kinds of flying bombs appear to have been introduced by the enemy, according to some of the latest reports from the affected areas. Various people now tell of flying bombs which streak through the sky trailing two lights instead of the usual one. These people say that they observed one of the lights go out whereupon the missiles changed course. Experts say that it is very improbable that the second light has anything to do with the change

of course, unless there is some new development of which we are at present unaware.

Other people now appear to have witnessed flying bombs which can crash through far more buildings before exploding thus causing a great deal more destruction. The damage caused by these bombs would indicate a directional blast of the explosive charge in a backward direction. These missiles, according to experts, may be fitted with an armour-piercing nose similar to those used on shells which are intended to penetrate deeply.[61]

There is some evidence that propaganda of this type may well have been having some effect in Britain. At the end of June, Home Intelligence noted that the habits and effects of the flying bombs were the subject of widespread and exaggerated rumours. London was said to be a 'heap of rubble', damaged much more severely than in the 1940 Blitz. Casualties were said to be immense: 1,200 in Ruislip alone; 600 dead in one area in one day; 1,000 in one dance hall; 300 killed by a bomb near Buckingham Palace. By early July, there were rumoured to be 250,000 casualties in London.[62] No less than 283 flying bombs were said to have fallen in Croydon in one night; 300 were said to have fallen in one area all at once. One bomb was said to have reached Leamington and another to have dropped near Wigan. The rumours were said to be aggravated and often caused by: lack of information resulting from security measures; the tales of evacuees from – and visitors to – London; letters and telegrams from Londoners, in many cases frantically seeking accommodation in safe areas; and German radio accounts. Many people blamed official reticence for leaving the way open for exaggerated accounts and for leading people to accept German claims. And in spite of the continuing good news from France and Russia, spirits in London were said to be lower than at any time in the previous two years.[63] There was even a minority who were said to be ready for 'peace at any price': 'after five years of war, there is a limit to what people can stand'. The official suggestion that morale had not been affected had irritated a number of people considerably. 'Why are the Government telling people that the Germans have failed to upset morale, when everyone who knows people in bombed areas knows this is a lie?' People were beginning to ask why the papers were allowed to publish German claims: 'people who read that the enemy claim that Southampton is in flames may not believe all of it, but they think there may be some basis in fact.' There were, again, reports of increased listening to German broadcasts.[64]

And once again, the secrecy which shrouded casualty figures from flying bomb attacks gave rise to a new wave of Haw-Haw rumours. In June, a rumour was widely circulating that Haw-Haw had threatened that Merton and Morden were to be bombed, a rumour which like so many of its predecessors was groundless.[65] In the same month it was also rumoured in London that the German wireless had claimed that a direct hit was scored on Victoria Station.[66] At the end of June, Major Rowan Robinson, of SHAEF reported that an unnamed gentleman, 'very high up', had reported hearing in a German broadcast in English the names of future targets of the flying bombs. The response from the BBC's Monitoring Service was that no such threats or warnings could be found, but that it was possible that the story had its origins in someone listening to but not monitoring the NBBS, which had mentioned Woolwich Arsenal in connection with a flying bomb.[67] On 1 July, another rumour had it that Aldershot was to have a heavy attack, while another on the same day cited Norwich.[68] In another rumour, Haw-Haw had said that 'he was sorry about the people killed at Highbury Corner, but that he meant to get Cossor's factory'.[69] On 2 July, an official of the Ministry of Home Security rang the Monitoring Service to say that he had met at least four people who had heard in a German broadcast that flying bombs would no longer be directed to London but to the North (specifically Blackpool). Other flying-bomb stories were in circulation in or about Selsdon, Croydon, Streatham, the West End of London, the Midlands, Ashstead, Leatherhead, Welwyn Garden City, Hitchen and the rest of Hertfordshire, Sussex and Newhaven. Haw-Haw was supposed to have said that a small arms factory in Eastern Enfield was to have been bombed but instead a school was hit, and that people of Walthamstow could come out of their shelters as it was now the turn of Enfield.[70]

The whole process of rumour-mongering, whether or not instigated or encouraged by German propaganda, began afresh when the V-2 rocket attacks began in September. The first of the new weapons fell on Chiswick in West London in the early evening of 8 September, with devastating effect on a quiet residential street, although fear and rumour of a 'V-2' had been widespread since July.[71] No official explanation for the terrific explosion was immediately forthcoming, however, and within days, as more rockets fell on the London region, the great majority of unofficial opinion had it that V-2 had arrived. Once more the country was awash with rumour.[72] Rockets were widely rumoured to have fallen at Chiswick, Kew and Dagenham, as well as at Nottingham, Newcastle and Belfast. Explosions were rumoured to be terrific and to cause enormous damage, including craters larger than the Houses of Parliament, hurling debris back across the Channel, blowing everyone and everything in a vast radius to dust. One explosion was rumoured to have killed no fewer than 5,000 people.[73] Official confirmation that rocket attacks were underway was not given until Churchill's announcement on 10 November.

One of the first propaganda items on the new horror weapons appeared at 13.48 on 9 November, on Transocean, the German telegraphic service for European news agencies:

The technical development of modern long-distance warfare has entered a new phase with the employment of V-2. This has been announced by informed quarters in Berlin on Thursday afternoon.

The new German long-distance weapon is certain to be able to cover far greater distances than has appeared likely from former German rocket weapons. It is useless to puzzle over the launching places of German long-distance weapons as it is impossible to discover the extremely carefully and cunningly camouflaged launching ramps of V-1 and V-2. According to reliable information technicians had to overcome greatest difficulties in improving the aim and accuracy as compared with the first German long-distance weapon V-1. On the basis of the experiences made, it proved possible to invent an improved aiming mechanism and an improved apparatus for guiding the new flying dynamite charges.

Rather more alarming details were given out on the Persian service on the same day, and flashed from the Monitoring Service to the Ministry of Home Security:

4. Lisbon. It is reported from London that frightful bodies with enormous explosive power descended on London. It is also said that Euston station was razed to the ground. The British police have thrown a cordon round the damaged parts and nobody is allowed to go near them. All officials have received orders to keep silent on the subject.

5. Berlin. Well informed German circles make the following statement on the development of missile throwing machines:

These machines hurl many missiles at the enemy in one stroke. In less than 10 seconds over 10 tons of high explosives are hurled at the enemy. It can be said that in a single instant a whole train load of high explosives can be showered on the enemy.[74]

The NBBS, with its customary brass-necked remarks about 'the enemy', had its opinions on the new weapon which it shared with listeners on 10 November:

Now that the Prime Minister has personally seen fit to lift the ban on V-2, the *New British Broadcasting Station* from now on will also endeavour to enlighten its listeners on the enemy's long-range rocket attacks against this country. Determined, however, to prevent the enemy receiving information, of which he would otherwise be unaware, this station will comply with the Government's restrictions.

The new fly bomb, mentioned by the enemy a day or two ago, is causing a great amount of talk amongst the neutrals. Nobody seems to know many details about the latest whizz-bang, although the opinion of one Swiss engineer is rather interesting. He points out that if, as some people suspect, the new weapon is the much-vaunted long-range monster rocket, then not only London, but the whole of the British Isles may soon become affected.[75]

The German Telegraphic Service Venus transmitted the following article in English on the 11th:

For three weeks now V-2 which, according to British sources seems to be a kind of monstrous rocket-bomb, has been hurtling silently down out of space to deal death and destruction in addition to that caused by V-1. Naturally, the German authorities are not interested in making public any particulars regarding the construction of V-2. They are content to listen to what the British say about the effect. And the effect is such as to make H. G. Wells wonder whether one of his 'Things to Come' hasn't prematurely come to life in Germany. The most remarkable thing about V-2 seems to be its enormous speed which exceeds that of sound waves. The result is that V-2 crashes down without preliminary warning. There is no way of defence, no alarm system to enable a defence if such a thing is possible to get into action. A period of horrible and silent death has begun for Great Britain. England is reaping the reward for its merciless slaughter of German civilians and countless German towns and cities. And there will be other V weapons even more mysterious and horrible.[76]

As late as the end of February 1945, the NBBS was still trying to whip up anxiety about the threat from V-2, and in its final fling in March, introduced yet another new terror weapon:

The one man bomb is the latest surprise to be sprung on our forces in the west by German scientists, and according to all reports it has a nasty effect. The bomb is piloted to a great height and when over our lines is aimed downwards on its objective. The pilot drops by parachute. The enemy may be preparing to use these weapons on (?a big scale). All that is known is that the bomb is two or three times bigger than a V-projectile.[77]

Again, the question needs to be addressed whether this type of material was having any effect in the UK. It might be thought that with the war so evidently running against Germany, Nazi propaganda of any sort was more or less irrelevant by this stage. It might also be argued that the material on V-2 especially, as in the NBBS broadcast cited above, was not particularly well-handled. The propagandists obviously knew next to nothing about the true nature of the weapon, and rather silly talks about 'whizz-bangs' and 'fly-bombs' seriously underestimated the truly terrifying potential of this awesome weapon. On the other hand, Home Intelligence reports indicate that by the end of 1944, the public optimism of the late summer had evaporated, in particular after the failure of the British expedition at Arnhem. It was noted in November that 'people are said to be settling down to the old routine, as before D-Day, and resigning themselves to another war winter and the possibility of another war spring – a depressing prospect for many.'[78] Later in the month, 'war weariness and lack of interest in the fighting' were fairly widely reported.[79] Home Intelligence noted in December 1944 that 'people are generally described as depressed', keenly aware of 'the likelihood of the war in Europe continuing for many more months'. Depressing too were 'signs of disagreement between the Allies, the prospect of endless unrest in Europe and – not least – the housing and unemployment situations at home'. Rumours of the effects of rocket attacks continued, as did the general belief that rockets were causing a lot of slaughter and damage and that the truth was being withheld or minimised.[80] As we have seen too, Home Intelligence had noted during the V-1 and V-2 raids that there was a minority in the UK by 1944 who were ready for peace 'at any price'.

However, it is important not to overdo the significance of the 'peace at any price' brigade, whose numbers even during the worst of the renewed blitzing seem to have been quite small. Home Intelligence also noted that at the time of the July 1944 assassination attempt upon Hitler:

> People are unanimous that there must be no negotiated peace, no matter what moves are made inside Germany for the overthrow of the Nazis. They feel that now is the time to be most careful, or the Germans will trick us again; the German generals are as dangerous as the Nazis; and our best line is to go on hitting hard again and again. Only a complete military defeat of Germany can convince the German people they have really lost the war.[81]

Hatred and bitterness against Germany and the Germans was very intense by the summer of 1944, feelings only aggravated and intensified by the V-1 and V-2 raids, and by renewed revelations about German atrocities and barbarities in occupied Europe. In September it was noted that 'the recent revelations about the "camps of annihilation" at Lublin and Maidenek have staggered people; some find them too disgusting to read. The only other reactions are increased hatred and an intensified desire for retribution. Their truth is not doubted.'[82] Rather than wanting to settle for a negotiated peace with the Germans by 1944, many Britons were demanding their total annihilation.[83] It is hard to see that propaganda could do much to mitigate the effects of a hatred of such intensity.

Notes

1 Goebbels, *Tagebücher*, entry for 28 February 1943.
2 Semmler, *Man Next to Hitler*, p. 76. Semler's name was incorrectly spelled by the publishers of his diary.
3 Semmler, *Man Next to Hitler*, pp. 76–7.
4 The actual number of bodies was around 4,000.
5 PRO WO 204/6225, *Summary of Psychological Reactions*, 5 April 1943.
6 PRO WO 204/6225, *Summary of Psychological Reactions*, 16 April 1943.
7 BRES IEFUK 22.30 15.04.43.
8 PRO WO 193/453, *Morale Report – May to July 1943*.
9 PRO INF 1/292, *Home Intelligence Weekly*, 3 June 1943.
10 PRO INF 1/292, *Home Intelligence Weekly*, 26 November 1941.
11 PRO INF 1/292, *Home Intelligence Weekly*, 1 October 1942.
12 PRO INF 1/292, *Home Intelligence Weekly*, 11 November 1943.
13 PRO INF 1/292, *Home Intelligence Weekly*, 22 April 1943.
14 PRO INF 1/292, *Home Intelligence Weekly*, 6 May 1943.
15 PRO INF 1/292, *Home Intelligence Weekly*, 21 January 1943.
16 PRO HO 199/394B, *Notes for the Week*, 5 April 1943.
17 PRO INF 1/282, *Home Intelligence Weekly*, 14 October 1943.
18 PRO INF 1/292, *Home Intelligence Weekly*, 18 February 1943.
19 PRO INF 1/292, *Home Intelligence Weekly*, 11 March 1943.
20 PRO INF 1/292, *Home Intelligence Weekly*, 25 March 1943.
21 PRO INF 1/292, *Home Intelligence Weekly*, 15 April 1943.
22 PRO INF 1/292, *Home Intelligence Weekly*, 6 May 1943.
23 PRO INF 1/292, *Home Intelligence Weekly*, 26 August 1943.
24 RN IEFUK 20.50 21.10.43.

25 CAL IEFUK 16.30 31.12.42.
26 PRO INF 1/292, *Home Intelligence Weekly*, 7 January 1943.
27 PRO INF 1/292, *Home Intelligence Weekly*, 26 November 1942.
28 PRO INF 1/292, *Home Intelligence Weekly*, 24 February 1944.
29 PRO INF 1/292, *Home Intelligence Weekly*, 2 June 1944.
30 PRO INF 1/292, *Home Intelligence Weekly*, 16 November 1944.
31 PRO INF 1/292, *Home Intelligence Weekly*, 6 May 1943.
32 PRO INF 1/292, *Home Intelligence Weekly*, 3 June 1943.
33 CAL IEFUK 22.30 29.7.43.
34 Balfour, *Propaganda in War*, pp. 275–6.
35 PRO FO 898 184, PWE, *German Propaganda and the Retreat in Russia in 1943*, 10 February 1944.
36 PRO WO 204/6312, *German Propaganda and German Summary for week ending 2nd January, 1944.*
37 Cited in Bergmeier and Lotz, *Hitler's Airwaves*, p. 52.
38 PRO WO 204/6312, *German Propaganda and the German, Week Ending 16th January 1944.*
39 PRO WO 204/6312, *German Propaganda and the German, Week Ending 16th January 1944.*
40 PRO INF 1/292, *Home Intelligence Weekly*, 3 December 1942.
41 PRO INF 1/292, *Home Intelligence Weekly*, 16 September 1943.
42 PRO INF 1/282, *Home Intelligence Weekly*, 11 April 1944.
43 PRO INF 1/292, *Home Intelligence Weekly*, 24 December 1942.
44 PRO INF 1/292, *Home Intelligence Weekly*, 7 January 1943.
45 PRO INF 1/292, *Home Intelligence Weekly*, 16 December 1943.
46 PRO INF 1/292, *Home Intelligence Weekly*, 11 March 1944.
47 PRO INF 1/292, *Home Intelligence Weekly*, 15 June 1944.
48 DES IEFUK 22.30 7.6.44.
49 DES IEFUK 19.30 20.6.44.
50 DES IEFUK 22.30 22.6.44.
51 PRO INF 1/967.
52 George, *Propaganda Analysis*, p. 141.
53 PRO INF 1/282, *Home Intelligence Weekly*, 25 November 1943.
54 PRO INF 1/282, *Peck to Radcliffe*, 26 November 1943.
55 PRO INF 1/292, *Home Intelligence Weekly*, 9 December 1943.
56 PRO INF 1/292, *Home Intelligence Weekly*, 22 June 1944.
57 NBBS IEFE 21.30 17.6.44.
58 RN IEFE 20.55 27.6.44.
59 RN IEFE 20.55 8.7.44.
60 DES IEFUK 22.30 24.6.44.
61 PRO HO 199/466.
62 PRO INF 1/292, *Home Intelligence Weekly*, 6 July 1944.
63 PRO INF 1/292, *Home Intelligence Weekly*, 29 June 1944.
64 PRO INF 1/292, *Home Intelligence Weekly*, 6 July 1944.
65 PRO HO 199/466, *Jellicoe to Monitoring Service*, 28 June 1944.
66 PRO HO 199/466, *Monitoring Service to Home Security*, 28 June 1944. No mention of a direct hit on Victoria was actually made on the German wireless, although hits were claimed on Waterloo Station and High Holborn.
67 PRO HO 199/466, *Monitoring Service to Home Security*, 29 June 1944.
68 PRO HO 199/466, *Jellicoe to Monitoring Service*, 1 July 1944.
69 PRO HO 199/466, *Monitoring Service to Home Security*, 6 July 1944.

70 PRO HO 199/466, *Monitoring Service to Home Security*, various, 2–28 July 1944.

71 PRO INF 1/292, *Home Intelligence Weekly*, 3 August 1944.

72 PRO HO 262/15, *Daily Report on London Opinion*, 16 September 1944.

73 PRO INF 1/292, *Home Intelligence Weekly*, 21 September 1944.

74 PRO HO 199/374.

75 NBBS IEFE 21.30 10.11.44.

76 PRO HO 199/374.

77 NBBS IEFE 21.30 8.3.45. The station did not explain the likely fate of the pilot, dropping to earth in the wake of his massive bomb.

78 PRO INF 1/292, *Home Intelligence Weekly*, 2 November 1944.

79 PRO INF 1/292, *Home Intelligence Weekly*, 9 November 1944.

80 PRO INF 1/292, *Home Intelligence Weekly*, 21 December 1944.

81 PRO INF 1/292, *Home Intelligence Weekly*, 27 July 1944.

82 PRO INF 1/292, *Home Intelligence Weekly*, 7 September 1944.

83 PRO INF 1/292, *Home Intelligence Weekly*, 31 August 1944.

7

An Assessment of Germany's Wireless Propaganda for the UK in the Second World War

William Joyce continued to broadcast from Germany to Britain until 30 April 1945. Until the very end, he continued to tell his listeners that Germany was undefeated and would recover the initiative, but to warn them that if Germany did collapse, 'the Soviet colossus' would devour all Europe, including the British Isles. The death of President Roosevelt provided only a temporary fillip, but in his last broadcast talk, Joyce finally admitted that the end of hostilities was in sight. The end, however, when it came, would bring neither security nor prosperity, and no more than a temporary respite from war. There loomed upon the horizon the growing threat to British interests from Bolshevik Imperialism:

> How modest, how harmless does Germany's request for the return of Danzig seem in contrast to the immense acquisitions of the Soviet Union and the further ambitions of the Kremlin. Stalin is not content with Poland, Finland, the Baltic States, Rumania, Bulgaria, Hungary and Eastern Slovakia. He wants the whole of Central Europe, with Norway, Turkey and Persia thrown in. And if these territories fall to him, his lust for aggrandisement will only be stimulated further . . .
>
> It might be said that on 31st August 1939, the atmosphere of Europe was explosive, but today it is supercharged with explosives of the highest power. The terrible war through which we have been passing is but the prelude to a struggle of a far more decisive nature.

Stalin, said Joyce, now constituted the greatest threat to peace that has existed in modern times. The Soviet Union menaced the security of the whole world. By contrast, Britain's victories were barren:

> They leave her poor and they leave her people hungry; they leave her bereft of the markets and the wealth that she possessed six years ago. But, above all, they leave her with an immensely greater problem than she had then. We are nearing the end of one phase in Europe's history, but the next will be no happier. It will be grimmer, harder and perhaps bloodier. And now I ask you earnestly, can Britain survive? I am profoundly convinced that without German help she cannot.[1]

Hyperbole notwithstanding, Joyce was right. Scarcely had the European war ended, than the Cold War began, or rather it recommenced, having been temporarily suspended until the common Nazi enemy was thoroughly crushed. Britain's economic position was now quite dire and never again could she regain her prewar global position in a world dominated by 'the rapacious giants of US imperialism and Soviet Bolshevism'. But what good did it do Joyce or his German masters to be right – in this respect at any rate – in the final analysis? Was anything achieved for Germany by the tens of thousands of hours of English-language broadcasts from Berlin, and the tens of thousands of marks spent by the Germans on producing them? Before addressing this question directly, perhaps it is worth summarising the findings of this study. We begin with the organisation itself.

As was made apparent in Chapter 1, to talk of German wireless propaganda in terms of what 'Lord Haw-Haw' did or did not achieve disguises the fact that Haw-Haw was not a person at all, but a fairly large and mixed collection of individuals of varying shades of ability and conviction. F. W. Ogilvie described Haw-Haw as 'a well-informed syndicate', although this probably overestimates the group's coherence and the extent of its access to information. In the course of this study it has been possible to identify about forty British persons about whom enough is known to make positive judgements on their motivations in pursuing the extraordinary step of traitorously broadcasting propaganda in wartime. Perhaps a quarter of them worked for the Germans because of prior political conviction. The rest did so from a variety of more or less discreditable motives of a self-serving nature. Their behaviour was hardly noble, but in the circumstances is scarcely inexplicable. Given the scale of Britain's predicament in 1940, and the large numbers of British prisoners in German hands, the wonder is that the number of volunteers was so small. Harder to explain is the shocking inconsistencies in the scale of penalties meted out to the broadcasters by the British authorities after the war. Severe terms of penal servitude and imprisonment were imposed upon those members of the Armed Forces who had assisted the enemy by broadcasting, although none of them faced a capital charge.[2] The civilians, on the other hand, received an extraordinary range of punishments. Some were not so much as charged when it would seem that they had committed identical offences to others who received stiff sentences. The contrast between the fates of Lander and Banning is especially bemusing. The treatment of the better known broadcasters, however, reveals the extent of political calculation behind an ostensibly independent judicial process, and whatever one's opinion of the individuals involved, suggests that a number of serious injustices were done. John Amery was probably as guilty of treason as it is possible to be, although there were suggestions that the execution of this well-connected but semi-deranged individual had as much a political as a judicial motivation. Baillie-Stewart, already notorious and unpopular in Britain, received a harsh sentence under the Defence Regulations, despite the acknowledgement that he had long since abjured his British citizenship. The wholly British nonentities, like John Ward or Dorothy Eckersley or James Clark, were leniently treated by contrast. The Joyce case is most controversial of all. The general public wanted him hanged, but there were those who felt that it was a shameful act to execute an American for acts committed in Germany on the pretext that he had travelled on an illegally obtained British passport. A member of the government prosecuted him and new case law was made to hang him. The contrasting failure to take any action at all against Edward Bowlby on the grounds that he was 'scarcely a public figure like Haw-Haw' reveals the final irony that Joyce the propagandist was hanged by the British in an act of political propaganda.

The evidence produced here on the functioning of the English-language services is consistent with the views of many historians on the arbitrary, internally antagonistic and chaotic nature of government and administration in the Third Reich. Organisational problems included the ramshackle systems of recruitment and supervision of staff; the tiers of conflicting hierarchies and authorities; the system by which *Themen* would be dribbled down from an unpredictable and not-well informed Minister, through levels of partly informed middle-ranking officials to the wholly uninformed jobbing propagandists, the majority of whom had no experience of propaganda work and little enough aptitude for it. The near total absence of mechanisms for the receipt (let alone the analysis) of feedback from Britain on the impact of propaganda, and the true nature of social and economic conditions there, was a serious difficulty which was never overcome.

As regards the content of Nazi wireless propaganda for Britain, four distinct phases have been identified here. In the first period, between the outbreak of war and the attack on Norway, the purpose of propaganda seemed to be to force the British to bring the war to an end by negotiating with Germany. The method to achieve this was to isolate them internationally and to undermine the solidarity of their home front by exposing and humiliating them with their history of duplicity and cruelty and the reality of their present social problems. Nowhere, however, is there any evidence that a well thought-out plan of attack had been drawn up. Instead, Goebbels' officials reacted to his off-the-cuff commands that a particular issue should be pressed or soft-pedalled, and so the command was passed on down the line. However, it is not clear that it was the aim seriously to hound the British to the negotiating table, since while Hitler talked peace he planned for war. Goebbels' view seemed to be that since Britain and Germany were at war, German propaganda must lacerate her enemy. The easiest targets were Britain's financial and imperial power and their contrast with her domestic social problems. It is not hard to understand therefore the emphasis on British plutocracy and German socialism in this period of the war. In the second phase, which ran from the spring of 1940 until the spring of 1941, propaganda was used directly as a weapon in support of armed assault. Goebbels believed that his wireless propaganda had undermined the French and that the same could be done for the British. The freedom stations were seen as an integral part of this campaign to disrupt the home front, through a campaign of terrorism by radio about starvation and invasion over the summer months, and another about starvation and bombing raids over the autumn and winter. Again though, it is not clear if a propaganda campaign was seriously intended to 'soften up' the British in advance of invasion, since it is not clear if invasion was ever seriously contemplated. Either way the aim of the propaganda was the same – to weaken British resolve to continue the fight by what we have called 'disintegration' propaganda, aimed at separating governed from government, class from class, and Gentile from Jew.

Hitler had given up on the British by the spring of 1941 and thereafter his attentions focused on the Soviet Union. Propaganda for Britain entered its third phase, and again the target was obvious. Churchill's alliance with Russia, as he himself cheerfully admitted, was an act of barefaced expediency, and it was easy now to portray him and Britain as the enemy of Christianity and the betrayer of European culture. Germany and Italy were creating a New Order in Europe, from which the British were to be permanently excluded. Not surprisingly, Goebbels seems to have lost interest in propaganda for the British at this point, and in consequence it merely continued in the same vein, more or less without direction. The fact that the freedom stations – which could only have been expected to be temporary operations – continued long after they had been rendered obsolete by events seems to prove the point. The *Christian Peace Movement* was still broadcasting in 1942, *Radio Caledonia* until 1943, and *Workers' Challenge* and the NBBS until 1945.

After Stalingrad, Germany was on the defensive. Hitler hoped to prolong German resistance until the Allies split asunder and he could come to a negotiated peace with the West, or until his secret weapons could come to Germany's rescue. As we have seen, Goebbels' task was to open this split in the ranks of the Allies by whipping up anxieties at the coming Bolshevisation of Europe. In this its fourth and last phase, the propagandists endlessly repeated the same story, that through his alliance with Jewish-Bolshevism, Churchill was leading Britain to her doom.

How does one begin – and the attempt must be made – to assess the quality of six years of daily radio broadcasts? As we have seen, opinions were divided during the war as to the quality of propaganda broadcasts from Germany – this is still so. One historian has recently dismissed them as 'Haw-Haw's strident pulpit-propaganda' in contrast to what she sees as the success of Priestley's low-key broadcasts and Churchill's 'grandiose radio orations'.[3] As has been shown throughout this study, however, Joyce was one broadcaster among many, and to use the nickname in this way merely obscures that fact. Eduard Dietze was probably a better broadcaster than William Joyce. His talks were well-delivered, sober in style, seemingly objective and seemingly reasonable. Edward Bowlby's talks were well-enough written and his broadcasting style was excellent. He had a good radio voice and used it to effect, although the content of his talks was based upon an obsessive and maniacal anti-Semitism which outdid even Joyce's overpowering fanaticism. Norman Baillie-Stewart was a success as a broadcaster in the early days of the *RRG*'s English service, and was highly regarded by the professional listeners at the BBC. He made no impact, however, on his return to broadcasting in 1942. John Amery had no talent for writing or broadcasting and, as we have seen, the chief impact of his talks seems to have been to excite sympathy for his parents. None of the other broadcasters on the official stations made any impression in the UK. From the freedom stations, Vincent Lander and Leonard Banning seemed to be fairly accomplished broadcasters and propagandists, albeit wholly untrained. Most of the rest of the *Concordia* crew, however, were weak and rather pathetic figures who spent much of their time in Germany trying to shirk their duties. Despite the occasional attempt by the British newspapers to create new 'Haw-Haws' from the cast of characters paraded on these stations, none of them ever rose above the level of obscurity in the UK.

Moreover, that Joyce merely indulged in strident ranting is as much a myth as the notion that the 'Haw-Haw' character was cleverly dreamed up by British counter-propagandists to undermine German broadcasts. Certainly it would be quite wrong to underestimate Joyce's intellectual gifts. He was a highly intelligent, articulate and well-read individual who by all accounts could be personable, thoughtful and humourous. And when he chose to keep his feet upon the ground, Joyce was capable of producing radio talks of high quality and cleverness. But there was another, deeply unattractive Joyce – the bullying fascist, the obsessive anti-Semite, the near-crackpot conspiracy theorist, whose bizarre ideas and flights of fancy must at times have made him sound absurd to all but the most disaffected Briton.

It should be recalled too that the German broadcasts consisted not just of propaganda talks, but of news and musical programmes, although the latter have not been considered here. As this study has shown, throughout the duration of the war, British listeners tuned in to German broadcasts for news which they felt was being withheld by the BBC. As we have seen, time and again the German stations were ahead of the BBC with major news stories, or produced fuller details than were available from British stations. The freedom stations had no regard for the truth and would lie when it was convenient to do so, but the official English-language stations produced news material which was largely true, probably to the same extent that the BBC's own domestic news was largely true.

Moreover, the BBC's self-image as the bearer of the beacon of truth, much admired throughout occupied Europe, was not one widely held in wartime Britain. Again and again we have had cause to cite here bitter complaints about the inadequacy of the BBC's news service, about its tardiness, about padding, about incomplete and over-optimistic reports. These attacks upon the BBC were not confined to the opening weeks of the war, as is often suggested, but continued through every major campaign until D-Day and beyond. Indeed, it is ironic that probably one of the more significant achievements of the German broadcasts to the UK is that they forced the BBC and the MoI to treat the British public with more openness and more respect.

It has been argued here also that the traditional interpretation of the extent of listening to German broadcasts needs to be revised, and there are good reasons for doubting the massive listening figures produced in 1939 and early 1940. There is no disputing that large numbers of people in Britain did tune in to the

Hamburg broadcasts, encouraged by the weak performance of the BBC and by the popular press which informed the public that they were missing out on a great national joke. But the methods of data gathering, and the national atmosphere in which they were gathered, almost certainly functioned to exaggerate the numbers tuning in at this stage. On the other hand, the traditional interpretation seriously underestimates the extent of listening after the phoney war had ended. It has been suggested here that the BBC's methods of data gathering were probably inadequate, and that, as Robert Silvey recognised in time, he faced the insurmountable problem of the unwillingness of the public to admit to listening to German stations at a time when it was regarded as unpatriotic to do so. Home Intelligence reports were produced from a much wider and more diverse information base than the BBC's, and were produced with greater regularity. They provide consistent evidence that listening to German stations did not cease in early 1940, but continued throughout the entire war and was geographically widespread. And it seems quite natural that this should be so. After the novelty of hearing the enemy speak in one's own front room had worn off, that section of the public who followed the war in detail, or who had an interest in current affairs, would be sure to want to listen in to German stations as a complement to the BBC rather than an alternative. This was especially true at times of particularly heightened excitement, and whether the news was good or bad, evidence would quickly emerge of increased listening to Germany. It is difficult, probably impossible, to produce any meaningful estimate of the numbers of listeners which the official German stations may have had at any given moment. However, the regularity and widespread nature of references in Home Intelligence and other reports suggests very strongly that estimates of 'negligible' listening produced by the BBC are far off the mark.

Of course, it is one thing to state that the German stations had an audience in Britain. It is another to argue from that that they succeeded in their intention of disrupting the British home front. However, as has been emphasised here, the traditional picture of wartime Britain is largely mythical. This is not to deny that the British showed courage, determination and resolution in periods of immense hardship – that they certainly did. However, at times, spirits in Britain were very low, class antagonism was very sharp, the government was deeply unpopular and Jews were widely disliked. Nor is it the case that low morale was confined to the Phoney War, and that the 'Dunkirk spirit' united the nation thereafter. There were periods in 1940 in 1942 and even in 1944 when a 'peace at any price' contingent was vocal in Britain, a group to which Nazi propaganda made a direct appeal. Anti-Jewish feeling was enduring and ubiquitous, providing a potentially responsive constituency for Nazi anti-Semitism. And there was widespread concern in Britain from as early as 1940, that after the war there would be a return to the depression and unemployment of the 1930s, again a theme regularly featured on the German wireless. In addition, from as early as 1942 and 1943, there were fears that after the war there would be serious tensions between Britain and the USA on the one hand, and Russia on the other, or that Britain would be dominated by America. Time and again, these same themes appeared in Nazi propaganda.

Is there any evidence that German wireless broadcasts had any effect in encouraging these sentiments? Did the stations achieve anything to justify the Germans' efforts in creating and maintaining them for the six long years of war? In the end, it is necessary to measure the success of propaganda against the hopes and expectations of its originators. Goebbels himself once said that 'if a brand of propaganda has won over the circle of people which it wanted to persuade, then I imagine it was good; if not, then I imagine it was bad.'[4] By these brutally simplistic criteria, German propaganda to Britain was bad propaganda since morale on the British home front did not break. However, in his less public moments, Goebbels was sufficient of a realist to expect less than total success or total failure. But what were Goebbels' expectations of his propaganda for Britain?

In the early part of the war they were certainly high, and he managed to convince himself that Lord Haw-Haw was brilliantly successful. Repeatedly he referred to the excellence and potency of 'our broadcasts' and, like everybody else, allowed himself to be swept along by the Haw-Haw myth. 'Our English radio broadcasts', he noted, 'are now being taken with deadly seriousness in England. Lord Haw-Haw's name is on everybody's lips.'[5] A few days later he wrote, 'Our broadcasts to England are having a great effect, according to all reports. We operate in tune with the principle: constant dripping wears away the stone.'[6] Hitler too was impressed: 'The Führer praises our radio propaganda, which has recently achieved some magnificent successes abroad. We concentrate completely on news and on objectivity in that area. This brings the most effective results.'[7] In March 1940, Goebbels again noted: 'I tell the Führer about Lord Haw-Haw's success, which is really astonishing. He praises our foreign propaganda'.[8] And that the material being produced by his foreign language services and the freedom stations was hitting home, Goebbels was in no doubt. Later in March he noted in his diary that:

> The indignation which we've been assiduously whipping up in Paris and London is growing. Lord Haw-Haw is the great spokesman for this consternation. Thus is the disunity amongst the English cleverly encouraged. This is all to the good and I encourage this tendency. We work so much more successfully in the background, and this is especially so of our secret English station, which still hasn't been unmasked as our work. Our foreign propaganda goes from strength to strength. We mustn't expect results too soon, but steady drops will wear away this stone too. We must be patient and with grim determination, concentrate our attentions on the single spot.[9]

But it was for Joyce that the Minister reserved his highest praise. 'The English are lying to the heavens again', he noted in February 1940, 'but our Lord Haw-Haw is always ready with an answer for them.'[10] In August, after reading another 'outstanding essay' by Haw-Haw, Goebbels wrote, 'That boy's all right! And besides totally incorruptible. He genuinely wants to serve

England.'[11] A few days later, upon reading a few more of Joyce's efforts, he described them as 'as always, excellent.'[12] And shortly after the heavy air raids on London had begun, Goebbels wrote that 'Lord Haw-Haw is magnificent. I read a few of his talks, which lay out the position for the English without a single psychological error.'[13] He was, wrote the Minister, 'the best polemicist in our foreign language services. One reads his talks with the greatest pleasure. We could do with a few leader-writers like him for our domestic press.'[14] Later on (in March 1941) after Göring had expressed great admiration for Haw-Haw's work, Goebbels described him as 'the best horse in my stable'.[15] On 1 September 1944, William Joyce was awarded the Cross of War Merit, First Class, for his services to Germany.[16]

Of course Goebbels, intelligent as he was, was not beyond self-delusion about the effectiveness of his propaganda machine. Given the lack of really accurate intelligence information about conditions in the UK, the Minister and his fellow propagandists had to rely upon speculation, supposition, extrapolation and wishful-thinking about the success of their material there. The continued references throughout Goebbels' diaries and in his ministerial conferences to British, American and neutral press reports reveals the weakness of German intelligence-gathering, as does the fact that only one case has ever emerged of a British resident attempting seriously to act as an agent for Haw-Haw in the UK.[17] In the absence of much evidence to the contrary, Goebbels believed Haw-Haw to be a magnificent success in 1940 and 1941, because he wanted to believe it. With the help of the British press, Joyce had made himself a 'world celebrity', as Goebbels called him, and night after night he churned out the polemics which the Minister would have written were he in Joyce's place.[18]

And it is true that in a strictly academic or rhetorical sense, many of the talks by Joyce, Dietze and some others were excellent propaganda. The exposures of Britain's military and economic weaknesses, her hypocrisies and her social problems, were often cleverly written and powerfully delivered with verve and searing wit. However, propaganda does not operate in a vacuum. Telling as many of the broadcasters' arguments may have been, the fact remained that even the least sophisticated Briton knew the broadcasters were German Nazis and their enemies. Goebbels was simply wrong to state that Joyce set out the position for the British 'without a single psychological error'. To be humiliated and exposed by an enemy will not necessarily endear him to you, or make you want to negotiate with him. The process may on the contrary merely make you angry, especially so if he is raining bombs on your cities at the same time. Joyce's repeated references to Britain in 1940 as 'this doomed island', to the Home Guard as 'a guerrilla rabble' and to Churchill as a 'Cockney guttersnipe' are likely to have generated as much resentment as fear.

But the German propagandists had a greater problem still than this in that for nearly the whole war their central message was fundamentally repugnant to the majority of the British people. In the first phase of the war, Germany's propaganda of social criticism was regarded by many Britons as quite telling, but the pre-war years of Anglo-German tension – to say nothing of residual antagonisms from the Great War – could not be so easily erased. In any case, Germany had probably alienated the pro-Hitler constituency by her pact with Russia, and no use could be made of the very widespread resentment against the Soviet Union following her brutal assault on 'the gallant little Finns'. In the second phase, the message of the broadcasts could be reduced to the simple formula, 'Surrender or Die'. This threat was accompanied from September 1940 by the bombing of British cities which generated a hatred for the German masses which did not exist in 1939. In the third phase, the theme was anti-Bolshevism, but the Soviet Union was now immensely popular in Britain, and the revelation of the butchery of the Polish officers at Katyn reverberated on the Poles not the Russians. In the fourth phase, German propaganda consisted of more threats and more insults, accompanied by more bombing. By this time, feelings against the Germans were so strong that even the attempt to murder Hitler by his own generals excited no friendly feelings towards them.

One other major problem was insurmountable. There is no doubt that in the extraordinary circumstances of war, the most fantastic claims and boasts will be believed by some individuals at times of crisis or sudden panic. However, if propaganda is to be effective on a longer-term basis it must be credible, and be seen to be at least in line with objective reality. Threats by a terrifying enemy that 'tomorrow you die' may indeed induce panic and even cries of surrender. However, if the same enemy threatens that 'tomorrow you die' every day for a year, the threat is seen as hollow and may even be used against the threatener. So it was with Nazi propaganda for Britain, and the chief culprit was not William Joyce, nor even Joseph Goebbels, but Hitler himself, whose frequent forays into propaganda often proved unwise if not disastrous. It was Hitler who was responsible for the patently absurd claim that the sinking of the *Athenia* was decided upon personally by Churchill. It was Hitler who in his Reichstag speech in July 1940 spoke as a victor, as if the war were already won – a claim no doubt effective in bolstering Germany's short-term confidence but a foolish error in retrospect. Hitler it was who in September 1940 promised the British that 'he was coming' for them – frightening for Britons, amusing for Germans in the short-term, the empty threats of a bully and a braggart in the long run. Exactly a year later, in September 1941, it was Hitler who claimed that the Russians were beaten and that the war against the Soviet Union was as good as over. While Hitler insisted on offering so many hostages to fortune, and fortune had turned against Germany, no amount of skilful propaganda from Goebbels' staff could restore Germany's credibility in the eyes of the world.

Of course, it was not necessary for Britons to become wholly converted to National Socialism for Nazi propaganda to have had some success. Any promotion of national disunity, of anti-Semitism, of anti-American sentiment or fear of the spread of Bolshevism would have been regarded by the Germans as a point well scored. As we have seen, the official British view as relayed to the general public was that the sturdy British were proof against Hitler's propaganda tricks. In private, however – in 1940 certainly, but at many other times as well – numerous individuals in official and semi-official capacities were alarmed at the impact which these 'skilful and highly dangerous' German broadcasts might be having on public opinion and the morale of British forces. Moreover, their concern was centred on the working classes, who were assumed to be most susceptible to Nazi propaganda. Here though was something of a self-fulfilling prophesy. The middle classes assumed that the uneducated workers would fall victim to clever propaganda, and when the workers grumbled and complained, and when morale sagged, the middle classes assumed they were right – the workers had fallen victim to Nazi propaganda. However, what seems more likely is that the average member of the working classes had no need of Lord Haw-Haw or any other propagandist to make him at times disgruntled and discontented. After all, the war into which his leaders had taken him had been one disaster after another until the end of 1942, the workers were the class bearing the brunt of the suffering, and it was only too easy to believe that when it was all over there would be a return to the social and economic depressions of the 1930s. However, there is little enough evidence that the working classes were particularly susceptible to German machinations. It is unlikely that the average British worker often had the stomach for a fifteen-minute talk on the capitalist manipulation of the international economy or the intricacies of Soviet-Polish relations or the Jewish domination of Wall Street. The letter-writers to the MoI were overwhelmingly middle class. Haw-Haw's audience probably was too.

Some thirty-odd years after Joyce's execution, James Cameron wrote that Lord Haw-Haw could at times be

> horribly persuasive [because] he was not a ranting Goebbels or a screeching Hitler; it was clear that he knew his way around the British psyche and could exploit it by translating the horrible Nazi dogma into something he reckoned might reasonably be accepted in English suburbia, and I dare say sometimes was.[19]

It would indeed be extraordinary if all the thousands of hours and millions of words of propaganda which Goebbels addressed to the British affected not a soul. But all in all, the British were probably too stubborn, too phlegmatic, too pig-headed to be propagandised by Germans in wartime. It was probably their pig-headedness which saved them.

Notes

1 DES IEFUK 21.30 30.4.45.
2 It will be recalled that a combination of contractual and judicial technicalities resulted in Roy Purdy's being charged with treason, a fact reflected in the relative shortness of his time served in prison.
3 Nicholas, *Echo of War*, p. 60.
4 Cited in Bramsted in *The Australian Outlook*, p. 69.
5 *Goebbels' Diaries*, Taylor (ed.), entry for 6 January 1940.
6 *Goebbels' Diaries*, Taylor (ed.), entry for 17 January 1940.

7 *Goebbels' Diaries*, Taylor (ed.), entry for 31 January 1940.
8 Goebbels, *Tagebücher*, entry for 15 March 1940.
9 Goebbels, *Tagebücher*, entry for 16 March 1940.
10 Goebbels, *Tagebücher*, entry for 6 February 1940.
11 Goebbels, *Tagebücher*, entry for 22 August 1940.
12 Goebbels, *Tagebücher*, entry for 26 August 1940.
13 Goebbels, *Tagebücher*, entry for 11 September 1940.
14 Goebbels, *Tagebücher*, entry for 22 September 1940.
15 Goebbels, *Tagebücher*, entry for 29 March 1941.
16 PRO HO 45/22405.
17 For details on the case of Anna Wolkoff, see Fleming, *Invasion 1940*, pp. 126–7.
18 Goebbels, *Tagebücher*, entry for 26 April 1940.
19 *The Manchester Guardian*, 19 February 1979.

Bibliography

Published Primary

Banse, Ewald. *Germany, Prepare for War! From the German 'Raum und Volk im Weltkriege'*, trans. Alan Harris. Lovat Dickson Limited, London, 1934.

Baumann, Gerhard. *Grundlagen und Praxis der internationalen Propaganda*. Essen Verlag Verlagenstalt, Essen, 1941.

Childs, Harold L. and Whitton, John B. (eds) *Propaganda by Short-Wave*. Princeton University Press, Princeton, NJ, 1942.

Farago, Ladislas and Gittler, L. F. (eds) *German Psychological Warfare, Survey and Bibliography*. Committee for National Morale, New York, 1941.

Friedmann, Otto. *Broadcasting for Democracy*. Allan & Unwin, London, 1942.

Fritzsche, Hans. *Zeugen gegen England. Von Alexander bis Woolton*. Völkischer Verlag, Düsseldorf, 1941.

Hadamovsky, Eugen. *Propaganda und nationale Macht. Die Organisation der öffentlichen Meinung für die nationale Politik*. Gerhard Stalling, Oldenburg, 1933.

Hall, J. W. (ed.) *Trial of William Joyce*. William Hodge & Co., London, 1946.

Heiber, H. (ed.) *Goebbels Reden*. Droste Verlag, Düsseldorf, 1971.

Huxley, Aldous. 'Notes on Propaganda', *Harper's Magazine*, Vol. 174, December 1936.

Joyce, William. *Fascism and India*. BUF Publications (undated, probably 1933).

Joyce, William. *Fascism and Jewry*. BUF Publications (undated, probably 1936).

Joyce, William. *Fascist Educational Policy*. BUF Publications (undated, probably 1933).

Joyce, William. *Twilight Over England. The Path to Democracy is the Road to Oblivion*. Originally Internationaler Verlag, Berlin, 1940; reprinted with a new introduction by Terry Charman, Imperial War Museum, London, 1992.

Kingsley, Martin. *Propaganda's Harvest*. Kegan Paul, London, 1941.

Knop, W. G. (ed.) *Beware of the English! German Propaganda Exposes England*. Hamish Hamilton, London, 1939.

Kris, Ernst and Speier, Hans. *German Radio Propaganda: Report on Home Broadcasting during the War*. Oxford University Press, New York, 1944.

Laski, Neville. *How Nazi Propaganda Works*. The Cardinal Press, Leicester, 1941.

Lavine, Harold and Wechsler, James. *War Propaganda and the United States*. Yale University Press, New Haven, CT, 1940.

Lean, E. Tangye. *Voices in the Darkness: The Story of the European Radio War*. Secker & Warburg, London, 1943.

Mass-Observation. 'Public and Private Opinion on Lord Haw-Haw', *Us* (Mass-Observation's Weekly Intelligence Service), no. 9, 29 March 1940.

Maugham, Frederick. *Lies as Allies, or Hitler at War*. Oxford University Press, London, 1941.

McKenzie, Vernon. *Here Lies Goebbels!* Michael Joseph, London, 1940.

Personal-Amt des Heeres. *Wofür Kämpfen Wir?* Berlin, January 1944.

Reichsverband Deutscher Rundfunkteilnehmer. *Rundfunk im Aufbruch: Handbuch des deutschen Rundfunks 1934 mit Funkkalender. Mit einem Geleitwort von Dr Goebbels,* ed. Reichsverband Deutscher Rundfunkteilnehmer (RDR) e.V. Berlin. Schauenburg & Lahr, Baden, 1933.

Rolo, Charles J. *Radio Goes to War.* Faber & Faber, London, 1943.

Sinclair, W. A. *The Voice of the Nazi, being eight broadcast talks given between December 1939 and May 1940.* Collins, London, 1940.

Sington, Derek and Weidenfeld, Arthur. *The Goebbels Experiment. A Study of the Nazi Propaganda Machine.* John Murray, London, 1942.

Thomas, Ivor. *Warfare by Words.* Penguin Books for the Forces, Harmondsworth, 1942.

The Trial of German Major War Criminals. Proceedings of the International Military Tribunal Sitting at Nuremburg, Germany. Part 17, 20th June, 1946 to 1st July, 1946. Published under the authority of H. M. Attorney-General by His Majesty's Stationery Office, London, 1948.

Memoirs & Diaries

Baillie-Stewart, Norman with Murdoch, John. *The Officer in the Tower: The Dramatic Life-Story of the Last Englishman to be Imprisoned in the Tower of London.* Leslie Frewin Publishers, London, 1967.

Delmer, Sefton. *An Autobiography. Volume II, Black Boomerang.* Secker & Warburg, London, 1962.

Goebbels, Joseph. *Die Tagebücher von Joseph Goebbels, Teil II. Diktate 1941–1945,* ed. Elke Fröhlich on behalf of the Institut für Zeitgeschichte and with the support of the Russian State Archive. K. G. Saur, München, 1996.

Goebbels, Joseph *Die Tagebücher von Joseph Goebbels. Sämtliche Fragmente, Teil II. Aufzeichnungen 1924–1941,* ed. Elke Fröhlich on behalf of the Institut für Zeitgeschichte and in association with the Bundesarchiv. K. G. Saur, München, 1987.

Goebbels, Joseph. *Joseph Goebbels Tagebücher 1924–1945,* ed. Ralf Georg Reuth. R. Piper GmbH, München, 1992.

Goebbels, Joseph. *The Goebbels Diaries, 1939–1941,* trans. and ed. Fred Taylor. Hamish Hamilton, London, 1982.

Goebbels, Joseph. *The Goebbels Diaries: The Last Days,* trans. and ed. Hugh Trevor-Roper. Secker & Warburg, London, 1978.

Hitler, Adolf. *Mein Kampf,* trans. Ralph Manheim, with an introduction by D. Cameron Watt. Pimlico, London, 1992.

Nicolson, Harold. *Diaries and Letters 1930–1964,* edited and condensed by Stanley Olson. Collins, London, 1980.

Shirer, William L. *Berlin Diary. The Journal of a Foreign Correspondent 1934–1941.* Alfred A. Knopf, New York, 1941.

Silvey, Robert. *Who's Listening? The Story of BBC Audience Research.* George Allen & Unwin, London, 1974.

Semmler, Rudolf. *Goebbels – The Man Next to Hitler, with an introduction by D. McLachlan and Notes by G.S. Wagner.* Westhouse, London, 1947.

Newspapers & Periodicals

Bath Chronicle and Herald
Daily Express
Daily Mirror
Daily News
Daily Telegraph
Daily Worker
Empire News
Frankfurter Zeitung
Huddersfield Daily Examiner
Jewish Chronicle
Life
News Chronicle
Radio Times
Reynolds' News
Sunday Dispatch
Sunday Pictorial
Sunday Telegraph
The Listener
The Manchester Guardian
The New York Times
The Star
The Times
Völkischer Beobachter
World's Press News
Yorkshire Observer

Secondary Sources

Books etc.

Addison, Paul. *The Road to 1945: British Politics and the Second World War.* Pimlico, London, 1994.

Ansel, Walter. *Hitler Confronts England.* Cambridge University Press, London, 1960.

Baird, Jay W. *The Mythical World of Nazi War Propaganda, 1939–1945.* University of Minnesota Press, Minneapolis, 1974.

Balfour, Michael. *Propaganda in War 1939–1945: Organisations, Policies and Publics in Britain and Germany.* Routledge & Kegan Paul, London, 1979.

Bechhofer Roberts, C.E. *The Trial of William Joyce: With Some Notes on Other Recent Trials for Treason etc.* Jarrolds, London, 1946.

Bergmeier, Horst J. P. and Lotz, Rainer E. *Hitler's Airwaves. The Inside Story of Nazi Radio Broadcasting and Propaganda Swing.* Yale University Press, London, 1997.

Boelcke, Willi A. *The Secret Conferences of Dr Goebbels, October 1939–March 1943.* Weidenfeld and Nicolson, London, 1967.

Briggs, Asa. *The History of Broadcasting in the United Kingdom: Volume III The War of Words*. Oxford University Press, London, 1970, revised 1995.

Buchbender, Ortwin and Hauschild, Reinhard. *Geheimsender gegen Frankreich: die Täuschungsoperation 'Radio Humanité' 1940*. Mittler, Herford, 1984.

Bulloch, John. *Akin to Treason*. Arthur Barker Ltd., London, 1966.

Bullock, Alan. *Hitler. A Study in Tyranny*. Penguin Books, London, 1990.

Calder, Angus. *The People's War*. Jonathon Cape, London, 1965.

Cesarani, D. (ed.). *The Final Solution: Origins and Implementation*. Routledge, London, 1994.

Cole, J. A. *Lord Haw-Haw. The Full Story of William Joyce*. Faber & Faber, London, 1987.

Cole, Robert. *Britain and the War of Words in Neutral Europe*. Macmillan, London, 1990.

Crone, Michael. *Hilversum under dem Hakenkreuz: die Rundfunkpolitik der Nationalsocialisten in den besetzten Niederlanden 1940–45*. Saur, München, 1983

Davies, Andrew. 'Cinema and Broadcasting', in Paul Johnson (ed.), *20th Century Britain: Economic, Social and Cultural Change*. Longman, London, 1994.

de Jong, Louis. *The German Fifth Column in the Second World War*. University of Chicago Press, Chicago, 1956.

Diller, Ansgar. *Rundfunkpolitik im Dritten Reich*. Deutscher Taschenbuch Verlag, München, 1980.

Edwards, John Carver. *Berlin Calling: American Broadcasters in Service to the Third Reich*. Praeger, New York 1991.

Fleming, Peter. *Invasion 1940. An Account of the German Preparations and the British Counter-Measures*. Rupert Hart-Davis, London, 1957.

George, Alexander L. *Propaganda Analysis: A Study of Inferences Made from Nazi Propaganda in World War II*. Greenwood Press, Westport, CT, 1973.

Gombrich, E.H. *Myth and Reality in German Wartime Broadcasts*. Athlone Press, London, 1970.

Graves, Robert & Hodge, Alan. *The Long Weekend: A Social History of Great Britain 1918–1939*. original 1940; reprinted Sphere, London, 1991.

Hale, Julian. *Radio Power: Propaganda and International Broadcasting*. Paul Elek, London, 1975.

Harrisson, Tom. *Living Through the Blitz*. Collins, London, 1976.

Jones, Stephen G. *Workers at Play: A Social and Economic History of Leisure 1918–1939*. Routledge & Kegan Paul, London, 1986.

Kushner, Tony. *The Persistence of Prejudice: anti-Semitism in British Society during the Second World War*. Manchester University Press, Manchester, 1989.

McLaine, Ian. *Ministry of Morale: Home Front Morale and the Ministry of Information in World War II*. George Allen & Unwin, London, 1979.

Nicholas, Siân. *The Echo of War: Home Front Propaganda and the Wartime BBC, 1939–1945*. Manchester University Press, Manchester, 1996.

Pohle, Heinz. *Der Rundfunk als Instrument der Politik: zur Geschichte des deutschen Rundfunks von 1923/38*, Verlag Hans Bredow Institut, Hamburg, 1955.

Reuth, R. G. *Goebbels*, trans. Krishna Winston, Constable, London, 1993.

Schnabel, Reimund. *Mißbrauchte Mikrofone: Deutsche Rundfunkpropaganda im Zweiten Weltkreig. Eine Dokumentation*. Europa Verlag, Vienna, 1967.

Selwyn, Francis. *Hitler's Englishman. The Crime of Lord Haw-Haw*. Routledge & Kegan Paul, London, 1987.

Taylor, P. M. *Munitions of the Mind. A History of Propaganda from the Ancient World to the Present Day*. Manchester University Press, Manchester, 1995.

Welch, David (ed.). *Nazi Propaganda: The Power and the Limitations*. Croom Helm, London, 1983.

Welch, David. *Propaganda and the German Cinema 1933–1945*. Clarendon Press, Oxford, 1983.

Welch, David. *The Third Reich: Politics and Propaganda*. Routledge, London, 1993.

West, Rebecca. *The Meaning of Treason*. Original Macmillan, 1949; reprinted Virago, London, 1982.

West, W. J. *Truth Betrayed*. Duckworth, London, 1987.

Wheatley, Ronald. *Operation Sea-Lion: German Plans for the Invasion of England 1939–1942*. Oxford University Press, London, 1958.

Wolf, Joseph. *Presse und Funk im Dritten Reich: Eine Dokumentation*. Verlag Ullstein, Berlin, 1989.

Journals and Periodicals

Boyer, R. J. F. 'The radio factor in international relations', *The Australian Outlook*, Vol. 4, no. 4, December 1950, pp. 207–13.

Bramsted, E. 'Joseph Goebbels and National Socialist Propaganda 1926–1939: some aspects', *The Australian Outlook*, vol. 8, no. 2, June 1954, pp. 69–93.

Bruner, Jerome S. 'The dimensions of propaganda: German short-wave broadcasts to America', *Journal of Abnormal and Social Psychology*, vol. 36, no. 3, 1941; reprinted in Katz, Dorwin Cartwright, Eldersveld, Samuel and Lee, Alfred McClung (eds), *Public Opinion and Propaganda*. Henry Holt, New York, 1954.

Charman, Terry. 'The number one radio personality of the war: Lord Haw-Haw and his British audience during the phoney war', *Imperial War Museum Review*, no. 7, pp. 74–82.

Childs, Harold L. and Whitton, John B. (eds). 'The political use of radio', *Geneva Studies*, vol. X, no. 3, August 1939.

Church, George F. 'Short waves and propaganda', *Public Opinion Quarterly*, April 1939, pp. 209–22.

Clark, James C. 'Robert Henry Best: the path to treason, 1921–1945', *Journalism Quarterly*, vol. 67, no 4 Winter 1990, pp. 1051–61.

Doherty, M. A. 'Black propaganda by radio: the German *Concordia* Broadcasts to Britain, 1940–1941', *Historical Journal of Film, Radio and Television*, vol. 14, no. 2, 1994, pp. 167–197.

Durant, Henry and Durant, Ruth. 'Lord Haw-Haw of Hamburg: 2. His British audience', *Public Opinion Quarterly*, September 1940, pp. 443–50.

Fowles, Jib. 'Three who truly made radio: Ken Burns, "Empire of the air: the men who made radio" (PBS)', *Historical Journal of Film, Radio and Television*, vol. 14, no. 2, 1994, pp. 219–224.

Freifeld, Sidney A. 'The war of nerves in the news', *Contemporary Jewish Record*, vol. 5, no. 1, February 1942.

Gillespie, R. D. 'German psychological warfare: an American survey', *British Medical Journal*, 4 April 1942.

Graves, Harold N. Jr. 'Propaganda by short wave: Berlin calling America', *Public Opinion Quarterly*, December 1940, pp. 601–19.

Hillgruber, Andreas. 'England's place in Hitler's plans for world domination', *Journal of Contemporary History*, vol. 9, no. 1, January 1974, pp. 5–22.

Horten, Gerd. 'Radio days on America's home front', *History Today*, vol 46, no. 9, September 1996, pp. 46–62.

Kirwin, Gerald. 'Allied bombing and Nazi domestic propaganda', *European History Quarterly*, vol. 15, no. 3, July 1985, pp. 341–62.

Marquis, Alice Goldfarb. 'Written on the wind: the impact of radio during the 1930s', *Journal of Contemporary History*, vol. 19, 1984, pp. 385–15.

Orr, Stuart. 'A vain and silly man', *CPS Journal*, May/June 1994, p. 16.

Pronay, Nicholas and Taylor Philip M. ' "An improper use of broadcasting . . .", the British government and clandestine radio propaganda operations against Germany during the Munich Crisis and after', *Journal of Contemporary History*, vol. 3, 1979, pp. 357–84.

Rubinstein, W. D. 'The secret of Leopold Amery', *History Today*, vol. 49, no. 2, February 1999, pp. 17–23.

Speier, Hans. 'The radio communication of war news in Germany', *Social Research*, vol. 8, no. 4, November 1941, pp. 399–418.

Uzulis, André. 'Psychologische Kriegführung und Hitlers Erfolg im Westen. Zur nationalsozialistischen Rundfunk- und Flugblattpropaganda gegenüber Frankreich 1939/1940', *Zeitschrift für Geschichtswissenschaft*, vol. 42, no. 2, 1994.

Warlaumont, Hazel G. 'Strategies in international radio wars: a comparative approach', *Journal of Broadcasting and Electronic Media*, vol. 32, no. 1, Winter 1988.

Wilkinson, Richard. 'Hore-Belisa – Britain's Dreyfus?', *History Today*, vol. 47, no. 12, December 1997, pp. 17–23.

Index